THE MIRROR OF LIGHT AND OTHER WORKS

—ɯ—

Rodney Collin

Edited by Robin Bloor

KARNAK PRESS

THE MIRROR OF LIGHT
AND OTHER WORKS

Rodney Collin

The cover was designed by Robin Bloor

ISBN 978-1-957278-18-6

Printed in the United States of America

KARNAK PRESS
Austin, Texas

Dedication

To the pupils of the first rank

"There is a phase when one has to go away from external knowledge and find everything in oneself"

~ Rodney Collin

Contents

THE PREFACE

To understand the trajectory of the Fourth Way, one must eventually and inevitably grapple with the figure of Rodney Collin. In the history of the Gurdjieff Work, there are those who maintained the form, those who preserved the word, and those few who attempted to breathe life into the cosmic scale of the ideas themselves. Collin belonged to the latter group.

He was not merely a student of P. D. Ouspensky; he was the primary architect of what we might call the "cosmological bridge"—the intellectual and spiritual span between the rigorous psychological observations of the early Work and the vast, terrifyingly beautiful mechanics of objective science and the universe itself.

The Intellectual Inheritance

When Rodney Collin first encountered Ouspensky in London, the Work was already transitioning into a more structured, perhaps even rigid, phase. Ouspensky, the master of the intellectual center, had devoted himself to distilling Gurdjieff's "Fragments" into a coherent system. However, systems have a tendency to become closed loops unless they are fed by fresh observations and an expansion of scale.

Collin's importance lies in his refusal to let the ideas become stagnant. He took the "Ray of Creation"—that vertical map of descending consciousness from the Absolute to the Moon—and did something Ouspensky had perhaps been too cautious to do: he looked at it through the lens of modern science, biology, and astronomy.

In his seminal work, *The Theory of Celestial Influence*, Collin attempted to provide a scientific scaffolding for Gurdjieff's cosmology. He understood that if the Work were true, it must be true at every level of reality. If man is a microcosm, then the laws

1

governing the solar system must be visible in the human bloodstream, and the laws of the galaxy must be reflected in the human psyche. This was not mere philosophy for Collin; it was a matter of objective measurement.

The Scale of Time and Influence

One of Collin's most profound contributions to the Work was his exploration of the "Time Scale." He recognized that different entities exist in different dimensions of time—that what is a "life" for a cell is a few days for a human, and what is a "life" for a human is but a "moment" for a planet.

His articulation of such ideas changed the tenor of the Work. It moved the practice of self-remembering from a purely psychological activity to a cosmological necessity. By understanding our place within the "Great Organic Film" of life on Earth, Collin showed us that our efforts to "wake up" were not just for our own benefit, but were part of a larger metabolic process of the Earth itself.

He described the Work as having both biological and astronomical application:

"Man is a miniature of the universe, not in a poetic sense, but in a literal, structural, and functional sense. The same laws that rotate the planets operate the endocrine system."

This perspective is what makes Collin so vital to the modern seeker. He bridged the gap between the ancient tradition and the burgeoning "Electric Universe" of the twenty-first century, intuiting connections between plasma, magnetism, and consciousness long before they became topics of contemporary debate.

The Transition to Mexico

The death of Ouspensky in 1947 led to a bifurcation in the Work. While many of Ouspensky's senior pupils remained in London or moved to Paris to join Gurdjieff, Collin took a different path. He moved to Mexico. This move was symbolic of a broader "westward" shift of the teaching, but it also represented Collin's belief that the Work had to be lived in a new way, away from the shadows of old European intellectualism.

In Mexico, at the Lyceum, Collin focused on the "Harmonious Development of Man" in a literal sense. He became fascinated by the "Mirror of Light"—the idea that the teaching could be reflected through a group of people working in a specific, intentional environment. His writings, particularly those assembled in this volume, moved beyond the complex astronomical tables of his earlier work toward a profound, almost devotional simplicity. He began to emphasize the role of the "higher emotional center" and the necessity of love and sacrifice in the Work.

The Importance of Reinventing the Work

We are now several generations removed from Gurdjieff and Ouspensky. The danger for those who now follow the teachings of these two gifted individuals is that the Work itself becomes formatory.

Rodney Collin serves as a case study in how to avoid this difficulty. He showed that a Work student could, through intense personal effort (conscious labors and intentional suffering), connect directly with the source. He did not just repeat what he was told; he verified it, expanded upon it, and then risked everything to implement it.

Sadly, his life ended abruptly in 1956, when he fell from a cathedral tower in Cuzco, Peru. Whether this was an accident or a symbolic "exit" remains a subject of much debate among students. However, the manner of his death is far less important than the trajectory of his life. He was a man who lived at a high state of tension, constantly trying to reconcile the "Absolute" with the "Individual".

Why This Book Matters

The publication of this volume is timely. In an age where information is abundant but understanding is scarce, re-experiencing the writings of Rodney Collin provides a welcome influence. He reminds us that the Work is a science of the soul that demands a total commitment to the reality of one's life.

Here, we have assembled all of Rodney Collin's "minor works"—those that lie beyond his more familiar volumes: *The Theory of Celestial Influence*, *The Theory of Eternal Life*, and *The Theory of Conscious Harmony*.

We will not attempt to introduce or discuss the six works that comprise this volume here, as we have included a specific foreword for each of the texts: *The Mirror of Light*, *Hellas*, *The Mysteries of the Seed*, *Lessons in Religion for a Skeptical World*, *The Christian Mystery*, and *The Herald of Harmony*.

Ultimately, the writings collected here represent more than a historical record; they are a testament to the possibility of a living transmission. Collin's life was an arrow shot into the unknown, and these works are the sparks trailing in its wake. As you read these texts, do not look for a museum of ideas, but for a mirror of your own potential.

Collin's legacy reflects from the pages that follow.

THE MIRROR OF LIGHT AND OTHER WORKS

THE MIRROR OF LIGHT

From The Notebooks Of
Rodney Collin

*He shall bring forth
Thy righteousness of the light and
Thy judgement as the noon-day.*

PSALM 37. 6.

THE MIRROR OF LIGHT AND OTHER WORKS

FOREWORD TO
THE MIRROR OF LIGHT

In the vast and often labyrinthine literature of the Fourth Way, the voice of Rodney Collin stands apart—resonant with a distinct, almost crystalline clarity.

Placed alongside the deeper, more elusive currents of the Gurdjieff-Ouspensky tradition, Collin provides a rare synthesis. He bridges the analytical and the devotional, the laws of physics interwoven with the laws of the spirit. The *Mirror of Light* is not merely a book; it is a transmission, a series of emanations captured from the notebooks of a man who was striving, with every fiber of his being, to wake up.

The central metaphor that anchors this work is optical, a concept that appeals to the scientist as much as the seeker. Collin proposes that "we live our life in a mirror; everything is reversed". Just as the physical eye receives a scene reversed and the brain must right it, our spiritual perception is inverted: we mistake cause for effect, and the physical for the real, when in fact, "the life we live, the world we live in, is a mirage".

The task of the seeker, then, is to find the focal point where the rays cross—the elusive point of Reality. In these pages Collin treats human interactions as an energetic phenomena. He speaks of "irradiations" with the precision of a physicist discussing electromagnetism.

"The living body emits irradiations. They are electrical," he writes.

We are depicted not as isolated psychological islands, but as transmitters and receivers—radios tuning in to the "accumulated negativity" or positivity of the world. These are the mechanics of the soul. When we understand that "one unit of positiveness reflects one hundredfold, but one unit of negativeness reflects a thousandfold", the terrifying responsibility of our daily moods becomes clear. We are responsible for the weather of the human atmosphere.

This text also marks a transition in the language of the Work. While it is rooted in the "Fourth Way," Collin boldly reframes the Work for his era as the "Work of Harmony". He moves us toward a "New Christianity", stripping away the calcified layers of religious institution to reveal the raw, vibrating core of the teachings.

He urges us to understand that "religion is a virtue to bring us near Our Lord; a science to strengthen us". It is a call to a practical sanctity where "cleanliness" and "neatness" are not bourgeois habits, but spiritual imperatives, because "God only comes into clean things".

Perhaps most urgent for us, living in times of acceleration and chaos, is Collin's concept of kairos—a "time of exceptional opportunity". He reminds us that we are often asleep to our own possibilities, waiting for a moment that is already here.

"Kairos time is the proof of unlimitation", he asserts. It is the intersection where our inner possibility meets the possibilities provided from a higher level.

In reading *The Mirror of Light*, one encounters the "Work" not as a dry system of cosmology, but as a living, breathing demand for love and harmony. It challenges us to "project positiveness" by will, to turn the "heavy matter" of our mechanical suffering into light, and to finally recognize that the Master we seek is already within, waiting for us to simply be "at home".

This is a book for those ready to stop looking at the reflection and start looking at the Light itself.

INTRODUCTION

We live our life in a mirror; everything is reversed. When we see a scene it is received in the brain reversed. The rays go out, cross and are received in reverse. Reality exists in the place where the two lines cross, if we can find it.

The same takes place in our thoughts; we think that cause is effect and effect, cause. For us, the physical is more real than the spiritual. That which our senses perceive we call objective, while all that is imperceptible to our physical senses we call unreal or imaginary. We think sowing and reaping are essentially different and fail to understand that they are the same. We regard birth and death as antitheses and have altogether forgotten that to die is to be born. The life we live, the world we live in, is a mirage.

If we understand a mirage we understand a miracle. We should study more about the mirror. It is the key of the book that should soon be written.

Rodney Collin, 1955

I

Every living body emits irradiations. They are electrical. Whenever anything is touched it collects irradiations. We would understand this better if we remembered the idea of the mirror. Everything reflects back. Places where people have had strong emotions are full of strong irradiations, either negative or positive. Inanimate objects reflect the irradiations of living creatures.

There is an exception to this. In ultra-heavy matter energy has become condensed to such a point that it escapes. Ultra-heavy matter is dangerous because instead of reflecting irradiations, it emits them. The earth needs a minimum of emissory material, but men are accumulating too much of it. This is why this is a kairos time, a time of exceptional opportunity for those who want to acquire will, love and reason.

A great change is approaching in which positive forces must balance negative ones. The positive irradiations emitted by people of good will collect the neutral irradiations emitted by ultraheavy matter and form them into a protective barrier like a kind of jelly that absorbs and neutralizes negative irradiations. We project all the time, either negativeness or positiveness. To positive irradiations are added neutral irradiations, in proportion to the strength of the positive ones.

It does not matter what we think about other people, but it does matter what we project. To think good or bad about them affects nobody; it neither helps nor hurts. But we do not realize how much our projections affect other people. If one says: 'So and so is ridiculous', that will not hurt him. But if one says: 'I love you' with a negative feeling, that will do harm. We do not realize the responsibility we have for everything we project.

We have to project positiveness. Negativeness flows out of us and reflects on other people. It affects thousands of people all over the world. If we have positive irradiations they help not only us but other people, also all over the world. We must be very careful to project sincerity and strength. If we project positive irradiations we can leave their distribution to God. Those who have seen truth irradiate goodness; we cannot imagine how strong these irradiations are nor to what tremendous distances they can reach.

We are like radios. The moment we are negative we may tune in to the accumulated negativeness of someone, perhaps thousands of miles distant, who has been negative for years. There are many, many different wavelengths, but there is always someone who has the same wavelength as our own, whom we affect and who affects us if we let him. That is one reason why it is so necessary to guard against being negative, in order not to collect the negativeness of other people and add it to our own. And think of the responsibility if we send negativeness to someone else. It might be someone who is just getting out of a negative state and whom we push back again by our negativeness.

Some people are built so that they collect negativeness and others positiveness, so we cannot judge them. We must just be careful not to send out negativeness, but positiveness instead. When we are in harmony with each other we produce a very high energy that goes hundreds of miles to people who need it. If we have no harmony inside us we cannot project it. Positive irradiations are made by will. When we have found our real selves we will be able to irradiate positiveness.

We can find proof of the strength of our irradiations in the way they can change the weather. Sometimes in a drought people carry the image of a saint in procession and pray to it for rain. When the rain comes they think the saint has worked a miracle. In reality the force of their concentrated irradiations changed the atmospheric pressure and enabled moisture to be precipitated. People with faith knew this long ago by experience and science is beginning to find it out.

One unit of positiveness reflects one hundredfold, but one unit of negativeness reflects a thousandfold. When reflected, each is magnified. That is why, when we turn negativeness into positiveness, the result is two thousandfold. Negativeness is much stronger. Bless negativeness that makes positiveness. It all depends on the level of the person how negative thoughts are used. A person of low level uses them negatively, in a very low form; one of a higher level can turn them into positiveness.

If we are absolutely positive ourselves we can turn negative irradiations into tremendous force. We have to collect them first by attention. To turn negative irradiations positive we must be completely positive ourselves. If we doubt, even for a second, nothing can be done because we are already negative. If we see something unpleasant or gruesome we must find something funny in it and laugh, and point it out to other people if they are being affected by the unpleasantness. If we see someone reacting negatively we must try to make ourselves positive by laughing or not believing it.

That is why it is possible to collect energy at a movie when the audience is horrified at a murder film. We have to be strong enough not to let the negativeness make us negative too. But then we become much stronger by turning it. Once we start turning it we can keep it turning; it keeps turning almost by itself. If we can be positive for an hour and then another hour and then another hour we purify our instincts and reactions. When we catch a bad thought in ourselves we can check it, change it and make it into a much stronger and good thought.

If we are completely positive we can counteract someone else's bad thought, no matter how bad it is, and turn it to good. We are connected with everyone we have met or talked to or felt, because we have given them part of ourselves our irradiations. It is not performance but irradiations that matter. Our reactions are physical; we have to make them positive. If we think of ourselves everything goes wrong. If we forget ourselves we can do right.

We cannot love everybody, but we are here to project harmony. If we have harmony we grow. To collect positiveness we must love people, really love them. Just love them. Everyone is in need of love; it is spiritual food. When we love people we give them our flesh and blood. Blood is emanations, flesh means our real self. To love is not an emotion nor a sensation nor an idea; it is the particular kind of irradiation that only a certain type of action can produce in us.

If a person feels affection for someone but is too lazy to help him, he does not love him. On the other hand a person may feel very irritated with someone, but if in spite of his impatience he makes an effort to help him, that is loving him. He projects to him irradiations that probably are of more help than his action, but which can only be set in motion by action with the intention to help. The only way to love our neighbour as ourself is to learn how to communicate with God. Then we have the grace to love both our neighbour and ourself.

All functions are biological. Just as the body's functions are biological, so emotions have a biological basis. There are two kinds of negativeness. The kind that comes from inside is meanness; this is bad. But the negativeness that comes from outside is reaction; this is not bad. Often when we react irritably it is because we have an accumulation of body acids that need to be eliminated. We need to have an elimination of these acids at least once a week, in anger or tears or strong laughter.

The mistake is when we identify ourselves with these eliminations and mix them with feelings. It is wrong to stop anyone from this kind of elimination; it does them harm in the same way it would do harm to stop a physical elimination. Babies are very wise; they know about this. They will cry till they are red in the face. Mothers should not pick them up till they have finished, though they must not be left to cry too long or they will form the habit.

We must learn how to get rid of our emotional waste. Once a week we should run, shout, laugh, cry, put it out of us. We should get rid of our physical reactions, but not against other people. We must know the difference between physical reactions, and feelings. We must never hurt anybody; apart from that it does not matter how we work off our emotional waste. When we have eliminated it we will be clean.

The cleaner we are outside the cleaner inside. If we are clean the pores of the skin are ready to get rid of acids and we will be more healthy. Cleanliness depends on how we were brought up. We have to be clean as a base, to be virile, strong. Our houses should be clean. There is a Russian saying: 'Where there is dust there is a devil'. God only comes into clean things.

When we understand cleanliness we have to cultivate neatness. We should always be aware of neatness, for it helps very much with self-respect. After neatness comes smartness, a combination of quality, suitability and fashion that is within the reach of everyone with taste and intelligence. It does not of necessity mean being dressed in the latest fashion, for often fashion means making oneself look ridiculous in order not to be thought ridiculous.

When instead of saying: 'I feel so lazy today', we turn our lethargy into positiveness by saying: 'I must do something to get out of this', we find that we have more energy than if we gave in to it. We must try to convert our negativeness into positiveness. We must make everything positive by our wish, by our strength, by our efforts.

If there is one person who is depressed in a gathering of people he can make everyone else depressed too. But if we come in and say to ourselves: 'This cannot go on. I am strong; I can change it by being positive', the atmosphere in the room will change. We must not allow negativeness. The stronger person wins. If the stronger person projects negativeness, negativeness wins. Whatever is strongest affects whatever is weakest.

A crowd can be on the verge of panic and one strong person, by projecting confidence, can stop it. In a group of people who are trying to work one person can raise the whole level. We can never make the excuse that there are some in the group that keep the whole on a low level, because one person can change the rest—just one person. Supposing you come into a room and find four people quarrelling. You go to one of them and say 'hello'. You can say it in such a way that it changes his mood. Then you go to the next one, or even smile at him. If you are sufficiently strong and positive yourself you will change him, and so on with all four.

People cannot be negative in the presence of someone who is really positive. Negativeness comes when we feel or see something ugly or dirty or mean and let it come into us. We should recognize and measure negativeness but not let it come into us. If we prevent negativeness from coming inside it becomes less and less. We should never be depressed about things we have done that seem to us now were bad. Nothing is bad in itself.

Life is a ladder; we must put our feet on each rung and step up from it. Bad is down a rung, good is up. But no rung is bad or good in itself. There is nothing good or bad; there is positive and negative, whichever we make ourselves. We must not think so much of

16

ourselves and of the past. Feel how exciting is the coming. That really is exciting.

Energy is like small cells in the air which attract others of the same kind. There are two kinds of energy: negative and positive. We know what is negative and what is positive. We must face what we are thinking. If it is negative we must say to ourselves: 'This is a negative thought. It may be pleasant, but I don't want it.' Then if we think about something else, or read a book, the thought will go. Up to the tenth time it will be hard, but the eleventh time it will be easy. We must make good habits. It is just as easy to make good habits as bad ones.

We cannot know what is good or bad, but we can recognize right actions and wrong actions. People often blame their state of mind on external influences. There are no external influences, only internal ones. If someone is negative towards us it cannot affect us as long as it remains outside. It can only affect us if we let it come inside, bring it inside us. How else can someone else's negativeness affect us? It can only affect us if we allow it inside us by making it our own. Then what was external becomes internal because we ourselves make it so by giving it our attention.

If we relax we will never get tired, but if we try to control our attention we get tired very soon. If we do not try to force our attention it will not wander; we will collect our energy instead of losing it. Relax and everything will come. We relax when we forget ourselves. We can rest by smiling; immediately the whole body relaxes and rests. We must learn to relax our muscles, especially at the back of the shoulders. We should try to feel our spine from the skull down to the bottom—feel it and have control over it. Then we will not be tired.

We know that our body has a limitation and will get tired if it goes beyond that limitation. We know that if we do not sit straight we will get tired. If we do not sit straight it is our fault if we get tired. Either our body commands us or we command our body. By will power we can train our body to do more. We have to go little by little. It makes us tired to draw in again the air we breathe out. When we are tired and depressed it is because we are getting back the same energy we are expelling.

17

The remedy for this kind of tiredness is to move, move mentally, that is, direct our attention away from ourselves and make it follow a definite line, and if possible move physically with a purpose. We must collect our feelings. When we try to collect ourselves, our aura grows stronger. When it does that, the negative feelings of other people cannot reach us. They can only penetrate the outer fringe of our aura. If we collect ourselves frequently and strongly we cannot be touched.

It is said that by concentrating himself Cagliostro could throw somebody down a yard away by the force of his aura. There are strange stories in the Acts; when somebody did something against the Apostles they would suddenly be struck dead. Perhaps their own negativeness was thrown back at them. Every energy we project comes back. When we are tired we cannot project clearly.

The most powerful projection and terrible force in the world is fear. It compels men to seek happiness, develop civilizations and start wars. Fear is behind all the irrationality and chaotic emotions that dog mankind. The old prophets knew the power of fear; all the holy books recognize it. We must understand what it means to leave fear behind. To understand the big work we must not have any kind of fear. It is the mother of hatred. Little hates grow into big hates. We cannot allow them any more.

We may call them misunderstandings or by any other name we like. Out of them come wars and all awful things. We must get rid of them. Then will come harmony. Even if a person is negative now, probably one day he will grow out of it and understand. It does not matter what we see in other people, what horrible things we see in them. There is only one way to help people who hate: to show them real love and humility. But by actions, not by words. Probably there will be a strong reaction, but in the end it will work.

There is a heart in everybody; if that is touched, they understand. When they see someone sincere they hear what he says. If we project sincerity, truthfulness and honesty, they will feel it. They may not recognize it at the moment, but one day they will. If we are honest, truthful and sincere with ourselves we will be the same with other people and something of that they will feel. Some day they will recognize it. We must reach people more by feelings than by words.

There is a good side to everyone; there is no one who is completely bad, as there is no one who is completely good. No one is perfect or he would not be here. People do not understand the tremendous force of negativeness because they do not want to be responsible for it. We must not feed any negative emotions. If we take our difficulties seriously we feed them. If we say to something we do not want, such as vanity: 'Excuse me!' it will leave us. We must try to float over the top of difficulties, not wallow in them.

It is very important to stay above all annoyances. If we feel light and happy we will be ourselves. What is it to be oneself? It means to be one's positive self. People say: 'I was born with a bad temper; that is how I am.' That is exactly not being oneself. To be means to be positive. To be negative means not to be. Negativeness, zero, a minus quantity by definition is not. A positive force by its very nature gives out.

To be ourselves we must give—give attention, give interest, give whatever we can at every moment. Then we are ourselves, we have being. First comes respect, then love, then harmony. First we must respect ourselves. Charity begins at home; that means in ourselves. Someone who says: 'I am stupid, I am vulgar, I am bad' is blaspheming God, because God is in everyone. It is true that we are all temples of the Holy Ghost.

When we realize that we have done something stupid or vulgar or wrong we should say: 'This is in me; I will take it out of me because it does not belong in me; for my own self-respect, because my real self is not like this, I will not act like this.' When we act wrongly we are acting, behaving in a way that is not in accordance with what we are. We cannot act rightly; we can only be right, and then our behaviour is in accordance with what we are.

We should not try to do things—just be. Be ourselves, love God, be friends with our neighbour. Friendship means being alert to the needs of one's neighbour and ready to help him. To say: 'What can I do for my neighbour?' is to think of oneself. To be alert, open, loving, is all that is necessary. Then one will act rightly without trying to do right.

To be oneself is to obey one's conscience. Conscience is our alarm clock. Everyone has three kinds of time: his own, that of nature and that of the sun. We have to check our clocks by the time of the sun. Conscience means relating our time to the other two times of nature, that is, of the world in which we live, our neighbours; of the sun, that is, God. Time exists only on this physical level.

When we have reached being there is neither past nor future; there is only being. When we are, we are every minute. Then we have found liberty, happiness, beauty. And beauty is love. Where there is love, God is within us. Wherever we see something beautiful, God is there. God made all that is beautiful; it is man who makes ugliness. Real love does not stop at a person or an object; if it is real it goes on to God.

Nothing real ever disappears. If it disappears it is not real. What is not true always disappears for it has never been. We must forget ourselves. When we find something beautiful we should lose ourselves in it; this is ecstasy. Ecstasy is the contemplation of reality. It is real emotion. Ecstasy is the opposite of imagination. If we see something beautiful we are experiencing something real. We are seeing a fact.

If we take things into ourselves we make them small and lose them. If we lose ourselves in things bigger than ourselves, we lose our small selves and find our real selves. To be ourselves we must have courage of will. We are so full of our own acting we do not notice it ourselves and forget that everyone else can see that we are putting on an act. The only ones we deceive are ourselves.

If we do not act we can be ourselves. That is more comfortable, because we do not have to remember what role we played before. We should come back to ourselves every day, be ourselves without imitation. Everyone should find in himself what he can do, even if it is done badly at first. Everybody must work and make the best of his work. Everybody must be something through his work.

First point: to aim to know oneself; second point: to know that one does not know oneself; third point: to know oneself, to be oneself. To find something that does not change, that is to find oneself. How to find it? By what we see in other people. That which shocks us in other people is what we have in ourselves; that which we respect in other people we have in ourselves too.

If we recognize a quality in someone else, that means we have it ourselves. If we have a fault we know someone else has it too. If we feel that someone is negative it means that we are feeding our own negativeness. When we label something we are not labelling it but ourselves. If we speak negatively about a person we are really talking about ourselves. We paint ourselves with the colours we paint other people.

When people say something nasty about us, it is never really about us; it is themselves they are talking about, because they only see in others the reflection of themselves. So if people say unpleasant things about us we can only be sorry for them, sorry that they are so small, even if our conscience tells us that we caused their talk by something we did. We identify with what they say because our conscience tells us we caused it.

That is why fear of people is imagination. One reason why it is so important to find our real selves is that no one can hurt us. No one knows who we are. Others can see the outside but not the inside, the real self. We must be individual, to make our souls strong. Your soul can make mine stronger, mine can make yours stronger. Twenty strong people could change the world—pure, good, strong individuals. There could be peace, always peace and harmony if there were only twenty men who understood and practised harmony.

Everything is so simple, within our reach. We are the ones who complicate it. Why is it we do not understand that being ourselves, being real, is everything? But even those words we do not understand. To be ourselves, this is the work. Work begins when we learn to separate ourselves from what we are not, when we get the taste of our true selves. Why do we do that? Not to please ourselves, but to have something real and clean to offer to God.

Christ said: 'Leave all you have and follow Me.' That did not mean that we should leave all the circumstances of our lives. It meant leave the falseness in ourselves and be our real selves. Only the real self can follow Him.

II

M arriage is a cross, and a very heavy one. It is by no means all sweetness and there is much work to be done. Both partners have to break their habits; their work is to adapt themselves to each other. True marriage is a state of perfect polarity of the individuals, for the woman, if she works on herself, becomes more a woman, and the man, if he works too, becomes more a man. Anyone who has been married knows how difficult it is to make a marriage harmonious and produce the true spiritual union that lasts for ever. Physical union loses its attraction in three or four months when it has become a habit, but on the level of the spirit ever new bonds of union are created, which become a source of constantly renewed happiness.

When she marries, a wife has the duty and obligation to make her husband completely happy, and the husband has the duty and obligation to make his wife completely happy. Both are responsible for the happiness of the other. The home should be pure and holy. How is this accomplished? The work of making a home harmonious and happy is not for or by the husband or wife; it is the work of God. Because of this, those who marry take great responsibilities, but receive blessing and grace that is, if they do the work of God, a work that is truly holy. Married couples have the obligation of teaching their children how to project harmony, but by deeds and not by words.

When a woman marries she ceases to be Miss So-and-So and becomes Mrs X. She has to forget herself in order to live for her husband. Here true work begins—to forget oneself. The wife should never separate herself from her husband. She must guess his thoughts and fulfil his wishes even if she is worn out with fatigue and to do so means more work and further efforts for her. And the more a husband is a real man the more he will cherish his wife, respect her and protect her.

How many young people in love want to get married, but she has family problems and he, economic ones? They take these questions seriously and quite rightly so, but which is more important, to work for a salary or for that which brings no money but is the work of God? When there is real love there are no problems; they are only created by vanity and selfishness.

When two people marry they make a promise to God. If they divorce they not only break that promise made to God and to each other but they break something that has grown between them. A woman who gives herself to a man gives him something more than her body; she gives him part of herself for always. What she gives her husband and he to her binds them into one.

Our irradiations are 'coloured' by the chemics of the body. Each person has different chemics. This accounts for the attraction, repulsion or indifference between people. We should remember that, to people whose chemics we do not like, ours are equally repellent. We must go beyond them, then the difficulty will not come back. People are attracted to each other if their chemics are different and complementary. Particles of their chemics interchange until they have become balanced. Then the attraction ceases and the two people are indifferent to each other.

This is why marriages based on physical attraction always come to grief. If a marriage is the result of only physical attraction the sexual feelings that marriage arouses are attached by association to chemical reactions. When the husband and wife no longer exchange chemical particles through irradiation they become attracted to other people and their sexual feelings follow. If, however, people marry because they have attraction for each other on a higher level, really love each other, their sexual feelings become attached to real love and not to chemical reactions. They increase and become more natural and the two people help each other to grow.

When sexual feelings are aroused before or outside of marriage they must be controlled. And yet sexual feelings should never be controlled because it is dangerous to do so. All kinds of physical and emotional disturbances result. Sexual feelings do not depend on chemics. The fact that the man is a man and the woman is a woman is enough to arouse them. Naturally this does not mean that people should marry although their chemics repel each other. They should obey their instinct about this, while remembering that imagination can easily make them believe that physical attraction is mental and spiritual affinity, whereas it has no connection with them whatsoever.

It is very important that young people should be taught about irradiations. If they understood the real facts of marriage they would not later have to control their sexual feelings in relation to others who are not their marriage partners. Husbands and wives who have sexual relations with others than their marriage partners do themselves great harm. They divide the flow of their finest irradiations and receive mixed irradiations in return, with the result that their soul is weakened. At death their spirit will have an inadequate vehicle in which to adjust itself to its new conditions. Besides damaging themselves, unfaithful husbands and wives damage each other, for they steal from the reserve of subtle energy accumulated by marriage.

The negative force of instinct is promiscuity. It is connection with that which is low. Real sex produces a tremendous connection with that which is high. When man and wife are one it is the biggest connection, the biggest act of creation that could take place because it is a pure connection for a real purpose. We have to be pure to create something pure. Chastity is the careful and constant watch over our physical and spiritual senses, in order to keep them pure and immaculate before God. The married should be careful not to become drunk with the wine of their own barrel.

When we make real connections with people and our influence helps them, if it is a man who does so he becomes more manly and if a woman, she becomes more womanly. A man who helps his wife and children to develop can say: 'This is my wife, these are my children.' A woman who helps her husband and children to develop can say: 'This is my husband, these are my children.' She cannot say that she formed them, but everyone knows it. If we make a real connection with someone, no matter who it is, every influence we put into him is ours, although we cannot say: 'I did it!' We cannot proclaim the fact for others to hear, but we have the internal satisfaction of knowing it. It is a spiritual satisfaction. Each slightest influence lasts; we cannot know how many people we can influence nor how far our influence can reach.

To receive real inspiration it is necessary to purify one's thoughts of everything heavy. It is hard work, but then our mind rises to a point where it can be touched by thought from a higher level. But if our thought is not purified, that which may seem like inspiration will only be imagination. In a normal, healthy person sex supplies the energy for all creative work. It should flow directly into some creative work without being recognizable as sex energy. Recognizable sex energy is the result of laziness. It means that we have not given ourselves enough work to utilize our creative force.

Creative work does not necessarily mean composing music or painting pictures. A housewife who cleans a room is doing creative work, for she is creating order and harmony in her home. It is as important a work as that of an artist, for though the latter may affect a wider immediate range of people, nothing is more intense than the influence of a home. The influence of a woman affects not only her husband and children, but everyone with whom they also come into contact throughout their lives. This is why it is so important that the woman should herself reflect only pure and harmonious influences. She is the selector of the influences that pour onto the home from its surroundings; she selects and reflects those that correspond to her own quality of being.

God created everything clean; it is man who makes things dirty. Adam and Eve were pure because they were made by Christ. The fruit of the tree was dirt. The knowledge of good and evil means that they learnt what was clean and what was dirty. Nothing and nobody can destroy what is pure in us. The light will bring it out and keep it warm. We must never work in the dark. Dirty things are done in the dark, clean things are open.

We must not base our lives on physical things since the result continues after we have left the physical. Spiritualism is criminal for this reason. When anyone who is very attached to his physical body dies, his soul is attracted by its chemical irradiations and stays tied to this level without disintegrating, thus preventing the spirit from being liberated. People who practise spiritualism call these souls and bind them even more firmly to this level by giving them opportunities to manifest themselves. This chains their spirits. The only spirits who can be called to manifest on the physical level are those who are identified with the physical world. They may be identified by a desire to help, not having discovered in this life that no one can help anyone through identification.

This accounts for the high moral tone of many spirit messages. Many so-called spirit messages come from the subconscious of the medium, and if this is an altruistic person the 'messages' will be elevating in tone. Nine tenths of 'spirit manifestations' are due to trickery, sleight-of-hand, suggestion or hypnotism in one form or another. But in cases of genuine manifestations the only way we can 'prove the spirits' is not, as many people think, by whether their messages are elevating or not, but by whether they have been provoked by séances or mediumship, or whether they have come as a response to prayer to God alone.

Spirits should go up, not be held down. If a spirit is held down, when it goes higher it can get lost. We can help spirits by praying to God for them. Our prayers are food for spirits. We must help them and pray for them but never bring them down. We must not disturb them from the place where they should be. Only free spirits, saints, higher men, can speak to persons who are still alive. They come as revelations. Real revelations by free spirits are never made in the dark or involve loss of consciousness in the person receiving them. This is why in every religious representation of spirit manifestations the 'vision' is surrounded by a bright light or halo and the person receiving the vision or communication is depicted in a state of heightened consciousness.

There are plenty of low spirits trying to get in touch with people on this earth. They can only do so through the medium of low-level people and only if they are called. They do not have permission to do it unless they are called, but because God gave us free will, if we want them and call them they will come. If we call a high spirit or think of one, the thought goes first to God; then, if it is His will, He sends it to the spirit.

We can understand this if we think of God as the brain of the universe. In the human body any stimulus is reported to the brain, which then sends out a message to the area which was stimulated and sometimes also to a corresponding area. All thoughts, good or bad, go straight to the mind of God and stay there for ever, to be used for our judgement. All that the human brain receives is stored on the rolls of memory, forming the basis of our subsequent reactions or judgements. Man was formed in the image of God in many more ways than we realize.

Free spirits can go up and down between heaven and earth like the angels in Jacob's dream. How often do we realize that we exist within their consciousness? The fourth dimension interpenetrates the three dimensions[1] in which we have our physical existence, the world of limitation and illusion. The fourth dimension is consciousness, light, reality.[2]

---

[1] *Matter, space and time.*
[2] *See the introduction to* A New Model of the Universe *by P. D. Ouspensky.*

III

There is a work that has had many names. In the first century it was called the Work of Faith, in the twelfth century it was called the Work of Works, in the sixteenth century the Work of Laws, in the eighteenth, the Work of Reason. In our time it should be called the Work of Harmony. It is much greater than any one man's work; it is the work of all the high ones put together. Each contributed something.

Our work is harmony in all things; to be honest, truthful and sincere. Truthfulness must come from us. Sincerity must come from others. Honesty comes from above. Truthfulness is everywhere except in us, so we have to work to gain it. Sincerity must come from others, for we must enable them to be sincere with us. Honesty is from above; it is the strength God gives us.

Honesty is consideration and will. Consideration for others must be our first measure. Consideration is like a plate onto which everything we eat must first be served. To think that others have the same possibilities and the same failings that we have—that is honesty. Being truthful, sincere and honest we become humble, for we realize that we are nothing and at the same time that we have everything.

Sincerity is recognition of our true feelings. This does not mean that we have to disclose them to other people, for often to do so is not honest. Honesty is dealing with people in such a way that we do not hurt them. To hurt people and to hurt their feelings is very different; sometimes we have to hurt their feelings in order not to hurt their selves.

Truthfulness is understanding laws and living in accordance with them. It is necessary to be truthful in order to find the real meaning of things. Only by truthfulness can we find our being or significance. By discovering our own being we can discover the inner sense of everything else. Veracity is the instrument by which we discover higher truth, therefore the way to the truth of life is truthfulness.

And then? To know what lies on the level of truthfulness it is necessary to have reached it. We all have powers that we can use when we love the truth. Our work is so pure that we must free ourselves from this present of material things. We must always try to feel up, in space. When we have that sensation we will never lose it. It is a wonderful work; it fills us with joy. If the work is not joyful it is not right. It is beautiful because it links everything and brings it higher.

The work is the truth; we do not realize how high it is. We are here to give it simply. We still complicate it. Every question is answered in our work; it is simplified for us to understand. If we are open and objective we will see how very simple it is. Work is becoming sensitive to and fulfilling the requirements of ordinary daily life.

There is only one school: the school of truth. Sects use labels because they know only half the truth. The real truth has no name. The truth is in everything. Our work is all religions; it is real understanding. What is the difference between early Christianity and the way today? It is the same. The work cannot be new, but truth must always be expressed in new language.

The words of Christ have waited two thousand years to be understood. They can be understood at once with clear thoughts and clean minds. The Gospels were not written only for people two thousand years ago. They are always a new force, and it is our duty to relate the situation of each individual to every passage of the Gospels, interpreting it not only with the mind but with the emotions of our hearts.

The work is always there; it cannot change. It is ourselves who must change, to find a way to express it. Everybody has the truth of God in himself, but the trouble is that everybody believes the truth he sees is the only one. As long as we know that our vision is limited, we see more. Why do people want to impose their ideas on others? They even want to impose their own ideas of taste on others.

When we try to force our thoughts onto a person we are not teaching; but if we try to hear what he does not understand, we are learning; then we can feel the person and can teach him. There is

29

only one truth and people must come to it in their own way. If intellectual people are imposed on they go away; if simple people are imposed on they follow blindly, and that is no use either to themselves or to others.

If we want to help we must do so; we can teach, help, but not impose. In order to teach others what to do, we must first know what we should do ourselves. He who does not know how to swim cannot plunge into the water to save others. To teach is to understand, to understand is to accept, to accept is to realize, to realize is to find truth.

The mind must be used to find truth in us, not pictures of truth. The way to truth is sincerity and honesty. Truth is recognized by its clarity. Everything confused is a lie. But we have to find truth in that which is confused. Everything true is simple. The simple things are the real ones. We complicate everything to suit our personality, because we think things are too simple for our great minds.

It is enough really to want to be honest, truthful and sincere. If we say we are so, we are judging. But if we want to be so, we are asking for help and we know that help will come. Mankind has always been inspired since the beginning, helped towards its goal. There is a place which echoes that inspiration, but we cannot search for it outside ourselves. It is within that we must look. We must find the place.

Then we must give, give and give. What can we give? Faith and constancy. Our work is to find and help those who do not yet know what harmony means. If we give truth and sincerity those who want it will hear. Millions of people everywhere are waiting, asking for truth. They feel it, smell it. They will come. We must not be discouraged because of those who do not come, for we have no right to impose anything on anybody.

We must be tolerant and kind to everyone; it is our obligation. Our real work is with patience, tolerance and constancy. People come to us hoping that we will tell them what in their hearts they already know. If we let them talk they will say what that is and see it clearly for themselves. If we tell them our own ideas we will be telling them what we need, not what they need, and they will be disappointed.

The right way to help them is to tell them what they want, to give them confidence so that they will find for themselves what they must do. We will never know what people are if we do not observe what they say. If we think: 'I have to listen to them' we will never know. If we think: 'What are they trying to tell me?' then we will know.

We can say so much by one word. One word has many meanings. We can make people happy with a word and hurt people by a word. We must never tell a person what he really is only what he is pretending to be, or is not. No one can trespass; what a person is in himself is sacred. We must talk in a way that everyone can understand.

When we talk with people we must work very fast. We must get used to feeling whether or not they are ready for what we want to say, whether they can accept it at that moment or whether it will do harm to say it. When we want to say something we must ask ourselves: 'Is this honest? Do I really know his state of mind at this moment?'

It may be sincere to speak sharply to someone, but if we feel that he will resent it we are not being honest if we speak to him in such a way. When we want to help others and know at the same time that it might disturb them, we must forget ourselves and speak to them for their sake only. It is true that we must render good for evil, but nevertheless we must be careful not to give too much to those who have done us wrong, because if we do so we harm them by making them believe it is our obligation to do them good.

It is not an obligation. We can meet everyone, but it does not mean that we must invite everybody to live in our house. We must help people with pure feeling, but it does not mean that we must be sympathetic. Nobody grows by apparent kindness, for that makes people weak. Real kindness is when we push people upwards. They may call it roughness.

How often we scold our children, then go out and laugh. But what good would it do them, when they have done something wrong, to make them feel we were pleased with them? That would not be real kindness. To them, our scolding was not kindness; from our point of view it was, but from theirs it was not. We must be alert all the time.

If a person cannot digest more knowledge it is no use giving him any more. But if the next person is hungry we must give him what he needs. When we want to give someone an idea we must know how prepared he is. If we are going to plant a seed we must know if the land is fertilized or not. If it is not, we have to fertilize it first.

We see someone pass; we must give him understanding. It is easy enough to give him money or an old coat. Desire to help others grows by seeing their need. When we really see their need, then we cannot but long to help. We must work to be attuned to others. If we rest in other people's words we can help them. When we talk to people we must try to give them the impression that everything we say comes from them.

We must never impose, never command, never force. If we feel that something is needed and try to give it, that is different. Love is the only power that can make help real. People do not understand each other. They do not see that they are all the same all passing through the same difficulties, problems, diseases. Nobody is any better, nobody is any worse. We all have to pass through it all. We are all balanced the same.

Everything we give we will receive. In the way we give, in that way we will receive. If we respect others they will respect us, if we understand others they will understand us. Everything we give we collect the same size, the same colour, the same quality. We have to learn to give and take. It is more difficult to take than to give, but we have to learn.

Every contact should be a bargain. If we smile at someone and he smiles back it is a bargain. It is the same with being sincere. We have to be honest in these bargains; we should be very careful to weigh them, but we do not, because we waste so much time thinking of ourselves. We can help when we are sincere, when we say what we really know. If we know more than others it will help them, if we know less it will help them too.

To help is a cycle; we can only help people if they help us. We must all work, work with love, work with harmony. But it has to be real harmony, not just words, not by preaching but by action. To love our neighbour is easy, but to make our neighbour love us, to act so that he can love us, is not at all easy. We cannot give till we have. Harmony is peace. We must feel peace in order to give it.

We have not only to work spiritually but in every way that is needed. We must love, and love rightly and simply. It is not enough for one man to show love; many must show it. And how can we show what we have not got? That is why we must forget ourselves and give. We must not think about ourselves, about whether we are saying the right thing.

We can be more open to people by thinking of them. We must feel them, feel what they need. There is a masterkey that will open everyone: kindness, just kindness. It is not our fault if we do not understand other people's points of view, but we have to respect them. We must be kind and tolerant with everyone. That is our duty, our real work.

There is always something right, good and clean in everyone. We must find it but not force it. We must try to bring it out. The only way to bring out the good in people is by not thinking of ourselves. We must remember that our work is to bring out the best in everything. If we are positive everything surrounding us can be used for that.

Where there is argument there are idiots. The wise man gives his wisdom little by little and if it is not accepted, becomes silent. We have to accept our neighbour's mistakes in order to be able to accept our own. For example, a wife who sees the mistakes and faults of her husband has to accept them because they are in her, in her imagination. Perhaps they are not faults at all, but something very big that she does not understand.

God gave him to her that they might go through everything together. If there are mistakes it is not his fault nor her fault. She must help him go out into life by accepting him as he is, with all his defects, in order to accept herself as she is. We must accept everyone, accept them with our hearts. Villon said: 'This is my monarchy: I have swallowed all my shame.' He had accepted himself. That is the sly man's pill.

The greatest happiness is acceptance. It is to be so humble that nothing that is said, no criticism or praise, can hurt us. To be able to accept everything with humility, that is the greatest happiness. We must make everything our own. If a husband is annoyed with his wife and she makes his annoyance hers, accepts it, they become closer. If he shows her affection and she makes that her own, the same thing happens.

We cannot judge, for we do not know what is good or bad. If we make everything of others ours we will be happy; no one can take it from us because it will be ours, we will have made it ours. We will be able to do everything, for we will be near God. We should never go to sleep until we have forgiven everybody, even our own temptations, even ourselves. We must always go to bed clean by forgiveness.

When we die we shall not be with the saints and angels; we shall be with the people we have forgiven and who have forgiven us. Where there is pardon there is love. Forgiveness is humility. Where there is humility there is love. Where there is love there is no condemning, because we feel there is nothing to forgive. Remorse and love are the same. Remorse is real love, or rather love is the pleasure, remorse the pain. If we are really awake we feel remorse in proportion to the injury we have done others; it is payment.

When there is separation there is no knowledge. Civilization grows when people combine in order to see what is lacking and to provide it according to each other's needs. Now there is no civilization because people combine to harm each other. If we act in accordance with a role we will not hurt anyone. For instance, when a painter comes to teach us and says it is useful to hold the brush in a certain way and that the principal lines should go in such and such a way, he is acting in a role towards us and we will not be hurt by anything he says.

Then afterwards we paint our picture ourselves. When we talk and exchange ideas it is in order that we may all grow. If I am wrong tell me so; if you are wrong let us discuss that too. Between our wrong ideas and our right ideas we will come nearer the truth. We must learn not to take discussions personally. When we are talking together we must be like chess players, watching for opportunities to learn, watching which move will teach us best.

We must avoid being personal and hurt if people do not agree with us, for if we are, we are tying ourselves down, making ourselves terreneal, earthly. If we are really positive in learning we feel much better than if we reject our opportunities. We may feel that we are not helping someone, but how do we know if we are or not? Even if we cannot think of anything to say, how do we know that our smile, the projection of our longing to help, just listening with attention, is not help?

34

It is help. Probably when we can think of nothing to say, when we feel most helpless, we are helping most. For then we pray to Our Lord to help through us. When we talk with a person and do not know what to say, it is not the language in any sense that matters; it is not even experience of what he thinks or how he lives, but the real feelings we have for him that matter. Results will come when we have been open and giving of our real self.

When we have felt a tremendous longing to help other people, no matter how, and then have forgotten ourselves, afterwards they may tell us that they have been helped, although we may not remember what we said and feel that we did nothing. Even if we do not understand someone, but think: 'This person needs something; what can I give him?' we have already given him love. And there is nothing that real love does not cure.

We cannot tell what people need. We cannot know how we can help people. But if we give positiveness we will help in a way we will never know. We can collect material things, but we cannot collect love. If we receive it we have to give it again. Many people say they are tired of giving. We all want to receive. We all say that we have given and not received, instead of saying that we have received and so must give.

In harmony there is no discontent. Harmony is perfect freedom. Real freedom is real love. Love is liberty. When we demand we do not love. Nobody in real work demands anything for himself. Always beware of those who demand for themselves, no matter what reason they give. In this world no one can become perfectly selfless, but when we are really strong, really ourselves, and help others, then we are near selflessness.

Nothing is done by ourselves; others help us in everything we do. When we understand that we have to help other people, give to other people, then we are safe, for we are already stamped with what we have to be. The divine in us wants to become what it is supposed to be. The divine in us realizes itself in wanting to help others, and this is love.

IV

Nothing belongs to us except the love of God. If we have that, we have won it for ourselves by loving our neighbour. Everything else is lent to us to use for others. Even the food we eat goes to make our blood, which together with oxygen creates the irradiations which go to other people. For this reason we have to take care of our things so that when someone else needs them they may be available. We shall have to give account for everything we have not taken care of.

We have the obligation to require of others that they respect our things in the same way that we respect them. If we arrange our house for ourselves, saying: 'This is my house' it will not be arranged right. But if we remember our responsibility, that we have to project something, give something through the impression that our house gives to those who come into it, our house will be arranged with good taste. We have to connect everything. If we want our house to be harmonious we have to connect the things in it with their purpose and with their surroundings. The key to everything we do is attention to the intention. Then the smallest detail will be right both in relation to our physical surroundings and our actions. Then we will never do anything to impress. 'Let not thy left hand know what thy right hand doeth' means if we do something good we should do it for the sake of the good and not that men may say that we are good.

Everything must be done from the heart, sincerely. Because God knows all that is hidden and from Him alone we will have our reward. If we do something good and tell about it, we have lost it; anyone might have done it and we reap no benefit. If we try to keep something for ourselves we lose it. This applies to everything, including money. We only have money if we spend it, for money in itself is worthless. But it must be spent wisely. We have no right to waste it, because our money does not belong to us any more than anything else. If we really belong to this work we do nothing for ourselves and nothing belongs to us. Everything we have belongs to God, to God's work.

When we know that, we are free. Freedom means belonging to God. If we wash our bodies, it is not for ourselves; it is because our instruments have to be kept clean for God's work. We have to keep our bodies biologically clean, and that is not for ourselves either, but for God's work, since our bodies belong to God. We should look after our bodies, remembering that they are sacred, that they may serve God. If one has an illness, it is an obligation to try to cure it and if it is not cured, accept it. Asceticism can be of different kinds; it can be a sacrifice to God, with pure intention, or it can be through hate of oneself, which is a vice. There is so much suffering in this world as it is, that needs to be absorbed, that to want to create suffering for oneself is unbalanced.

There is negative suffering and positive suffering. Positive suffering is to absorb the mechanical suffering of others, take it so effectively that they do not have it. Negative suffering involves further suffering by others in one form or another and always results from psychological sleep. Positive suffering implies a level of consciousness on which negative suffering cannot exist. Pain lies between negative and positive suffering and can be absorbed by either. 'Leave thy body and come' does not mean that we have to forget the body. We must make good use of it but remember that we have to leave it. The body will take us to God or prevent us from going to Him, depending on the use we make of it.

People who voluntarily suffer pain do so in order to put the physical body in its proper place and rise above it. In order to stand the pain they have to be on a higher level. Liberty means making the body obey the spirit. God is not displeased when we try to obtain benefits for the body as long as those benefits are placed at the service of the spirit. Sacrifice does not mean giving up something one likes in order to please God; it means getting rid of the false. The reason why many people are fascinated with the idea of sacrifice is because they confuse it with mechanical suffering, which they are not willing to sacrifice. They would have to admit that it was nothing praiseworthy, but on the contrary simply the result of sleep.

How little we think about death or what is going to happen to us after death. We know quite well we are not going to take this body with us, so we should think about the part of us that will go on after death. Our body is not nearly as important a part of us as our soul, yet we take care to feed our body. If we feed a body that when we die is only going to feed worms, how much more should we feed our soul, to enable it to be strong when it leaves that body.

Everything real begins from something real, but imagination corrupts reality. Imagination plays a very strong part in the physical body. If we imagine we are tired, we are tired. We must remember the part the mind plays in the actions of the physical body, especially in sex. We should not confuse real emotions with imaginary emotions. People often study, then add imagination to what they have learned. If a person has really believed for a long time that he will see a doll walking, in time he will come to see it. If we have prejudice, have already imagined what we will see, then we cannot be open. We must be open, otherwise our imagination holds our prejudices and preconceptions round us. They stick to us and we will see our imaginations and never be able to see real things.

There are three kinds of imagination: negative, mechanical and positive. Negative imagination is daydreaming about something that has no possibility of being put into fact. Mechanical imagination is making an image of something automatic that we are going to do, such as driving a car. Unless we imagined it first we could not do it; we can make no intentional movement unless we imagine it first. Positive imagination is creative, as when a painter imagines the picture he is going to paint and paints it. If he does not paint it he was daydreaming and his imagination was negative.

We can control our feelings by connection. We can make our circumstances, and feelings, come by connection with circumstances. Many of our feelings are brought by ourselves, by what we choose to think about. There are always many kinds of feelings in us; which we recognize, which we encourage, is for us to choose. We must not lose by laughter what we have gained by tears. It is difficult to generalize about feelings, for they depend on sensitiveness. There are people who can burn their fingers and not feel anything; others have only to hear fire spoken of and they feel burned. Many feelings are caused by imagination. Feelings are functions. If the organ is clean the function is clean. The organ is the container for something given from above.

'I' is a sacred word. Usually we mean 'us' a whole row of 'I's. We must learn to put them on shelves. One 'I' feels something; if we say to ourselves: 'That "I" feels such and such', it is as though we put it on its shelf. Another 'I' feels something and we put it on its shelf. When people keep talking about their I's they do not grow. With 'I said this', 'I showed that', 'I did the other' we will never grow. If a drop of water falls into the sea, is it the drop which gives its name to the sea or the sea to the drop of water?

Vanity is negative. If we recognize something positive we have done and are vain about it, the positiveness is lost. But if, when we recognize that we have done something positive, we immediately think of using it for others, we continue turning it into positiveness. When we attempt to do something, say, write something for ourselves, for our own pleasure or vanity, inevitably something goes wrong, something is wrong with it. But when we try to do something for the sake of others, write down something that it may be available for others, then we are open and receive help. When we do something good we should ask ourselves why. When we do something wrong we know it. It is when we do something good that we have to be alert, because we often do what appears to be good through self-righteousness or vanity.

We can do everything with vanity or without vanity. There can be vanity in our recognition of our obligations to others. Even if we work for money that is not for ourselves but for others, it can be for vanity. Many people with money are not real; they want to make themselves out to be what they are not. Their mind does not go with their circumstances. They travel but do not know how to find, because they do not know how to be alone. We notice nothing that goes on around us if we are resting on the feathers of our vanity.

We all feel very lonely sometimes by vanity only. For we are not alone in anything. If we loved others and understood them we would never feel lonely. To ourselves we feel very important. We think: 'I want.' If we felt our real positions then things would come to us. We should let them be and not try to hold them. If we forget ourselves things will come to us. Self-importance is always binding us, hindering us in every thing. We must break the chain of our importance.

He who thinks himself important has no importance; he who thinks himself completely unimportant begins to have importance. We should never remember that we are 'James' or 'John', only that we are 'we'. Then we will never be embarrassed, for embarrassment is false personality. We should be very careful not to be embarrassed, because it is vanity. It is imagination and an old habit. Most of our fears come from vanity. We fear that others will find us stupid, that they will understand more than we do. We can understand anything, if we are willing to study. Everyone has a mental picture of himself. When we see ourselves in a photograph or a mirror we say: 'I am really better than that!' We take ourselves very seriously. If we forgot ourselves a little we would have some knowledge.

Worry is the worst prejudice we have, because it comes from vanity. Bad temper is a compound of vanity and imagination. We get cross with circumstances because we cannot cope with them. We get cross when we do not want to make an effort to cope with them. Vanity is our worst enemy. Vanity does nothing for the thing itself, but for the effect it will have on others. When we cease to think of ourselves, of what impression we give, then we will be free. When we are thinking of other people, not of ourselves, the rest will take care of itself. When we learn to listen to others and forget ourselves, then we already are something. We think that to forget ourselves means giving up something pleasant. We do not realize that to do so means entering into a new state of happiness.

Everyone is basically alike. We all have the same problems; they all come from vanity. We know the cause, but many do not. They feel that the illusion is really true and we know it is not true. Tolerance kills vanity. Tolerance does not mean condoning things that seem to us to be wrong. It means not reacting mechanically to them. If we face everything in ourselves and do not make excuses, then we are tolerant. If we make excuses we are reacting to the unpleasant things we see in ourselves. To speak of mysticism in order to impress, to speak for the sake of speaking, is as bad as prostitution.

We should ask ourselves every day why we are here, why we have been given this responsibility, why we meet together, why we are connected so strongly. It is a grace that we are together, that we are in the Work, the Work of Works. The Work is in each one of us, in himself. Many people think they are in the work who do not understand it. Others supposedly not in the work have always been in it. We are not in the work yet; we have not begun. There are many people in the work, but they are invisible. If someone really and truly is in the work he is invisible.

We can understand the opposite of vanity if we think about the process of blending tobacco. A blend has a better flavour than any one of its components. Each individual loses its own particular flavour and acquires the better flavour of the whole. If we really understand this we may feel a pang at realizing that our 'I' has to die in order that the greater I, which is included in 'we', may be born. Only our intelligence can tell us that this is wholly desirable, that nothing real will be lost, that on the contrary illusions and imaginations prevent us from experiencing a happiness far greater than any possible for our many and petty I's.

The greatest happiness we can experience on this earth comes from humility so complete that nothing said to us or about us can make us react either with pleasure or with pain. When we accept whatever comes to us as an opportunity to learn, as an opportunity for being positive, then we will be really happy. When that point of humility is reached there is no longer 'I want', there is only 'we are'. This is self-remembering. Blessed are the pure of heart; blessed are the humble; blessed be those who speak the word of God; blessed be those who are united in the name of the Lord; blessed be those who leave fears and vanities.

V

R eligion is a virtue to bring us near Our Lord; a science to strengthen will. It is a science of many things. It is love, it is self-remembering. It is to be able to see from outside to inside. It is not a word which we can understand in our imagination; we must practise it by loving people. We must lay down our imagination and practise religion by being truthful, honest and sincere. Religion is connection with God by ethics. Our conscience tells us not to hurt other people. That is religion. We may not talk of God, but if we live by ethics we are religious.

Harmony and beauty go by taste into ethics. Taste can be developed with attention and knowledge. Many circumstances can develop taste. A person with good taste will never sin. When we have taste we want to learn and go by the highest to perfection. We give the exact value to everything: we see things as they are. We learn how to measure. We measure our words and have taste because we do not condemn. When we have taste we are living outside ourselves, seeing, hearing, touching everything. We are really living. We are no longer in imagination because there is no more exaggeration. We are balanced.

The better taste we have, the better conscience we have. Conscience is a faculty possessed by everyone, but we must realize that there are undeveloped consciences. If we feel something is honest we should do it. What was honest a month ago may be dishonest today, because our conscience is developing. Conscience is the best faculty we have. Everyone has the same conscience, but in some people it is more developed than in others. For instance, one person may think it is dishonest to cheat by a shilling but not by a penny; to another it may be dishonest to cheat by a farthing, because his conscience is more developed.

The only way we can develop our conscience is by wisdom. Understanding is like light; it is a very big word—it means knowledge, tolerance, conscience, wisdom. Wisdom is understanding how to turn circumstances so that they are useful. Facing them makes us grow—facing them with everything that is in us, looking with both eyes. Usually we look at things with one eye only; prejudice makes us shut the other. We are more clean when we have temptations. When we notice that our hands are dirty we wash them; then they are cleaner than they were before. No one is ever free from temptations. A man reaches the level of divinity by the force of the human world. Blessed are temptations, because they make us strong.

We should face our responsibilities, take our responsibilities. Responsibility is like a string of which we can see only the middle; both ends are out of sight. The man who is reliable in small things is reliable in big things. If someone says he will post a letter for you and does not do it, no matter for what reason, he has shown himself to be unfitted for responsibility of any kind. If we cannot be trusted with the little things of this world, how can we be trusted with celestial treasures?

One of the most important things for us is consistency. If we were consistently good we could be used as instruments; if we were consistently bad we could be used also, in a different way. But we are unreliable. We can be useful to others if we know how to say clearly what we think. A person who can express himself clearly thinks clearly. A person who thinks clearly acts consistently. If people say they feel but cannot express what it is they feel, they are not feeling but identifying themselves with it.

We have to do right in all conditions. We have to do our best. If we are doing right we should never feel hurt. If we are not doing right, not doing the work of Our Lord, then we should feel hurt. We must not imagine we are hurt when we are not. Let the small things be small and the big things big. We must not do good that looks bad nor wrong that looks right. We must try everything, think, accept, think for ourselves, measure for ourselves, eliminate what we do not think is right.

Consciousness and conscience are the same. Consciousness is awareness of our surroundings and of ourselves in them. Conscience is awareness of the effects of our actions on our surroundings. It is alertness to right and wrong. Alertness, awareness, both mean being awake, remembering oneself. Conscience is alertness of mind, of the three parts of the mind that come together in us and make consciousness. Conscience is incorruptible, the best that we have. It is the continuity of this life to eternity. It means thinking, projecting.

We are not here to do anything physically; we have to develop our minds. That makes us grow spiritually. We must develop our minds, for the more developed the mind the more developed the conscience. If we use our minds there is nothing in this world that we cannot understand if we have the will to discover it. We have a conscience and a will. Conscience may tell us not to do this or that, but without will we cannot obey it. Will introduces conscience into thought.

As we are, what we do is predetermined, but if we acquire will, what we do is not predetermined. Our physical movements are predetermined; if we walk it is predetermined that we move first one foot and then another. If we decide to sit, it is predetermined that we bend our knees. If we are dirty it is predetermined that we will continue to be dirty until we make an effort to be clean and predetermine that we will be clean. We control our breathing by a clean mind. If our conscience is dirty we are disturbed and our breathing becomes disturbed. Conscience is the voice of the spirit.

The recognition of conscience is in the soul. The body cannot recognize conscience because it is physical. The bridge between conscience and the body is recognition, soul. The soul accepts, looks. If we see something beautiful and realize it, that is the operation of the soul. That is self-remembering. It is necessary always to make the connection between spirit and body, otherwise we just exist without being.

The first step is to know that we are, that we have a mind. The second is to have a conscience, to acknowledge conscience. The third is to know our aim. The fourth is to know ourselves and to be humble. That is real self-remembering. At first we can be guided, but after the first or second step we ourselves have to decide whether we will go up or down. For God has given us free will and even He Himself cannot compel us to go in any direction. We ourselves have to decide. We have constantly to make decisions because we lack will and a permanent centre of gravity.

44

Our possibilities are the greatest assets we have. In order for them to be realized we must not strengthen our weaknesses. Every action without will is negative. There is only one will; it is like a light that we must always follow; it has to be vibrating all the time. We make it by wanting it. Will is essential for everyone. Without it we can go nowhere. With will we can make ourselves be. Nobody can give us will but ourselves. Since God gave us free will even He cannot touch it.

Free will means the ability to choose whether or not to exercise what little will we have. Spirit and body do not belong to us, but the soul does, because it is will. The only thing that really belongs to us is our will. Everyone has a will, although we may think we have none. An action is brought to completion by one of two causes; either the impulse which started it is strong enough to carry it through, or we have sufficient strength of will to do so. We are constantly completing actions by our own will, but they are so small and insignificant compared to the actions completed by the strength of the original impulse that we do not notice them. Further, we are much more apt to notice the instances where our will was not sufficiently strong to complete an action than those in which it was strong enough to do so.

Will is the strongest thing there is—the right will. We cannot be perfect; that is impossible. But we have to be strong. We have the key: honesty, truthfulness and sincerity. The way to be alive is to help others to be alive. If we forget ourselves in order to help others we have attention. Attention necessitates will. Ourself and the object of our attention are two factors; will is the third. When the three factors come together the result is we are more live, we are ourselves, we have being.

We can lose our being through the habit of mechanicalness. If the will is attached to the body, our being becomes less. Will has to obey our being and not the body. If we act from being we act rightly, but if our 'I's get in the way we are not right. We can make our essence grow and develop our being. If we have being we have soul, because with being we have will. It is the work of the will to make essence reach being. By will we can develop greater being than that with which we were born.

We feed the seed of essence with little wishes until they become desire. Whatever we want we get. If we really want to be clean we will be, in that instant. We have every possibility. Everything is there if we want it with the real centre of ourselves, not the left side, not the right side, but the real centre of ourselves. We can do everything by will. If we have will we have grace. We can do anything by ourselves, by effort. Not, of course, on a physical level; for example, if we do not eat we have no strength in our minds.

The word 'difficult' should not exist in our vocabulary. Immediately it introduces imagination and limits us. Nothing is difficult. There is nothing difficult for the human being. Every possibility is in us, only we say: 'Oh, no, that is impossible!' To be transformed we must stop thinking of 'buts'. So many things in our lives are 'but but but'. If we stop saying 'but' we will be ourselves.

We must try by will to collect more will. We must not just worry about it. By worrying we limit ourselves. We are the ones who limit ourselves. We are all in the same position. Worrying helps nothing; it means that we are uncertain. Nothing right can come of it, for it closes our sense perceptions. Exaggeration by worry brings instability. We have tremendous possibilities, with no limitations except those we impose on ourselves. We must break these limitations.

We are the image of God. We are unaware of it; that is why we limit ourselves. God made us in His image to be free, to be clean, to be happy. Because God made us in His image we can do everything. We make things wrong by limiting ourselves. The only way to be really happy is to be really free, and the only way to be really free is not to have imaginary fears. Fears are only imaginary, never real. They are outside us, not inside. It is we who build up imaginary things to fear.

Imagination is very fast. It is imagination that brings fear. Immediately we must say: 'I have will power and I am going to project something real. There is nothing to be frightened of; this is a waste of energy.' Will power is completely effective against imagination; just will. Each morning we should set ourselves an aim for the day, a particular aim, and try with all our strength to realize it. We may forget it after an hour, we may forget it after ten minutes. But if for ten minutes each day we really tried to carry out our own aim we set ourselves, then we would be making something of our own that nobody could take away from us. Then we would go forward.

To examine our conscience does not mean to try to score up against ourselves all the times we have failed to carry out our aim. That only increases our self-importance. To examine our conscience means to go through the day and see how many people have taught us something, to how many people we should be grateful. To say: 'What have I done wrong?' is to think of oneself. Think of 'them', not 'I'. 'I' is worth nothing. But the aggregate of 'I' and 'them' is worth something.

There are three stages in this work: surprise, fear and understanding. Surprise is the delight we feel at finding something new. We have fear when we see that we have to give up all human feelings, frictions, worries, prejudices; fear of really recognizing the truth, of having to kill the wrong 'I': 'I like, I need.' Understanding is knowing what is our real 'I'. To realize harmony we must forget personality and think only of cause and effect. He fulfils himself who in the highest possible degree fits his word with his thoughts, harmonizes his thoughts with his conduct and conforms his conduct with the intimate reality of man.

VI

If we find peace in ourselves we will be at peace with heaven and earth. Real happiness is to be free on a higher level than that which we usually call happiness. We call many things suffering because they last longer than happiness, which goes fast. Much of the time we think we are happy because our bodies feel well; for instance, if we have had a toothache and it stops, we think we are happy. Pain exists only in the nonexistent. Sadness and happiness are much the same: a circle. Freedom and happiness are again a circle, only a higher one. We cannot be ourselves on a low level; to be ourselves we have to be on a high level.

We must not be attached to things inside time, but to things that are out of time. We have to work for out of time. Our work is in time; we can choose whether to take it slowly or to hurry. This is not a work for a few months. It is for ever. Once we really enter the work we cannot go back. Those who stop on the way are immediately lost and unhappy. They have nothing to hold to any more. They cannot go back to where they were before. As long as we are occupied, looking and moving forward in this work, we are happy. As soon as we fall back there is great suffering. And the further we have gone the more painful and terrible it is to fall.

For that reason it is never right to urge people too much at the beginning. People with energy and determination always want special conditions, special exercises. The problem is that they can manage them once, even get interesting results, but they cannot do it again. Then they become disappointed and lose faith. If a person leaves the work it does not only mean that he goes out of it. It means that he changes the work to suit his own ideas.

We all have a role to play. There is nothing really frightening but this: to let our chances go, our real time. Time is opportunity. We are given so much time, just so many years. In that time we can do something, make something. If we do not use this time there is no other. Opportunity is coincidence; the way into higher worlds. It means our own inner possibility concurring with the possibility provided from a higher level. Real time is when everything is clear and possible for us. Then we must use it. We must not go back. We must gain time, not kill it. We must use it by acting towards other people according to the possibilities of the time.

Everyone has a kairos time, when great things are possible for him, only he does not know when it is. If only people understood about kairos time it would make them stay alert always because they never know when it is coming. Kairos time is the proof of unlimitation. We should be aware of all the processes, watch everything moving in us, be aware of every movement. 'When the eyes are shut the windows are shut; when the mouth is shut the door is shut; when the heart is closed the door is closed.'

When the mouth is shut is when we do not know how to express what we know. How do we know that we are alive? Not by consciousness, because that does not die. But we can tell by mind that we are alive. We must learn what it is to feel, to give and collect at the same time. We must feel ourselves alive, feel everything living around us, really feel it; feel that we are alert, feel ourselves a fragment of our surroundings.

This is another meaning of self-remembering: to remember that greater self of which our own self is but a tiny part, in fact as zero to infinity. That is why to remember ourselves means to forget ourselves, to shift our gaze from one factor of a dimension to the dimension as a whole, where there is no separation between the component parts. For when we say 'myself', we usually mean 'myself-but-not-you'. We must feel what we can see and touch, but recognize that they are fragments only, because we cannot feel all.

Why cannot we always see the colours in everything, really see things? The problem is to be alive. When we are alive we see and hear. We are alive when we connect our eyes with our real 'I'. Then we connect our 'I's with our real 'I'. We do not do it because we have the habit of laziness. To do it requires will; to do it requires the development of will, little by little, day by day. We develop will by bringing our attention to the intention of whatever we are doing at the moment. But we do not do this because we are lazy and excuse our laziness by saying that we have no will.

Consciousness is a deed with attention. No one can eat our food for us. Everyone can tell us of beautiful things, but until we kill our ignorance and find them for ourselves we will not see them. We develop only by diminishing our ignorance. Ignorance obscures everything, makes it negative. It is our greatest enemy. We have to digest everything. We have to combine emotions, logic and psychology. We must go step by step to the inner part, and it is emotion that connects all parts together.

We have to understand everything that is on this level. If we do not understand things on this level we cannot expect to understand those of a higher level. If we do not break prejudices we will not understand things that are on this level. First we have to reach a logical mind and then a psychological mind. We have to go through logic and illogic, go through them and be free of them so we can go to the next phase, Logic is putting thoughts into words. We have come to think of logic as reason, but it is not; it is the science of speaking reasonably.

Psychology is the knowledge of the soul. Logical mind recognizes the psychological, psychological mind recognizes the esoteric. When the mind includes the heart, then it is psychological, because heart and mind have been harmonized. If this does not seem logical we must remember that it was not by logic that America was discovered, for by logic no one could suppose that a continent existed where people walked with their feet upwards. It was not by logic that the planets were discovered, for not by logic could men have known that there were stones in the heavens.

It was by something in their hearts. All discoveries have been made by something in men's hearts. We think we know, but we know nothing. The day we accept the fact that we know nothing, we will have wisdom. We are all on the same level of ignorance. None of us knows where others are wrong. We have to accept them as they are in order to accept ourselves as we are. Then we shall have understanding and wisdom and love: or rather charity, which is the approach to love.

That which we transform with love we can project to others and so help them without criticism. If we just say someone's name with feeling we help them. Logic and feeling together is something real. We have reached the psychological level when we know that everything we do by ourselves is not enough. When we try to describe a miracle with logic it is no longer a miracle. It is the same with mysteries; they cannot be described logically, only psychologically.

And a secret is a secret only as long as it is kept; as soon as it is divulged it is not a secret. If we are told to do something, we must think. This is real self-discipline; to verify, to make ourselves find seven or more reasons why a thing is right or not right. If we cannot find them it is because we have not learned to think quickly. If we have read a book and only learned it by heart we have not assimilated it. If we limit ourselves to words we will never progress.

To receive real inspiration it is necessary to purify one's thoughts of everything heavy. It is hard work, but then our mind rises to a point where it can be touched by thought from a higher level. But if our thought is not purified, that which may seem like inspiration will only be imagination. Thoughts are a grace; they are given.

The mind is like a cup into which water is poured from above. If the cup is clean the water is clean. We can make our container better. If our cup is copper, we can make it silver; if it is silver, we can make it gold. We can make energy by having pure thoughts. But we must not fight bad thoughts. Everything we do has its repercussions and bad thoughts are repercussions from things we did in the past that we have grown out of doing. Everything has its repercussions, but they are not real. We must not fight things that are unreal; it is a waste of energy.

There is a very simple way of getting rid of negative thoughts: just by thinking of harmonious colours. If we concentrate our thoughts sufficiently strongly on another person it affects him. For instance, if for a certain reason we concentrate on a person the thought that he is going to drop something he is holding, he will drop it. He may think we have supernatural powers. It is only that we have the quite natural power of concentration.

The trouble is we do not develop this natural power. In order to concentrate, in order to be able to project our thoughts to other people, we have to be harmonized ourselves. That means we have to know that we are doing right, that we have the right motive for doing it. If we have any doubts at all, if even a tiny part of our conscience is in doubt that we are doing it in order to help the other person, we are not harmonized, we are not acting as a whole. And if there is any division in us we cannot be concentrated and so have no power of projection; our thoughts are not projected, they are just diffused.

We make what we think. The mind is very strong; it is the strongest part of us. The thoughts that we feed come alive. If we want to go higher we have to go through where we are now. So we must feed nothing but clear thoughts, so that our minds will be clean, with the thoughts that our conscience tells us are clean. Thus we shall live in reality and truth. We must not permit a dark thought to stay in our mind, because dark thoughts are dead and if we do not feed them we will not have to pass through dead moments.

We must not criticize nor say anything of others that we have not made our own, made our own by clear thoughts in a clean mind. Concentration is a sense which prepares for thought. Reason is the container of thoughts. We should listen with logic, feeling and intellect harmonized by attention. The truth in ourselves is real feeling complemented by logic. To learn is to enter into the new. Often what we take to be thoughts are only a collection of mental impressions. Real thoughts are creative.

New things can only come from ourselves. A change of level can only come from ourselves. We cannot be told anything new because we would not hear it. We have to have it already in ourselves in order to hear it. There are seven circles in learning. The first is that of a very little child who sees the world without realizing that it has to learn anything. The second is when the child is learning the alphabet. The third is when we have learned to read. The fourth is when we realize that there are other people who can teach us besides our mother. The fifth is when we see the difference between teachers. The sixth is when we choose what we want to learn and choose our teacher. The seventh is when we become interested in philosophy.

After that we must find everything in ourselves; we realize that we cannot learn from any teacher. The only teacher is God. When we know that, we are shepherds. Up to then we are sheep. Many people never reach even the fifth circle. When we have passed through the seventh circle there is neither good nor bad for us. We do things because it is our duty to do them, not from likes. On that level the only thing that counts is serving our neighbour; nothing else.

When we consider people we see their characteristics but we no longer say: 'That is good that is bad.' We just see people as they are without judging as to whether or not they ought to be so. When we have reached that level we know that for us there can be no human teacher. We receive everything direct.

People go from one teacher to another, from one school to another, because they do not put together for themselves by themselves the different parts that the first school gave them. Of course they go from one to another because the whole is not given them. Only by themselves, looking up but not looking down, can they grow. We must look down to help but not to be helped. Everything that is ours has to be won with effort. By that means it belongs to us and no one can take it away from us.

All work must be for ourselves; it must pass through us for us to give out again in irradiations. It is our business to digest, to work by ourselves with enthusiasm, with love, with dedication. If we do not understand we cannot digest. Our job is to raise ourselves, to connect with the high, so that we can be used.

Love is real humility. Obedience is the greatest grace of humanity; it is all love. Humility, love and obedience are the three forces that, brought together, make grace. There is nothing we cannot do by obedience. If we were really obedient someone could say to us: 'Write a poem!' and we could write a poem. We could be told; 'Dance!' and we would dance even though we had never danced before.

Obedience means hearing. There is nothing mysterious anywhere. What appears to be magic, when people do things or have powers that appear to be supernatural, is only that they can see more than we can, just simply notice more than we notice. Then they can do more than we can do.

If you really notice someone else, notice his face, his expression, his movements, the lines round his eyes, the way he sits, the way he moves his hands, you will see what he is. You may say to him: 'You are thinking so and so, you have such and such a difficulty', and he may think you are clairvoyant. But it is simply that you notice him. Everything we do and think has to come out, show itself in some way or other.

Drops of water may be seeping into a wall; at a certain moment they have to come out. One person will notice that the wall is damp, another will not. We have great wisdom that could be developed if we could lose our mechanicalness. But we lose ourselves through abstract memory: this is memory unconnected with anything real. We can use our memories if we understand things, feel them and sense them.

What is life? To see the consequences of our actions. We really possess that which we accept consciously. To accept consciously is to understand. Our work is real understanding, to prepare for peace. The gift of understanding enlightens us. It throws a living, penetrating and extraordinary light upon revealed truths. It brings to us a sure means of knowing the real meaning of the divine word.

VII

There are so many grand things to think about there is no time to be muddled, there is no time to think about ourselves. We must think: 'I am doing this for those who are to come.' Then our thinking is unlimited. But if we think of ourselves and say: 'What have I done! What mistakes I have made!' we limit ourselves. We must not be limited. We must realize that we are instruments and that there is no limit to what can be done through us if we do not think it is ourselves who are doing.

None of our errors have killed us. If we take them to learn from it is good. Ignorance means that the light has not come to us. Sleep means that we have not sought the light. We never pay for the mistakes that are done through ignorance. But we do pay for the mistakes we make through sleep. If we make the same mistake twice it is because we have gone to sleep. The lazy man loses both this world and the next. Ignorance kills innocence. Evil kills innocence. Vanity kills innocence. Hypocrisy is lying to oneself. There is always hope of salvation when we recognize the truth about ourselves. But the difficult thing is to forgive ourselves. When we admit a mistake openly we do not do it again.

We must face everything in ourselves. We know we have negativeness. God has allowed temptations in order to see how strong we are. If we do not make excuses, but face temptations without allowing them to come inside us, they come less and less often. We stand our ladder of progress on experience. We fall again and again, but our mistakes push us up. We would make more mistakes if we had no experience. Unless we are very much awake we cannot profit by someone else's experience.

Nobody was ever killed by problems. If we could not deal with everything that comes to us, God would not allow it to come. It is not problems but self-pity and worry that kill people. Worry kills people because they allow it. They like to worry. There are no problems that are not imaginary, that are not in the mind. There are stages in our lives; sometimes we are not prepared for them. If we are awake there are no problems. There are many factors in the situations we think are problems, for example, our laziness. It is lack of understanding that makes difficulties. If they are under control they do not take us by surprise. We have to call them problems to give them a name to excuse our ignorance. Human beings love to make problems for themselves because they think it brave to have them. They do not understand that it is stupid, a waste of time.

We do not bear tribulations well because we do not know the right way of seeking spiritual consolations. For this reason he who faithfully works on himself, in himself and for himself more easily endures adversity. Prosperity causes us to fall more often and lower than tribulations. He whose gift costs him nothing will receive nothing of value in return. All the tribulations we have to go through are very important, for they make us grow. We have to take everything that comes to us as an instrument to grow.

We think we ought not to doubt. On the contrary, we must doubt. We must never accept anything till we really believe it because we have found out for ourselves why it is true. But we must understand what doubt means. We call many things doubts that are prejudices. We say: 'I doubt that statement' when we are not doubting at all, when it just means that we have already made up our minds that it is not true. On the other hand we should not accept something we are told because we want to accept it, because it would suit us personally if it were true. If we have doubts we should find out, prove to ourselves, whether we are right or not. P. D. Ouspensky always said: 'Don't believe what I say; find out for yourselves.'

Often what we think is a doubt is only vanity. We say: 'I wonder whether that is true?' Instead, we should say: 'This is something I don't know. Why don't I believe it? Because I don't understand it.' Then we could study and learn. We should face our lack of understanding and define it. We have to understand the difference between prejudice and knowledge. Finding four basic reasons for an opinion makes it clear whether it is prejudice or not. Refusing to accept something because it goes against our own type, taste or knowledge is not prejudice. Prejudice is insincerity. If we really analyse a prejudice we will find that it is not truthful. We must analyse each prejudice for ourselves.

We have to recognize why something is a prejudice for us. If I believe this, everyone else must believe it is a prejudice. Prejudice is limitation. We must not be prejudiced because prejudice means closing ourselves. It is more of a crime to act from prejudice than to kill without knowing. We can work as hard as we like, but if we have prejudice we will never have grace. To receive grace we must be open. 'If you do not believe that I AM, you will die in your sins—our ways of thinking, which cause our lack of being.

People think it is human to react with prejudice; it is not human, it is animal. To be human means to be open; it means to combine feeling with thinking, to feel other people's reactions and needs. It means being open to high influences and at the same time catching the lowest, heaviest vibrations and putting them together so that light may come. Like electricity, there has to be a positive and a negative pole for a spark to arc between the two. That is what it means to be human, to be real, open, alive to what other people are feeling; to be sensitive to them and at the same time know what is truth, know how to tell them what they need.

We will never be ourselves while we have prejudice, while we try to judge. We are all mirrors for each other. We see others in reverse to the way we see ourselves. That is why we cannot judge. We must always measure, never judge. What is the difference between measuring and judging? To measure is to observe, to judge is to say why things are and how they ought to be. If I see a fat man and say: 'He looks as though he weighed 200 lbs', I am attempting to measure. If I say: 'That man ought not to be so fat; evidently he eats too much through being greedy', I am trying to judge. How do I know why he is fat? He may be suffering from a glandular disturbance.

We must measure by our own highest standards. We can measure nothing that is inside ourselves. Unless something comes from outside we cannot measure. How to measure? To see, compare. It is truthful to notice that someone is going through a certain phase and why. Trying to find out why is measuring. But to say that the person is an idiot is judging. We cannot judge. In order to judge we would have to know every thing about a person, his complete heredity and all his environment and the influences that had affected him since

57

conception. We would have to have all this knowledge present in our mind simultaneously in order to be able to compare his action with his possibilities.

Even God does not judge people while they are still in this world. Something may be said that appears to us to be unkind, but we do not know the intention with which it was said, nor the effect on the person to whom it was said. If we said it, for us it might be negative, or the person to whom we said it might take it negatively. But we cannot judge whether it was negative between other people. We see that someone is worried and cannot understand how he could be worried by something that would not worry us. We cannot judge. All we can do is to help him turn it to find strength, to turn the situation that is worrying him so that he sees the way out.

We cannot judge and we cannot be judged. We can only respect all people, clean ourselves and let true feelings come. If we were wise we would not judge ourselves. We can judge nothing, because we are not complete. Only a complete being can judge. But we can measure. By measuring we can make comparisons, we can recognize, make contrasts, recognize polarity. By what standard can we measure? Not by anything solid. We have to measure spiritually. We must measure by real feelings, by what is in ourselves.

We must just see ourselves as instruments of God to help others. If we talk to others we will see how much or little both we and they know. We must always learn. acquire knowledge. To be awake enough to give attention to the person we are talking to, this is the work. So often we notice only our own reactions; this is sleep. To be awake means to be aware of ourselves in others. We only notice in others what we have in ourselves.

For example, if I see that someone else is lazy it is because I myself am lazy. If I were not lazy I would not see the laziness in the other person. I might see that he was slow and think that he was tired, or find some other reason for his failure to do things properly, but I would not see that he was lazy. We should feel that there is no badness in others, only in ourselves; that they do wrong through ignorance or blindness. We can never accuse anyone else of being bad for we can never know the real reason why they do what appears to us as wrong. But each person knows for himself that when he does something wrong he could have avoided it.

We can never judge others, but our own conscience can judge, not ourselves but our action in a particular case. If we measure and do not judge, others cannot judge us. Love is everything; it is understanding. We do not love other people for their virtues; how can we tell if a person does something right for vanity? We cannot judge, so we cannot know. We love people for their failings. We love one person because he is vain and needs taking down, another because he is weak and needs confidence. We love people for their needs. We must find the qualities of others and cover their defects with our sins. In this way we can learn not to judge.

VIII

Two men were going home when they met the Master without recognizing Him. He accompanied them on the road and taught them. When they arrived at Emmaus He entered their house and revealed Himself as the Divine Master. Those of us who go by the Fourth Way meet the Master without recognizing Him, and He teaches us. If we invite Him into our house He will manifest Himself to us. For this to happen it is necessary that we should be at home, that is, be present in ourselves.

Truth is to be oneself; when we are full of imagination and of judgement we are not yet ourselves. Everyone has a shallow side and a deep side. People can live from the surface or they can live from inside, from their true inner selves. For this reason each one of us must find his aim. Each individual must find his own aim. It will not be the same for everyone. It may change tomorrow, but it has always to be his own.

To find truth we must first know our aim. To know our aim we must first know what we want sincerely and simply know what we want. Without that, nothing is possible. It is not enough to know it one day and forget it the next. We must be able to express our aim in words, to fix it, to be sure of it. If our aim is vague it is not sure. If it is sure, we can always express it. Real words do not change; do the words of the Lord's Prayer change? Does the word we call our children, the word 'darling', change? We must be solid, we must know our aim and be able to formulate it.

We must always have questions about everything. As soon as we have no questions we stagnate. We must always have questions; whenever we have a question we have an answer. New circumstances and knowledge are developing at such a speed we have to be very alert to catch them. We can have ideas, but we cannot develop without school to help us digest what we already know, to be able to understand what is the Fourth Way. We cannot find it till we really self-remember. That is harmony. Without school, harmony is impossible.

Somebody has to explain it. The proof that the school of harmony is true is that it can be found everywhere. We can find it in books, in conversations, in films, everywhere. If we were clear about our aim we would understand harmony. We would remember ourselves. Self-remembering does not start within ourselves, but outside ourselves. Everything that starts within ourselves starts with selfishness. If I remember myself before I remember you, that is self-centredness. In self-remembering we bring what is outside inside, in order to collect. We cannot collect what is already in us.

If we were wise we would reflect that which comes from outside us. But not being wise, we cannot work on reflection because we do not know what to reflect. If we work always for our neighbour we will become wise and then we will know what is necessary to reflect. The Fourth Way is understanding, every moment and every situation. An understanding heart is self-remembering.

Real self-remembering is not the realization: 'I am here in these clothes, that man is over there in that coat.' Real self-remembering is to put all one's awareness into the needs of others. If, when we speak to someone, although our body remains where it is, our consciousness is with the other person, that is self-remembering. If we concentrate on ourselves we cannot be aware of other people. But if we are aware of other people that means that we are aware of ourselves. It is easy to understand.

If we try to look at our bodies we can see only part of them, and never our faces. But if we use a mirror we can see more of our bodies and our faces as well. If we use a combination of mirrors we can even see our own backs. In the same way, if we try to observe ourselves direct, we can see almost nothing, but if we observe someone else we can see more of ourselves reflected in him, and if we observe many people, really notice them, we will probably get a very good picture of ourselves indeed.

We can have many illusions about ourselves and our motives, but if we see other people's reactions to us, our illusions will disappear and gradually we will see ourselves as we really are. And when that happens we will see that other people are just like ourselves and that we are just like other people in fact, that we are all alike. Then we will no longer have the feeling of 'I', of separateness, either the proud feeling or the miserable feeling, both of which are only vanity.

To understand why self-remembering is not called 'remembering others' or 'remembering God' we must understand the idea of the mirror. People think that the words 'Thou shalt love the Lord with all thy heart . . . and thy neighbour as thyself' should read 'and thy neighbour and thyself', taking the last part to refer to self-respect. That too; but if we remember the idea of the mirror we will understand the original reading.

We must learn to harmonize body with spirit. We must remember our physical body, our soul and our spirit; remember ourselves. We cannot remember ourselves till we forget ourselves. If we are aware of our surroundings and of our eyes seeing them we are not thinking of ourselves. Our eyes that we see with are not ourselves. There is a tremendous difference between thinking about ourselves and remembering ourselves. We have not forgotten our name and address although we are not thinking about them all the time.

The spirit always knows and remembers it is in the presence of God. Not only the spirit; the body does too. Although it takes it for granted, it does not forget. Spirit is pure, the purest thing we have. We must purify our instincts. Little by little we have to take out what is impure in us in order to make room for the pure distillation from the spirit. We do it by self-remembering; that is, by being alert and open, using the whole of us, instinct, heart and intellect.

There is hypocrisy in all of us. We all have an enemy in ourselves. But we also have an angel on the other side. There is one person who will never fail us, our Guardian Angel, if we make the habit of asking him for help. We must choose which side we want to go, which way we want to lean. If we choose right we choose by self-remembering. It is a very wise work, but we must understand it right. Each person has to create self-remembering for himself in his own way, even in his own religion.

It does not matter what religion we have; Allah and God is the same person. The only Master is God, the only teacher is ourself. Nobody can force others to believe him. Everybody has to find his own way, his own understanding, his own alert conscience. We have to accept by ourselves, for ourselves, what self-remembering means for us. Self-remembering is the well of virtues, the food of the soul. Remembrance is everything. Self-remembering is divinity.

It is very important to know what is self-remembering, what is soul, what is conscience. Every individual should find out what it is for him, by developing his mind to accept, to recognize. Only by self-remembering can we dominate every circumstance necessary for the whole perfection of living. We can do it if we want it and aim for it. We must not jump to conclusions, but study thoroughly. Understanding takes away fear.

The first step in self-remembering is self-assurance. If we have self-assurance we do not mind the opinion of others. We must connect earth and sky, live between earth and sky. When we pray, when we help others, then we connect earth and sky. There is so much beauty in the world; when we look at all that beauty and perfection, how can we help self-remembering? When we self-remember we remember God. To recognize beauty is self-remembering; to communicate with the high, that is self-remembering; to feel beauty, to feel truth, that is self-remembering.

Self-remembering is not imagination. People think they are self-remembering when they control their feelings. That is not self-remembering. Self-remembering is awareness of the presence of God. We do not understand the big work of God. We cannot explain what white is or pure is; we have to be it and show it. When someone has really learned to do things for God and not for himself, he really acts for love of God and the devil cannot touch him.

The devil is not interested in people he is sure of, in the people who can be counted on to do wrong. It is the people who are really striving to love God that the devil is interested in. There is a personal devil, but he is in us. God is not in everything. He is only in clean things. How can we think He is in men when they are cruel? He sees it, yes; he sees everything, but is not in everything. Fear of God is recognition of our own level.

First must be fear of God. When there is fear there is purity. When there is purity, nonattachment to this world, there is charity. Fear of God does not come from Him but from ourselves, when we know that we are not clean. When repentance follows the fear of God, then we are clean and love Him without fear. Our whole being changes if we even think about repentance and try to understand what it means. Only people who are clean feel love of God; then there is no fear. 'Perfect love casteth out fear.'

God is justice and mercy. When we are judged it will be word by word, act by act and thought by thought, and we shall be paid with love. Otherwise we could never be forgiven and received into heaven. Christ threw the money-changers out of the temple because they were bargaining with God. Only God knows whether we are trying to bargain with Him. Often people go to church to bargain with God; sooner or later they get thrown out, in one form or another.

All the saints had strong tempers. By struggling with their tempers and turning them positive they became saints. Unless there is a temper to be turned positive, used positively, there is no strength of character. It needs tremendous strength of character to become a saint. Superstition is an insult to God because it denies our understanding that we are taken care of. If we want to go forward we must look forward with faith; nothing wrong can happen to us.

If we are really serving God our day-to-day needs will be provided for. If we want luxuries, that is different, but our needs will be looked after. If we give ourselves to this work our real needs will be looked after if we have no vanities. Generosity is the sister of charity. Charity is the transposition of love to the level of the spirit. Only a man who reaches that will be transported to the Kingdom of Heaven. Charity is quality, not quantity; it is intention, not extension.

Faith is love of God; hope is love of ourselves; charity is love of our neighbour. The more will, the more charity; the more charity, the more love. Faith is the acceptance of a reality which we feel but do not understand. Hope is confidence in the love of God. He has hope who has confidence, he who has confidence has love, he has love who gives his attention to others.

Love is not voluntary; it is a grace. He who has received the grace to pray has received no small mercy from God. We should pray for the grace to love God. There is no love that is not a grace—love of flowers, love of animals, love of people—all love is a grace. The greater the soul the more God's love can be transformed. Soul is will; it takes will to transform the love of God into charity.

When we are in love there is no sacrifice we would not make for the other person. Why do we not do the same for God? We are constantly thanking people for the things they give us, but how often do we think of thanking Our Lord? Dark moments only come when we have no faith. Dark moments only come when we shut the door on God. We must open the door and say: 'The Lord is there; blessed be the Lord.' To close the door and say: 'Lord, take away the darkness!' is an offence to God.

The sun shines and He made it; all the world testifies to the presence of God. He says to us: 'You have will; open your eyes and look at Me.' We do not need to say: 'I will seek God', when all the time God is seeking us. If I know that one day I shall see God, if I think of that, how can I help smiling with happiness? If I am shown day and night all the beautiful things there are in the world, surely I should smile. If I see children coming, and they are the true thing, life that is coming, the future, for that I ought to smile.

To laugh is not real, to cry is not real, but to smile is real. We should go through the work smiling. We are filled with the love of God when we feel happy. Happiness is the realization of the union of everything clean with God. Prayer makes us real, really clean. When we pray we are revealing our real selves, without hiding anything.

How should we pray? By real feelings. We must sincerely feel what we want. We must learn to harmonize our thoughts with our feelings and connect our feelings with the high. One of the ways we learn truth is by emphasizing our connection with a higher level. Thought is effective when it directs the irradiations caused by our feelings.

Prayer is good thought intensified by being sent to God. A good thought sent direct to someone helps him in proportion to the strength of the irradiations of our love for him; the same thought sent to God is intensified much as the rays of the sun are intensified by a burning-glass. Prayers are our highest irradiations magnified by God. That is why prayer is so powerful.

How should we pray? When we give our hearts to God then it does not matter what words we use; we are really praying. When we offer God our hearts with real attention to the intention, so that there is no wanting for ourselves and no not-wanting for ourselves when all we do is God's doing through us, then we are really alive. Then we see God; He ceases to be an idea that we think about, but a reality that we can see. Then we see Him and feel Him, for He is in our own heart.

Our heart is a mirror in which we see the reflection of the world; if God is in our heart, we see Him everywhere. Even if we do not know how to pray and we say: 'Help me, God!' we already have His help. Prayer does not have to be in words; there is prayer of the body and of the heart as well as of the mind. There was a man whose heart and mind were dry; he went into his garden and knocked two stones together, saying: 'I can find no other way to pray.' Do you not think God heard him?

Christ is so great, so high; sometimes we wonder how our prayers can reach Him. When anyone says the Lord's Prayer even the archangels withdraw so that the son may speak directly with his Father without anyone else overhearing. Sometimes when we pray we feel something. Then, next day by imagination we want to feel the same thing and so stop the new thing that we could feel. Praying is directing the heart to God. When we really pray we do not go into words, we go into God. We pray when we do not think of ourselves, but instead give ourselves wholly into the hands of God.

The path to God has been open since the beginning of the world. The Holy Spirit appeared as a tongue of flame over the head of each apostle. He hovers like a flame over each one of us. When we are negative we disconnect ourselves from Him; when we are positive we reach up and connect ourselves with the flame and its light shines through us.

Faith is connection with God, inspiration, grace. Grace comes from above. Christ came by grace. It was a grace that He came. He came from a virgin by grace. He came in a body by grace. We love by grace. By grace we can do anything. We have to keep ourselves in grace and keep our connection with Christ. By keeping our grace we leave all the heaviness of this world and keep the lightness of above.

And how do we do this? By prayer. To invoke the name of God is to pray. To invoke the name of God directly from the heart is to put ourselves directly in contact with God. May it be soon that we live with the name of God always in our hearts.

HELLAS

A Spectacle with Music and Dances in four acts

The Mirror of Light and Other Works

FOREWORD TO
HELLAS

R odney Collin was a man possessed by a singular necessity: to translate the precise, often arid cosmology of the Fourth Way into the language of the heart. In his *The Theory of Celestial Influence*, he mapped the mechanics of the universe; in *Hellas*, he attempts to map the soul of a civilization.

This work is not a play in the conventional sense. Collin himself subtitled it a "Spectacle with Music and Dances", but it is perhaps best understood as a mystery play—a dramatic ritual designed to demonstrate the laws of time, recurrence, and spiritual evolution.

To the student of Gurdjieff and Ouspensky, the structure of Hellas will be immediately recognizable as a study in scale. The drama unfolds on two levels simultaneously: the "Amphitheatre of Heaven," where planetary gods —Apollo, Hermes, Aphrodite—orchestrate the destiny of nations, and the terrestrial stage of Greece, where that destiny plays out in blood and marble.

Collin posits that a civilization is not merely a collection of historical accidents, but a living being, a "child" of the gods, with its own birth, life, death, and potential for immortality.

The protagonist of the play is "The Greek"—a single spirit who incarnates across four distinct epochs, evolving with the civilization he embodies. We first meet him in the archaic dawn of 700 B.C. as Homer, the blind poet whose inner vision births the culture. Here, the impulse is pure, instinctive, and creative.

By Act Two, in 399 B.C., the spirit has matured into the intellectual rigor of the Socratic era. We witness the tragedy of Socrates—portrayed here not just as a philosopher, but as a teacher desperately trying to wake his sleeping pupils before the mechanical forces of the state (the "Shadow") crush him.

In the third act, set in A.D. 33, the protagonist appears as Apollonius of Tyana, the magician-philosopher seeking to recover the lost wisdom of a world that has grown old and cynical. This act hinges on a pivotal cosmic moment: the "death of Pan" and the concurrent birth of Christ—a "fault in time" where the miraculous breaks through the mechanical laws of history.

Finally, in A.D. 268, amidst the chaotic collapse of Rome and the barbarian invasions, the spirit achieves its final synthesis in Plotinus. Here, facing the physical destruction of Athens, the protagonist transcends the material plane entirely, moving from philosophy to ecstasy, from the many to the One.

Throughout this journey, the character Hellas serves as the eternal feminine principle—muse, lover, and earth—grounding the soaring intellect of the Greek spirit.

But perhaps the most striking feature of this work is Collin's integration of "choreography described from actual dances".

These are clearly references to the Gurdjieff Movements. Collin understood that intellectual concepts alone are insufficient for transformation; the "sacred gymnastics" were intended to transmit knowledge directly to the body and feeling centers.

By embedding these movements into the dramatic structure of *Hellas*, Collin aims for "Objective Art"—art that produces a definite, calculated impression on the viewer, bypassing the subjective mind.

Hellas is a treatise on the escape from Time. Apollo's recurring command, "T-i-i-ime, STOP!" freezes the mechanical flow of events to reveal the vertical dimension of eternity. Collin is telling us that while civilizations, like men, must inevitably decay and die, there exists a possibility of "becoming solar"—of crystallizing a soul that can survive the wreck of empires. It is a work of profound optimism hidden within a tragedy, teaching us that the end of a world is merely the beginning of an ascent.

RB

Preface

THE ideas expressed in this play are not original. They have been expressed many times in history in various ways—now philosophically, now as poetry, and again in painting or even in architecture. I and others learned them as a system of psychology. But psychological language already has a fin de siècle flavour: as the author of that form well knew, when he declared before he died:

"I abandon this system. Try to reconstruct it all".

So much was put into the fashionable jargon of our day—in scientific terms, with electronic matter for divinity, and nuclear fission for its attainment. But not everyone is at home with molecules, and those that are grow tired of them at times. So now we return to legend, striving to reanimate a more attractive form. For myths defy fashion, and no matter how recast, like gold, will never spoil.

The choreography, however, is described from actual dances (once a true expression of ideas), brought from the East, and reconstructed some years since in Europe and America. These dances have not only a symbolic, but practical effect both on performers and on audiences. Unfortunately the knowledge of them, always precarious, may entirely disappear with the few who mastered them.

Should these dances, and particularly what lies behind them, be lost, then our play will certainly become—as, barring a miracle, it may be in any case—unplayable.

November 7, 1949

Olympians
> APOLLO CHRONOS HERA HERMES APHRODITE
> ARES SELENE THE SHADOW

Act One 700 B.C.

PROLOGUE ......The Amphitheatre of Heaven
SCENE I ....A hillside above Athens
SCENE II ....A village square in Attica
SCENE III ....A woodland glade in Attica, nine months later

> HOMER . . . aged twenty
> HELLAS . . . a shepherdess

Shepherds, shepherdesses, villagers, old men and women, a village elder, a carpenter, a captain, an innkeeper.

Act Two 399 B.C.

PROLOGUE .....The Amphitheatre of Heaven
SCENE I ....A gymnasium in Athens, evening
SCENE II ....The house of a hetaira, Athens, night
SCENE III ....A gymnasium in Athens, early morning

> PLATO . . . . aged thirty
> SOCRATES . . . aged seventy
> HELLAS . . . . a hetaira

Apollodorus, Thoas, Crito, Cebes and other pupils of Socrates, a jailer, dancing- girls.

Act Three A.D. 33

APOLLONIUS OF TYANA . . . aged forty

HELLAS . . . a Greek woman abroad

An old sailor, a Hindu fakir, a caliph, ministers, courtiers, dancing-girls, an astrologer, the captain of a caravan, bearers, muleteers, a Christian apostle.

Act Four A.D. 268

PLOTINUS .... aged sixty-five

HELLAS ..... his daughter and pupil

PORPHYRY . . . aged thirty-five, his pupil

Refugees, Gothic soldiers, pupils of Plotinus, a Christian fanatic, the mob.

ACT I PROLOGUE

O ut of darkness, faint blue radiance upon a long low amphitheatre, at the height of which huge Doric columns melt into a vast dome of starry night. Calm, immensity, timelessness and space.

As the glow gains, music—a rippling and strangely recurrent theme—grows audible and swells. It is a dance, some dance of worlds.

Shadowy movement upon the flight of stairs. Dancers are turning and weaving together in the dusk, their long robes like the petals of some great flower in growth. With each moment the light grows stronger. Now six figures are seen exchanging from place to place, three motionless between—and the whole always the same, yet always in motion and always different.

Behind the motionless figure at the head of the circle a warm golden light begins to grow, strengthening and strengthening like the rising sun. At the same time, so imperceptibly that one cannot tell their beginning, coloured spotlights begin to brighten on the individual dancers, a different colour to each, following them through the interweaving movement to make an ever changing, almost hypnotic pattern of colour and of light.

As one watches, the figures suggest angels, planets, Greek gods and goddesses. One seems to recognize Ares in his red radiance, green Aphrodite, Hermes pinkish-blue, Selene with pale moonlike glow, Hera amber, Chronos in sombre violet. While the motionless figure against the rising sun must surely be Apollo. Yet the movement and play of lights make it impossible to be sure.

Gradually the lights brighten, the music of the spheres grows stronger, the moving figures more brilliant and full of life against the outer dark and the dome of constellations.

Suddenly, in a tremendous voice, the motionless figure shouts:

T-i-i-i-m-e, STOP!

In the instant, the music ceases, the figures freeze motionless in the mid-postures of their dance. In the centre of the circle, about to pass each other, Hermes and Aphrodite are caught face to face. The spotlights die from the others, while their two join as a single sphere of brilliance in the immensity. Only the god and goddess, and beyond them the dark figure of Apollo against his sunburst, are visible.

How long the scene remains motionless, with only the sphere of light gaining in intensity, it is difficult to say.

Then Apollo cries again:

Apollo: Let there be pause from time!

The gods and goddesses sink into graceful positions upon the stairway where they are; they move, stretch a little, at ease; a warmer and more ordinary light embraces them.

Apollo: Hermes and Aphrodite, it is your turn. Through you shall be born on earth a new aspect of the eternal majesty and wisdom. Some race must choose, and from the numberless men and women in all its ages born, your love must create a child in your own images, and mine. This child shall be the genius of that race and age, and for mankind for ever a token of our truth. Art willing?

Hermes and With thy aid, father.
Aphrodite:

Apollo: The glorious being whom Chronos and Hera bore in Egypt has now grown old in time, though young in eternity. To whom shall his wisdom pass? Choose thy race, my children. 'Tis joy and anguish to have humankind for sons. They'll teach thee suffering, and make thee more than gods. Choose, then.

Hermes: O father, since endless ages we saw this moment come. And knew. though we spoke not, what race of men was ours. In the dark middle sea a rocky promontory lies

75

bathéd in thy light. It bears no cities, no weight of time or custom. All is sweet there and fresh. The men how innocent. . . yet quick, full of invention, nimble in mind and body, songful and gay—and so my sons.

Aphrodite: And loving beauty, mine. They love each other's bodies and their own. And sense our work in the sea and soft airs, swelling of fruits and cry of flocks at lambing time. What wanton children!

Apollo: Yes, I know that race, and love to shine upon them. They are not spoiled as yet. You'll enter into them, and so they'll be saved and spoiled. Thus it must be.

Hermes: Father, only thou canst save. Shine that we may give light—and beg for us thy other children's aid.

Apollo: I will not fail to love thy offspring no matter what ill they compass. And every god and goddess will shine upon them, each in the time appointed and at all times. My sons and daughters, what gifts lie in thy rays?

The music of the spheres becomes audible again in the background. A spotlight falls on each god and goddess as they speak.

Ares: Courage, passion in getting.

Aphrodite: Soft growth and sweet begetting.

Selene: Fickleness and sympathy, Water's mystery.

Hermes: Wit to fly, songs that perish.

Hera: Wisdom to heal and cherish.

Chronos: Mind and memory, Time's mastery.

Apollo: Just as one egg in millions grows to human child, so of all men and women in the womb of Greece, you must choose one on whom to engender and begin your offspring. One pure, straight, and strong—for the fire of gods' love burns all that is not echo of our harmony.

Aphrodite: How shall we choose?

Apollo: [*gesturing between the great columns on the left*] Look down upon this side. and you shall see all as it

76

was and is without your new creation—the men of Greece lying in nature's lap.

Hermes and Aphrodite rise and walk slowly hand in hand to the top of the steps upon the left, where they pause between two columns, and then, leaning upon a balcony, gaze far out and down, silhouetted against the sky. A pause.

Aphrodite: I see one who through all his time seems to gaze upward here. Others now look, now drop their heads and sleep. He not. He's comely, too, wellmade, with my seal upon him.

Hermes: Bears a lyre too, and sings, and by his music tries to wake his comrades. How nimbly his fingers play upon the strings, and his tongue upon their hearts!

Apollo: If him you choose, 'tis he must bear the token of your love and mine through all the age of Greece. He'll be immortal—yet with different immortality from that he has, and different from the gods. Hermes and Aphrodite, as long as your race shall live on earth, he'll live within it—now in this body, now in that—its very seed.

Aphrodite: How shall we know him and he us?

Apollo: If him you choose, he may come to you outside time. Here you may show him all. But when he returns to earth to do your will he'll fall within time again, a mortal man, born and decaying. Birth must dim his memory. Yet by your virtue he'll be born again, and die once more, and live and die, till he and Greece have grasped all they may: and even your child itself grows weary with fate fulfilled.

Aphrodite: Let him come to us.

A pause. Up the steps from a pit in the front of the stage a human appears. He wears a short light tunic, and seems very small, naked and vulnerable before the long-robed figures of the gods. He comes very slowly with his arm up and the back of his hand before his eyes, as though half- blinded—yet firmly and with courage. He passes up into the circle, and throws himself down before Hermes and Aphrodite.

The Greek: O most marvellous... master... lady... dear gods... I did not guess...

Aphrodite: You are dear to us, mortal, be still and feel our love.

Hermes: Immortal mortal, mortal immortal now.

Aphrodite: Do you love Greece?

The Greek: Next to the gods... with the gods even. How can I say it? I always felt all Greeks my brothers; all Hellene women my mother and my wife. As though bound to them all some bond you tied, and we could only be saved together from Nemesis and the Fates. . .

Apollo: It is more true than you could know. If you dare, go up and look where that which yet must be created, is.

He gestures between the columns on the right-hand. Slowly, and as though mastering an overwhelming fear, the Greek forces himself to climb the steps. It is as though he has to lift each foot by a separate effort to the next stair. His hands are clenched, sweat on his brow. There is utter silence. In what seems an immense time he reaches the top, draws himself up to his full height, and looks over. In the same instant he falls back, seeming to crumple, as he covers his face with his hands.

Aphrodite: Courage, mortal, our mortal.

With a great effort the Greek masters his body. He draws himself to his feet, grasps the balcony with both hands, and forces himself to look over into the void. This time he stands there, gazing steadfastly.

Hermes: What do you see, mortal?

The Greek: [*his voice trembling*]
It is more terrible and lovely than I guessed.

Hermes: Yet you can bear it?

The Greek: [*proudly*] I am a Greek.

Aphrodite: What is it like, our offspring? We too must learn to bear it.

The Greek: I see the past and future, the life and death of Hellas, all together, like some great being lying between the deep and Mount Olympus. Its belly the sea washes, in its heart the temples and mysteries, its head wreathed with the mists of Ida. And all the good and evil that the Greeks shall do are its joy and suffering for ever. ...

Aphrodite: And you, mortal, do you see yourself there?

The Greek: [*awestruck*] How strange! In every part I look I see myself—tilling and praying, committing every crime, myself peasant and priest and warrior and king. And infamous traitor. In this time, and forever, until the end of Greece. [*His voice breaks.*]

Aphrodite: [*aside*] The end of what's yet unborn; l am immortal—yet almost he makes me feel the pain of that which passes.

The Greek: [*turns to her*] And yet those countless figures that I see as I, do not exist. The light shifts, and they are but thy radiance reflected on the rocks of Greece. l am most terribly afraid . . .

Aphrodite: We will be with you, mortal.

The Greek: [*overwhelmed*] I see that I am nothing . . . nothing . . . Goddess and most holy Hermes, all Greece is thine ... I am thy child. Do as thou wilt with me. . . .

Apollo: [*in a tremendous voice*] In thy parents' name and mine, wake up thy fellows from their natural sleep!

The light behind Apollo swells to immense brilliance: there is a peal of thunder.

Apollo: [*shouts*] T-i-i-ime, ROLL ON!

The music of the spheres grows audible again, the gods and goddesses begin to move and circle; the play of lights weaves, interweaves and gains momentum. Light, colour, motion, speed, mount in crescendo. The whole earth and heaven seem filled with the rhythmic and repeating harmony.

And in the recurring figure of the dance, Hermes and Aphrodite once more approach. Not suddenly this time, but as if in a kind of swoon, the whole motion dies. The other spotlights fade, those upon

Hermes and Aphrodite join to a golden sphere against the darkness. A strange ringing grows about them. As this sphere of light grows more brilliant, the god and goddess, face to face, move imperceptibly together. Each puts out a hand. Their fingers touch. The light upon them, now blinding, seems suddenly to fuse. In the pitch darkness the ringing increases to almost unbearable intensity. It fills the whole air, the whole earth. Then gradually it diminishes. As it becomes tolerable again, the music of the spheres breaks in very faintly, and in the same moment sunlight slowly brightens on an earthly scene.

ACT I SCENE ONE 700 B.C.

A hilltop in Attica. early morning, the soft curve of the highest slope, turf dotted with narcissus, against a clear blue sky. Under a single olive tree a young man half-lying on one elbow, yet seeming to start up, his left arm reaching forward, eyes closed but with face thrown back and as if transfixed. In the moment the light brightens a girl is rising, very gracefully, from his side and out of his embrace. As the ringing dies away, but with the music of the spheres still audible, she stands looking down at him, tender, gentle and teasing.

Hellas: [softly] Did you enjoy me, Homer?

Homer: [under his breath, reverently] Enjoy?. . . Was that enjoyment?

Hellas: Tis you should say so, Homer.

Homer: How did it happen? Who are you?

Hellas: [tenderly] I am a woman: as you tune your lyre your lyre tuned me: I brought you my body tuned. You are innocent in your blindness, Homer, or you would not ask. Yet I am glad you are innocent.

Homer: [suddenly, passionately] I saw ... not with human sight . . . you made me see. . .but with gods' eyes. . . .

Hellas: [half-coquettish, half-wise] They say the gods hover near poets . . . but Aphrodite lives in women.

Homer: Aphrodite? Yes, she came to me. . . .

Hellas: It was I who came, Hellas.

Homer: [turning to her] Could you understand, if I told? If I dared to tell you, would you dare to bear it? Or would your own love swallow all, and Zeus blast me for the blasphemy. . . . Yet 'twas through you it happened . . . so you must know. . .

Hellas: I have Aphrodite in me, Homer.

Homer: [*seriously*] Yes, it's true. [*She kneels down a little away from him, and lays her hand gently on his knee.*]

Hellas: Make music of it, Homer.

Homer: [*his hand moves to the strings of his lyre, plucking them*] Later it will be sung. What song! Not a moment till the end of Greece but somewhere in Attica men will be singing it. . . . But now it is not time. It is too new. I do not yet know how.

Hellas: Just tell me then.

Homer: It is strange. Never since babyhood did I see the light, or trees, or women. Yet within me I knew it all. The dark sea, curling like cream upon the rocks: seabirds crying as arrows in the wind: the bleating of flocks of kids among the hills. Though I was blind, there was no scene in Hellas that was stranger to me. . . . [*He pauses.*]

Girls would sit beyond the firelight circle as I sang— sometimes they would call out to me, mocking yet tremulous. No woman ever came to me till you, Hellas. I could not take, and you were the first to give.

Hellas: [*she makes a movement of tenderness towards him*] Dear sightless one!

Homer: Yet within me I knew all women. All the soft corners of their bodies, and their caresses, and sweet words, and givings and withholdings, I knew already. How could that be, Hellas?

Hellas: [*whispers*] I do not know.

Homer: When you came, it was as though a song that one made became alive. All that I felt before as dream, I knew as real . . .all, all at once. . . . [*He makes a great blind gesture*] The gods . . . I saw the gods . . . their dance . . . they spoke with me. . . .

Hellas: Yes, Homer, sometimes it seems like that.

Homer:	[*astonished*] It seems? . . . Did you not see their motion, hear their wings, their voices, see what they showed?
Hellas:	I saw that I love you, Homer.
Homer:	Understanding was given me, and now I understand you too. I am blind, but I see; your eyes are open, but you dream. . . [*tenderly*] sweet dreams, tender dreams, Hellas, but wrapped in sleep.
Hellas:	[*dreamily*] I did not think of it before, but now I wonder. Suppose I were to be with child by you. . . a little chubby one, with your curls, your voice. . . [*Suddenly frightened, clings to him*] Would they kill it? No, they could not. Homer. You would save it, would you not? Say it was yours? Promise me you would?
Homer:	[*half to himself*] Hellas with child by me? That also I perceived. Yet was't by me, or by Hermes on Aphrodite? Something was conceived there, as the god and goddess wheeled together, a blaze of blinding light. Some new cosmos, some godling gotten. And in that moment you were in my arms. . . .
Hellas:	[*coming close to him*] What else did you see, Homer?
Homer:	I saw time open, and in its womb lay all of Hellas now unborn. Great marble palaces, exquisite temples, crowding streets, columns, bazaars and brothels rose and clothed this hill. Men swarmed like ants among the stone they quarried. Sang, quarrelled, cheated, fought, loved and tortured each other, and sold the very dead for profit. Slim ships flew out like needles to every coast on earth, bringing back wine and silk, wise men and bawds. The brotherhood of Hellenes was forgot, and while a few loved the gods, others invoked decay and rot, till the very stones grew putrid, and fell apart upon them. And deep in that womb of time the sky was red with fire and blood, and barbarians whom Pallas never knew thundered on shaggy horses among the abandoned tombs. . . .

As he has been speaking, shepherds, some girls, an old hag gathering sticks, two men with baskets of olives, have come over the hill and from the sides, and hearing him, sit round about to listen.

Homer:	And yet—most glorious and terrible—nothing grew nor passed: But all was there. The temples ever building, ever perfect, ever crumbling, and in ruins all at once. Those babes who fell to the hooves of savages at the end of time, forever screamed and suffered: and in the same moment others played careless with the young lambs on such a hill as this—but all eternally. And I was there in every scene, this morning now, the high hot noon of traffic, the bloody sunset. . . with some task laid on me. Ah, what weight of knowledge! Too much to bear. . . . [*A low sigh, almost a moan, goes up from those around.*]
A Young Girl:	[*breathless*] It's Orpheus.
An Old Man:	[*at the side, muttering*] Blasphemer, he speaks of the end of Hellas! May Pan pickle him! He spits, making the sign of the evil eye.
A Bearded Shepherd:	[*with his arm round a lusty shepherdess*] Tell us, No-eyes, the world will last till goatbranding? My wench has a kid to drop that month.
Hellas:	[*close to Homer*] You frighten me. Almost I see it too. The white walls in the sun; the blood. But it's only poetry, isn't it?
Homer:	[*tenderly and yet sadly*] Dreamer, I was sent to wake you.
Hellas:	[*passionately*] Then take me . . . away.
Homer:	Waking is only here.
Hellas:	It hurts. The old man has been muttering all the while, and it has spread to those near him, an ugly rumour.
Old Woman	And if the blind and cripples are allowed to get children on our girls, what kind of monsters shall we

have for Greeks? No wonder he sees gods' curse upon us. 'Tis he who brought it.

A Thin Elder: [*formally*] By the law, the offspring must be exposed to the eagles.

Hellas: [*cries out*] No!

A Shepherd: [*jerking a thumb at Homer*] He does no work. He breeds no goats, presses no olives. Lies around with his lyre and his girl all day. Much good is he to Attica — exposure's twenty years too late.

Conflicting Voices: [*There are muffled cries of protest.*] No, no. . . . The gods are with him. Play to us, Homer! [*But the angry voices drown them*] Blasphemer! Stone him! Her too! Blind man's moll!

Someone throws a stone. It hits Homer in the side. He feels about in the air, astonished. There is another and another. The shouting rises. A stone strikes Hellas in the breast, the belly.

Hellas: [*moans*] Ah, my young. . .

She drags up Homer, and half shielding, half pushing him, as the shouting and stoning rise to a roar, they pass off-stage to the left. When they are gone, the crowd pauses, baffled, uncertain what to do. There is a faint murmur of shame.

Conflicting Voices: She was hurt! Good riddance! What dream was that? A drunkard's nightmare! Let 'em fry in Hades! You heard how he lost his eyes? The poor creature, she's young yet. Pretty too. . . .

The Bearded Shepherd: [*above the turmoil, cheerfully*] Here, folks, we brought a barrel! Let's drink a cup, and give Dionysos thanks. They're not worth the worrying.

Old Man who muttered: That's right, the old gods are safest. [*He drinks*] Lovely Dion! Ah. . . !

Old Woman with sticks: Sure, the best times are past. When I was a girl, young Pan would come and kick the buckets over as we milked. And that weren't all. He'd catch us by the . . .

The Bearded Shepherd:	Drink deep, friends! That's the way to forget and feel. Last year's wine. . . and blessed by the elders, too.
The Thin Elder:	[*stiffly*] To Dionysos! [*Cups pass round. Someone has filled a basin. Men put their faces in to drink, roaring with laughter. Others begin singing. A shepherd catches at the young girl who spoke before.*]
Young girl:	Don't touch me! It was Orpheus, and we're bewitched!
Shepherd:	I'll bewitch you, witch. Come on, the shepherds' round!
Other Voices:	The shepherds' round! The shepherds' round!

The men and girls take hands in a circle, others strike up a gay tune on horns and guitars. The circle rocks from side to side, begins to sway then move, gaining momentum. Now they sweep into the centre, now back; now revolve. The circle whirls and shifts like a parody of the other. There are shouts above the din.

Man:	Drink to forget the future!
Girl:	Dance to return to the deep!
Second Girl:	Men for the dreams of maidens!
Second Man:	Woman the pillow for sleep!

The phrases, caught up by the rest and by the music, begin to repeat over and over again, until they are a roaring drunken chorus to the dance. The music grows faster, the dance dizzier, the din more deafening, until, as the whole circle begins to trip and tumble, the curtain falls.

ACT I SCENE TWO

A village square in Attica. Simple huts of timber and tile, fires burning, chickens and pigs wandering about, in one doorway a woman grinding corn, in another a man making shoes. Through an open door figures can be seen teasing wool, while in the garden before the same house girls spin on dancing bobbins as they laugh and talk together. From off-stage comes the cheerful tinkle and clang of a blacksmith's hammer.

In the shade of a big oak tree in mid-stage sits Homer, his lyre hanging from a branch, and a group of men and women squatting about him.

Homer: Carpenter, where is the auger we designed? Is it back from the blacksmith's yet?

Carpenter: [a nimble little man with sandy hair] Ay, Homer, it is that—and goes through boards of oak like a spoon through butter. For pegging beams there's been nothing like it. I can't wait to hear what the shipwrights at the Piraeus are going to say.

Homer: Let me feel if 'tis right. The carpenter hands him a large spiral auger of iron, which Homer takes and delicately feels, his fingers following the whorls from screw to shank.

Homer: [half to himself] Yes, thus it was. Thus the sun and revolving planets bore through the void of space, making a hole through which a wedge of time may enter.

Carpenter: 'Tis a real marvel.

Old Woman   Tell us more of what you saw, Homer.
with a basket:

Many Voices: Ay, tell us more. What else?

Homer:	[*to the old woman*] What have you in your basket, granny?
The Old Woman:	Sweet peaches, boy, all round and rosy—what a shame you'll never see 'em. Here I'll choose a good one for you.

She hobbles up to Homer, and puts a large ripe peach into his hand.

Homer:	Thank you, granny. [*He feels it delicately then holds it to his nose, savouring the scent.*] Ah, beautiful. . . . Like this was the very earth—turning in heaven, as a ripe fruit falls spinning from its tree. And all the forests and hills and living things we know were no more than this down upon it. And beautiful colours—rose and gold and green—shimmered upon its skin of lands and seas, as the sun sweetened it. And I knew— I know not how—that beneath this skin was flesh of marble and iron and gold that Zeus might eat. And in its inmost core, a terrible hard stone, black kernel that can come to nothing till the earth dies, when from it another earth might spring, and so eternally.
The Old Woman:	[*reverently*] The end of mother earth, mercy save us! It gives one gooseflesh just to think of it. And what would happen to the likes of us?
A Voice in the Crowd:	Don't worry, granny, you'll be wormfood long before!
Homer:	How to say what I saw? Yes, you'll be dead then—but alive elsewhere. For I saw the Fates spinning the lives of men on earth, as maidens spin thread upon their bobbins. They spun from the golden fleece of heaven. And there was no end to it. For as each single coil was spun, another followed and fell upon it, covering the last. To men the coil that disappeared seemed dead—yet 'twas but wound upon the bobbin of eternity, still there, and all alive. . . .

As he speaks, the three girls who were spinning in the garden have moved towards the centre of the stage, and begin to sway together in time, spinning their bobbins against their knees, reeling in the thread, and spinning again to a slow gentle rhythm, which they hum softly beneath their breath. Their swaying grows more rhythmical, and they dip from side to side, first left, then right—in a kind of spinning dance.

Homer: Most strange of all, I seemed to see that in the midst Apollo, crosslegged like a cobbler, sat, making some stock of unknown articles. All heaven was his workshop. He'd take the skin of earth, and stretch and knead it, softening, warming, giving it elasticity. Then, cutting certain shapes therefrom, would sew them up with the thread of human life. Each object was a soul— and somewhere had its mate. This was his work.

As he has been speaking four cobblers have gathered from their doors, and squatting cross-legged in a semi-circle before the girls, they begin to sway to left and right in the same rhythm, stretching the soft leather over their knees and between their hands as they move. The cobblers pick up the humming of the spinsters in a deep bass, and little by little this humming spreads through the whole crowd.

Deftly the maidens dip and spin: deftly the cobblers sew. For now the leather shapes are on their lasts. At their left side lies the awl; on their right knee, needle and thread. Rocking once they stab the hole, and rocking again they stitch. Gradually the rhythm takes possession of them. Other girls join the spinners, and the humming seems to spread to the whole village, so that the women grinding corn, the men teasing wool, and even the blacksmith's hammer sing to it. Somehow all the work of the village has become a single whole, all goes smooth and easily, and from this whole rises a throbbing murmur like a hive of bees.

Suddenly, in the midst of this activity one begins to hear, far off, the strong harsh singing of men's voices. Several are out of tune, some are whistling, the song is broken by shouts and catcalls. But there is vigour about it, an intoxicating swing and gaiety. The voices grow nearer and clearer:

> Agamemnon's body lies amouldering in the grave,
> Agamemnon's body lies amouldering in the grave,
> Agamemnon's body lies amouldering in the grave,
> While we poor devils march on top,
> March on top!

The band of soldiers bursts into the square with a roar on the last line. They are hot, red, sweaty and covered with dust. There suddenly seem to be a lot of lances among the crowd, glint of helmets, shouts, laughter, greetings. The spinning girls run for cover of their cottages, and the cobblers fish for their lasts and leather among trampling feet.

In a minute a wooden table and benches have been dragged under the tree near Homer, and jugs of wine, bowls of soup, and bread set there. The captain and a half-dozen soldiers throw themselves down, others have caught girls round the waist, or are unstrapping their shields and breastplates at the doors of the houses. Shouts and greetings are tossed above the hubbub.

Soldiers: Cheese and pickles, boys!

How many barbarians did you skewer, Jason?

Something to drink, for Pluto's sake!

Leave me be till you're washed and decent, can't you?

The Captain: [*between mouthfuls*] Well, we cleared the blighters down to the plain of Marathon. They'd had time to dig themselves in since spring, and we had to smoke 'em out like rabbits. There was a westerly breeze blowing, and we set the cornfields alight windward of their camp. The whole thing went like tinder. Then the stockade caught. That finished it. Some got away to the shore, where they'd left the boats they came in. Not many though. The rest'll stay till doomsday.

The Innkeeper: [*standing by, and filling his cup*] Good work, boys. My best calf to Athena tonight—and a barrel of wine in celebration!

Other Voices: A sheep! A jar of oil! A load of wood to fire the sacrifice!

The Captain: [*turns to Homer, wiping his mouth*] You're silent, poet. How about a paean of victory, eh?

Homer: I see them homeless in their little boats, fathers and children dead, adrift on the green sea. . . .

The Captain: Yes, it is like that. Might have been us instead. That's war, please Herakles.

Homer:	How many died?
The Captain:	A hundred, hundred and fifty maybe. Not so much, really.
Homer:	You gave them the rites?
The Captain:	Sure, we built a great pyre upon the promontory, tossed 'em all on, and offered up the prayers. ... [*He gets up, moves over near Homer, and his voice becomes serious suddenly.*] I wanted to see you, Homer. For you're the only one who can understand what this means.
Homer:	What does it mean?
The Captain:	Why, it's the biggest thing since Troy. Do you realize that today there's not a barbarian in Attica? From Eleusis to Marathon and from the crest of Parnes to Cape Sunium you'll not find a single bastard of them. Attica's ours! Pure Greek! Our land!
Homer:	[*slowly*] Yes, it was ordained like that.
The Captain:	You don't seem very pleased about it.
Homer:	Forgive me, 'tis your rôle.

Give me your hand, brother. The Captain comes over and shakes his hand like a pump-handle.

The Captain:	That's better, all Greeks together, eh? [*He picks up the auger which is lying there.*] What's this—a toy? [*The carpenter, standing by, makes dumb show of its use.*] By Zeus, I see—that's devilish ingenious. [*He starts to try the auger on the oak tree, gets stuck, and has to be helped out with it by the carpenter.*]
The Captain:	[*sitting down*] Gods' spears! if we'd had a few of those at Marathon we'd have shown them something. Under cover of dusk we could have crept to their boats, and in five minutes put half-a-dozen holes in them. They would have noticed nothing till they were out to sea—and that would have settled it.
Homer:	[*in horror, to himself*] O God, was it for this?

91

The Captain: [*noticing nothing, walks over and puts a hand across his shoulder confidentially*] Listen, Homer, why don't you invent such things for us? You're always turning out gadgets for folk in the village who'd get on just as well without them. There was that level with a bubble of air you thought up for Artimas the mason. And the spinningbobbin you made for the girls, and this auger here—and always you have some crazy story that 'twas the gods who showed you how. Of course I know you have to put it like that to keep your position with these dumbpates here. But you're a clever chap. What could you do for us? Now we could really use your help. At present we've just got the upper hand of all we meet. But it's damned hard work. If you could think of some way to cut down the weight of shield and keep the same protection, or lengthen the spear without spoiling the balance —why we'd run the country clear to Scythia. . . . Come, what do you say?

Homer: I cannot serve you. That is against the law. But what I give to others, that you'll soon take. And this I cannot stop.

The Captain: Well, I don't see why you're so standoffish. But maybe there's something in it. This auger now. . . . [*He picks it up again, and begins playing with it thoughtfully.*] If an arrow had such a twist. . . . [*There is a swirl of the crowd, and the captain disappears from sight as men and women surge in front of him. It is a kind of deputation.*]

The Village Elder: O wise Homer, let us weave the sacred carpet in celebration of this victory. Tell us how weave the Fates, and thus let us imitate them in the ritual. So will our good fortune be pleasant to the gods, and not draw Nemesis upon us.

Homer: It is well. Bring out the sacred loom, and I will tell you.

There is a great bustle of activity. For a moment the table is revealed, with the innkeeper pouring another cup for the captain

The Innkeeper: [*giving the inside story*] This is something new since you left. Homer's idea. You'll be surprised. . . .

92

Then the crowd swirls past again. From the left they are dragging on a huge vertical loom, built of wooden beams, on which half a great carpet with a strange pattern of circles and interweaving lines is already woven. The loom is set up in mid-stage, mats thrown down, and a dozen men take their places cross-legged before it, while the women bring out baskets of coloured wools and set heaps beside them. At either end of the loom is a man with a shuttle, and before it, in the centre, stands the master of the work, reading from a large parchment on which the whole scheme is drawn.

In a little, a quick gay music of pipes begins, and the weavers set to work. With each dip of the tune they pick up a loop of coloured wool upon their left, hook it into the warp, knot, and snip the end. When they have done this three times they beat the row down with a heavy brass comb, then run their fingers along to feel the evenness. When the row is finished, the tune changes, and the shuttle passes down the row from hand to hand, and back again. The music is quick, gay and intricate, weaving itself the pattern of the rug.

In the background, the teasers of wool have come out into the garden, and men are tending the vats of dye: others wash the yarn, girls spin, and even the soldiers are made to carry baskets or thrash the fleece. All is gay industrious and growing.

Homer: So I saw the pattern of our race . . . like a great carpet which the gods wove down the centuries. And each man and woman of the Greeks was a single knot therein, looped immovably within his place: the year, the city, fixed like warp and woof. And some were red like warriors, sailors blue perhaps, others white as priests, of many colours, grouped with their like and unlike in strange patterns that revealed themselves only as the ages passed. Pallas Athene, our godmother, knew this pattern well, and what it meant, and how 'twould be when finished. But we men knew it not, nor could know—for we are tightly fixed therein, and see no more than the nearest knots about us. Yet Greece is woven of us. and we in her, and shall forever be. And when the last row is finished by the Fates, all is not gone, as men believe— but revealed at last in all its form and beauty: and lies there, a delight and comfort

93

to the gods forever. For time is the warp, but the woof
eternity. . . .

*His words die away. The music gains strength, and the pattern of
movement grows and grows till the whole stage is a kaleidoscope of
sound and colour. At its height the curtain falls.*

ACT I SCENE THREE

A glade in the woods—Springtime. There are flowers in the grass, cherryblossom on the trees. At the rear centre of the stage is a kind of arbour, made by weaving the still-growing branches into three walls, a roof. In the arbour is a raised couch of woven branches, covered with straw, and lying on the couch—Hellas.

As the curtain rises, there enters from the left, hobbling upon a staff, the Old Woman with sticks of Scene 1. She hobbles, with the growing noises of age, to the arbour and the couch and clumsily falls on her knees, touching Hellas with her skinny hands.

Old Woman with sticks: Ah, mercy that I found you, dear. Heart gave me no peace these months, for the ill we did you. . . . All so alone, and alone . . . my, you're far gone, my darling. . . [*She is babbling.*]

Hellas: [*embracing her*] Oh, thank you for coming, granny. It's sweet to see another face. And very soon, very soon now I'll need you.

Old Woman with sticks: And what'll you be doing here—with no fire to warm you, no warm water to wash him, never a clean rag or wrap between you?

Hellas: It's a friendly place, safe—I love it now. There's a stream yonder, clean straw, and my cloak is warm enough for two.

Old Woman: [*bustling about gathering sticks together, to kindle a fire*] And were you not frightened, sweetling?

Hellas: More terrified than in all my life: more fearful than I thought one could be and still live. But it passed—and now I am not afraid.

Old Woman: What happened? Tell me.

Hellas: That day they stoned us. I knew I had to run away. Run from Homer even, to save Homer's babe.

Old Woman: And you came here—alone?

Hellas: Alone—something within me said, I must be weaned from weakness, to bear him strong. I must swallow fear, that he be born fearless.

Old Woman: Poor sweet!

Hellas: I brought a sack of beans, lived on berries, found wild honey. Heaven looked after me . . . heaven scared me too. . . .

[The old woman has a fire burning by the couch now, and is putting a pitcher of water to warm upon it.]

Now it is over I can speak about it, granny. Sometimes, those nights, as light died from the sky, and shapeless darkness crept from the rocks and trees, engulfing all in nothingness and night, fear would come upon me like a ravisher. All fears that ever were sprang from their lurking to possess me. Fear of robbers, demons. wild animals, wicked men; fear of every shadow, every branch that stirred; fear for my body, soul, fear for my mind and all the horrors lurking unknown therein; fear for Homer, for my babe, and every hurt that cruelty or wanton accident could bring them to. Sometimes I dared not stir for all the fears, like plague of spiders, that the movement of one muscle might release. Darkness was alive with them, and no grass moved but gave out terror. . . .

Old Woman: *[makes a sign against the evil eye, muttering]* Ay, 'tis strange what demons conjure 'gainst women in child-bearing.

Hellas: Do you know too? And that last hour 'fore dawn . . . when the moon's gone down, dew falls, and a terrible chill comes up from caverns beneath the earth. Then the hand of death seems laid on all the world. All's damp and darkness. One huddles within one's cloak. striving to fight off the dank of death, and cherish

within one's breast the last spark left from daylight.
That too was fearful, granny. . . .

Old Woman: [*soothing*] Ay, child, 'tis fearful . . . but 'tis over now.

Hellas: Yes, yes, 'tis over. And for ever. I thank the gods with
all my heart they sent great terrors on me, and alone.
For most men go through life the slaves of piddling
fears, small silly dreads of neighbour's tongue or their
own meanness being visible. They know not real fear,
but only fright of what fear might be; beset by crawling
terrors too mean to notice, too small and many for
mastering. So they go meanly fearful to the grave,
dreading the funeral more than death itself. . . .

*During these last speeches, the light in the wood has turned blue
and chill. But now it brightens again, the warm spring sunlight
reasserts itself.*

Old Woman: Tell how 'twas taken from you.

Hellas: One night when most was black, all on a sudden I felt:
'There's naught but this body and god— Apollo, light
himself'. Earth seemed to vanish, trees, people,
godlings even. Only my weak and tender body existed
in the universe, within it and without it light. . . . And
lo, there was no room for fear, no crack or cranny in
the universe where it could enter. For fear needs
darkness, and there was naught but light. . . . And in
that instant I felt the child stir within my womb, and
the babe too was light.

*The old woman with sticks comes to her, and begins caring for her,
smoothing her bed and covering, moistening her brow, combing her
hair, making her comfortable. As she does so a lark begins to sing in
the sky above the glade, high soaring trills that rise and hover, filling
the wood with joy. And after a little the lark-song takes on words.*

Lark-Song: The babe is light!
  The babe is light!
From realms of light
  To caverns warm,
Concealed from sight,

Remembering,
Remembering!

From thy retreat,
  From thy retreat,
So snug, so sweet,
  O babe, come forth!
The sunlight greet,
Remembering,
Remembering!

O babe of light,
  Concealed from sight,
Proclaim thy right!
  Come forth, come forth,
To find delight,
Remembering,
Remembering!

Hellas: *[as the song dies away]* How sweet the dawn after that night! What joyous birdsong as the last stars melted in the paling sky! Slowly the forms of living things emerged from darkness, took pale hues, the soft hints of colours. Low in the east the heavens began to glow, as Hermes rose to flee and announce the light. A hare started in the glade. Upon the mountaintops a pink wave broke, the valley still in shadow. At last upon the skyline, molten crescent shone; liquid fire burst upon the earth, o'erwhelming it with colour and with life. O what joy came with that sun! What happiness! The dew rose up to heaven, earth warmed, flowers opened, insects rose humming in the air, the young colts neighed and played for ever, upon the hill. All was joy and light. For fear was gone.

Lark-Song: The day has dawned,
  And night is scorned;
The earth adorned
  Awaits with joy
A babe newborn'd,
Remembering,
Remembering!

For light is here,
  Thy birth is near,
And banished fear
  With dark and night
Come, babe most dear,
Remembering,
Remembering!

Time, will and joy
  Make love's alloy,
The earth, gods' toy,
  Lacks but this thing—
Thy coming, boy,
Remembering,
Remembering!

Old Woman: [*bustling about Hellas*] Yes, 'tis the time and day for lambing. Last week my ewe bore four strong lambs at once: and gaffer's mare had a foal that galloped as he dropped. . . . Then the Captain's wife came down yesterday—sure soldiers waste no time, 'tis nine months to the day he came back from Marathon. A boy, ruddy, with freckles, it was, just like his dad. To-day she'll take him to the temple to be cleansed. . . . But you're shuddering!

Hellas: Quiet now, granny. My time is very near.

Old Woman: Hush then. Word spread you're here. Quite soon the boys and girls will come to bless you.

Hellas: [*cries out loud*] Sweet lord, my time has come!

Slowly from the left *enter ten young men, and from the right ten maidens, dressed simply in white tunics and loose trousers, bearing flowers. They close, facing the audience, to form a living screen before the arbour.*

A slow gracious music begins. Slowly and graciously develops the dance. Like young birches in the wind whiteclad dancers are bent by its rhythm to the right; they straighten, their arms like branches in the wind swing slowly over. They retreat; the rhythm bends them, slowly and graciously to the left, swings out their arms, makes them dip as they retreat and turn. They dip, dip to the very ground under the wind of the rhythm, turn, and advance again. Once more they are bent like birch trees to the right, and once more the wind of the music slowly sweeps their arms across.

The movement is slow, measured and gracious, the play of a strong silent wind among young bodies full of sap. Because the bodies are young and elastic they answer graciously the surge of the wind, and because they are young and full of sap the wind can possess them wholly and silently. For with all its silence and invisibility, the wind is strong and comes from far off, and there is no denying it.

So the white curtain bends, retreats, dips, billows and surges forward in the strong breath of the wind. There is nothing but the white motion and the slow swell of the music, which sweeps evenly back and forth, like a tide, irresistibly.

As the music dies away, the dancers slowly divide, parted by a last breeze to reveal the arbour. Utter silence falls. The earth is hushed.

For Hellas leans from the couch, holding a baby boy whose feet she lets touch the ground.

And the babe cries out.

In the same second, the dancers throw their flowers at his feet, lark-song soars up, the air is full of laughing and crying out, and nature stirs again - with happiness.

Hellas: A boy! He walks! The darling! What legs, what arms! A hero how he acts! Homer's son!

And in the same breath:

Lark-Song: O babe of light!
    O babe of light!
From realms of light
    Through caverns warm,
Into our sight,
Remembering,
Remembering!

From thy retreat,
    From thy retreat,
So snug, so sweet,

Into this earth,
Where all worlds meet,
Remembering,
Remembering!

O babe of light,
  Born from delight,
And heaven's might,
  Reveal to us,
What is thy right,
Remembering,
Remembering!

From the crowd detach themselves an old crone, a man in his prime, a young woman, and a youth, bearing gifts. They come forward, and kneel before the baby.

The Old Crone:	I bring thee earth, a platter of pottery. [*She places it before him.*]
The Young Woman:	I bring thee air, a breath of heaven's wind. [*She leans forward and breathes gently on the baby's brow.*]
The Man In His Prime:	I bring thee liquid, oil with hidden gold. [*He pours out a small jug of oil into the platter.*]
The Young Man:	I bring thee fire, to kindle and be consumed. [*With a pair of tongs, he places a red-hot coal upon the platter, beside the oil.*]
All four:	O babe, if holy breath thou use, To turn what moist and liquid is To fire, Then light will follow in thy train, Greece find her king, and thou thine own Desire.

The young woman bends over the platter, and blows upon the hot coal which, glowing white, kindles the oil, and this catching, transforms the whole into a dish of flame. The baby laughs and crows, warming himself. The four retreat into the crowd, and six others come forward, three men and three women, three from either side. They kneel too.

101

First Woman: I am a cook—my pot I give to thee. [*Gives it.*]

First Man: And I a minstrel—take my flute. [*Gives it.*]

Second Woman: I a shepherdess—all prospers 'neath my crook. [*Gives it.*]

Second Man: Thy friend's a soldier—make his sword thine own. [*Gives it.*]

Third Woman: A nurse am I—this vial will ease thy pain. [*Gives it.*]

Third Man: And I tell the stars—they're writ within this book. [*Gives it.*]

All six: The pot, the flute, the crook;
The sword, the vial, the book;
Master how and master why,
But first and foremost master 'I';
To rule thee wisely over men.
Master 'I' and master when.

The six melt back into the crowd, leaving their gifts. The baby laughs and crows over its new toys. But Hellas, gathering up the child, slowly rises from the couch and stands before them.

Hellas: Dear friends, I cannot thank you—for my heart is so full of joy that my voice breaks. In this day all is forgiven, all starts afresh.... [*The babe cries.*] And now I go to the temple to be cleansed with the babe. Let me be then, for it is the custom to go alone....

Slowly, carrying the babe, she walks off to the right, the crowd parting to let her pass, throwing flowers beneath her feet as she does so. The lark sings again:

Lark-Song: O babe of light!
  Born from delight,
And heaven's might,
  Reveal to us,
What is thy right,
Remembering,
Remembering!

When she has gone, the men and girls go off left, leaving the stage empty save for the Old Woman with sticks kneeling beside the couch. She is crying.

Old Woman with sticks: I see that the world of Pan is past—my childhood when elves came out of the earth to play with us. Then Pan possessed us, and blindly drunk we reeled and staggered, knowing not whether our bodies belonged to ourselves or the sprites that captured them. We lived in a kind of dream, innocent. There was no wrong, because we did not know ourselves, and could do no other than we did, like animals. How warm and easy was that world! Even dying was not difficult, for nothing was asked of us, but to sink back into the warm earth whence we came. . . . Now all is different— because of this babe men shall not sleep in peace; but toss and groan, feeling they should awake, and yet unable to. Something new came to our simple world, some new vision dawned. . . . And the brightness of that vision must blot the elves and naiads from our sight, poor shadowy beasties! So we'll be more lonely than before . . . more sad ... more thoughtful . . . more like the gods. . . .

She buries her head in the straw of the couch, and weeps, with the hoarse crackling sobs of age. Suddenly from the left, enters Homer. He feels his way with a big staff, yet agitatedly, in blind haste.

Homer: [*stops; in an urgent voice*] Is any here?

Old Woman with sticks: [*strangled*] Ay, granny's here. [*Homer feels his way forward, comes to the couch, touches it, seats himself at one end, as on a throne.*]

Homer: [*urgently*] I passed them on the way. They said Hellas was here, had borne a son. . . .

Old Woman with sticks: [*still kneeling by the other end of the couch, raises her head*] Ay, your Hellas bore your heir, 'tis right.

Homer: A son! . . . Then why's she not here? Where did she go—and why?

Old Woman with sticks:	From childbed she rose straight to bear your babe to the temple—to be cleansed as is the custom.
Homer:	Alone?
Old Woman with sticks:	Alone—so goes the Captain's wife today, also.
Homer:	[*softly*] I am afraid. I did not know. . . .
Old Woman with sticks:	[*half to herself*] I too am afraid . . . yet not for them, for us.
Homer:	Tell me. . . .

Suddenly, bursting down from the right, a shepherd breaks in, sweating, breathless, his clothes torn front rushing through the brambles.

The Shepherd:	[*breathless*] A terrible thing . . . terrible . . . from the top of my crag I see all down the valley. . . 'twas so clear one could see everything. . . .
Homer:	[*in a terrible voice*] What?
The Shepherd:	[*still panting*] Across the grassy hillside towards the temple . . . two women with babes were walking, innocent. . .so still it was, like a mirrored scene . . . they did not know. . . .
The Old Woman:	[*under her breath*] They did not know?
The Shepherd:	That's where the Captain's staked his range. . . to test out new weapons, so he says. He's got some twisted arrow that flies twice the old. . . .
Homer:	[*like a statue, very softly*] Well?
The Shepherd:	There was no warning. As the women walked, suddenly one fell—mother and babe transfixed. A stray arrow. There in the sunshine. . . . And the other walked on unknowing with her child. . . .

There is dead silence for a minute. Homer is frozen in his blindness on the couch, the Old Woman crouching on the ground. Then slowly he raises his head, half to heaven, half towards the audience, and in a terrible, tremendous voice, cries out with all his force, as though the shout were wrung from him:

Homer: O God, which? . . . which? . . .

[*Slow curtain*]

Act II Prologue

The *celestial amphitheatre. Again the divine dance in darkness, light growing, colour, music, interweaving figures, the interplay of the gods.*

But when the motion and brilliance is at its height, the rhythm most haunting, one feels that something has changed. Among the bright figures a kind of shadow moves. It is difficult to follow—a figure in black or grey which reflects no light, a kind of moving hole in the radiant pattern, which eclipses now one and now another of the angelic dancers. Somewhere behind the music is a strange elusive discord.

At a certain moment, as Hermes and Aphrodite approach the centre of the dance, the shadow moves between them and the onlooker. And in the same instant comes, like a crash of thunder, the tremendous voice:

T-i-i-ime, STOP!

The dance freezes—and the shadow is there, in the very centre of it.

Apollo: My shadow, with whom I eternally contend, it is thy hour! The pool of darkness seems to deepen, spread, while other darkness creeps in from the sides, from the front, down from the black night-sky. All is utterly still, and in the stillness the void seems to close in silently upon the shining circle.

The Shadow: [*deep and utterly flat*] And nothing shall move upon the face of the waters. I am that great nothing. Nothing I see, nothing I hear, nothing I know —for all that exists to me is nothing. Come to me, all who believe in nothing, for I will give you nothing. And wrap you in darkness and in silence as long as nothingness shall last. A heavy silence falls: the darkness deepens.

106

Apollo: Each being born of my bright children upon earth must one day look upon the face of nothingness— my child, my father, and my other self. This is their test. For till they can gaze on nothing unengulfed, they too are naught. Hermes and Aphrodite, let then thy son ascend!

Hermes and Aphrodite: Our most dear son! As the darkness gathers further, a dim light picks out a tiny human figure climbing up the steps from the front. It comes groping blindly, hands stretched before it in the gloom. Even as it comes, the shadow seems to grow before it, rising above the circle, growing, growing, until, with immense shadowy wings outspread, it hangs like a black cloud over the whole stage. Utter darkness.

The Shadow: Believe only in me, and I will believe in thee!

The Greek: [*cries out*] O woe, woe! I am utterly afraid. . . .

The Shadow: Dost thou believe in me?

The Greek: I do not know what to believe. All is taken from me. I am most terribly alone.

The Shadow: Wilt thou fear me?

The Greek: My blood is turned to water. I was afraid before—but this is different. In the darkness my heart is stolen from me, and even fear is but a shadow of itself. I vanish, disappear, my very senses are sucked out of me. I am afraid I am not. . . . Nothing . . . ah gods . . . nothing. . . .

The Shadow: Yes, thou shalt vanish. And I alone can save thee. Deny me, and thou shall be nothing. Accept me, and I will make thee everlasting as the rock.

The Greek: Ah god, what choice! Could I but see, but see! [*He tears wildly at his eyes, and falls sobbing on the ground.*] Nothing. . . nothing. . . .

The Shadow: Believe in nothing, and I'll make thee everlasting. I'll turn thee to crystal, and thou shalt outlive all living things, and never change—eternal as the earth. What dost thou say? Else must thou vanish.

The Greek: [*plunging blindly about the stage*] If I could see! My eyes are dead coals. Darkness, blackness. No form even. Nothing, nothing. If nothing exists, do I? If there's naught to perceive, what's this sweet body's use? If nothing made, then no creator.

The Shadow: If nothing exists, then thou art everything. Thou art alone in the universe. Thyself is god— the only god.

The Greek: No, no—somewhere there must be light. If not for me, yet somewhere. I may be dead, but not the gods. Not that, I could not bear it.

The Shadow: Think thou the void cares whether thou bear or not? Come, accept the void, and make thyself prince in darkness.

The Greek: I'd rather die. If in the living world is nothing, then let me die and find the gods in Hades. O let me die, let me but die. . . .

The Shadow: Do not blaspheme. Dare to live forever, dare to be crystallized. This is courage. Dare to believe in nothing, and nothing shall make thee everlasting and unique.

The Greek: No, no! [*cries out with all his force*] Dear gods. help me! Apollo, let me see thy glorious light again! Save me from darkness? Sweet Aphrodite, love me still! Hermes. my father, do not let me go! I love thee, I believe in thee. Save me from nothingness. . .

He throws himself upon the ground. And as he does so The shadow shrinks, the darkness recedes, the circle of gods begins to glow again, and the light of Apollo spreads till all the stage is filled with radiance once more.

Apollo: [*to Hermes and Aphrodite*] 'Tis well, thy son did not forsake thee.

The Greek: [*raising his head from the ground*] The light! . . the sun! . . .

Aphrodite: [*most gentle*] Dear son, behold that all grows, swells, blossoms, fruits. Unfolds in flowering lace, rainbow-hued, pregnant in curve, and so dies and is born again eternally—full of sap and sweetness. All this is I. Be comforted!

Hermes: Behold how fleet the motion of the stars, comets' and meteors' flight, the swoop of hawk and panther's leap, darting of thoughts which fly together in comprehension of the universe! All this is I. Be comforted!

The Greek: My father and my mother!

Apollo: But I will tell thee more. The fruit swells, falls and dies. The meteor's flight ends in disintegrated dust. Thoughts are forgotten as though they had never been. And thou, and all the crop of men, O Man, must wither equally. From this there's no redress—save one. To make thee a soul. For soul is a fragment of myself. From me must thou steal it, if thou canst.

The Greek turns beseechingly to Hermes and Aphrodite.

Apollo: In this, look not to them. Even my bright children too are transient. They'll cherish thy flesh and sinews. A soul is my gift alone.

The Greek: How to deserve it, O most mighty one?

Apollo: I told thee to wake thy fellow men. Thou triedst. In this thou shar'st my nature, who morn by morn shines down and wakes each man on earth anew. Continue so.

The Greek: I tried . . . and failed. Men laughed, or cried, or wondered and then forgot. And those that listened and began to stir—sometimes these made me feel most fearful of all.

Apollo: 'Tis right. There is a danger of which I did not speak. All men are transient, till a soul kindled from me is conceived in them. Then, like me, they begin to taste

109

Apollo... of immortality. But there's living immortality, and dead. Look yonder!

He gestures towards the night sky between the columns. And there, beyond the rim of the amphitheatre, strange frozen figures, glittering as though with moonlight, pass. A warrior, crouched, with lion pelt and mask across his face, sword set in frozen fury. Two lovers entwined, turned to statues as they melt upon each other. A jester, pointing in derision, the snarl of mockery fixed upon his face. And others. The silvery, half-transparent forms, glittering like glass, pass in an icy frieze against the cold blue sky.

Ares: Agamemnon was my son. Brave as a lion he fought— flashing sword, everdarting spear—dauntless against a score of men. Fought on when his flesh was torn and ragged with a hundred wounds; and by his very will and courage made him a soul to go on fighting with. Achieved immortality—but could not change his nature. And so fights on eternally, his soul in mid-thrust petrified for ever.

Aphrodite: Sappho my daughter. By loving she outgrew her body's self. Longed to have more to give her lover, and by giving gained it. Thus she too grew deathless. But deathless she could dream of nothing but more love. And so, embracing and embraced, her soul like a pretty ornament—turned all to glass.

Chronos: My son Epeias learned of me many things. He dreamed to tame the winds that work the universe, and turn the little windmills of men's minds. Tireless he studied, tireless observed, and came close to knowing. Voyaged the world of ideas till he found the idea of soul, and lived in that. Yet the more he learned, the more he laughed. All men seemed comic but himself. Their antics being the sport of gods, perceiving them he thought himself a god. And so the sea of eternity froze about his little bark, and froze his laugh with it.

The silvery figures move like dolls across the skyrim, and disappear.

The Greek: [*shivering*] They put a chill upon my blood!

Apollo: When they met my shadow, they did not wish to die. So my shadow, not I, gave them immortality.

The Greek: But if he is thy shadow. . . .

Apollo: He and I are one; yet woe to the mortal who takes one for other.

The Greek: What can be done for him?

Apollo: Wake him and remake him!

The Greek: HOW?

Apollo: Dismember and remember!

The Greek: And he?

Apollo: Must die and fly!

There is a sudden immense explosion of light, and all disappears.

Act II Scene One 399 B.C.

A sunlit open-air gymnasium in Athens. A courtyard, surrounded by a pillared colonnade, in which are vaulting-horses, parallel bars, trapezes, an occasional statue and stone seats. Beyond rises the Acropolis, stepped with arches, houses and temples to the white Parthenon against blue sky.

As the curtain rises, a band of twenty young men in white tunics begin to exercise to the music of three flutes and a drum. First they move their arms in a strange complicated order, all simultaneously; then their legs, then heads, then arms and legs; and finally their heads, arms and legs together. The exercise produces a strangely ungraceful, yet compelling impression, as of something unnatural performed by a great effort of will and attention.

In the foreground, on the step between the courtyard and the colonnade, two men are sitting, one squat, elderly, tough-looking, with an ugly yet attractive squashed face. The other is about thirty, tall, lithe, strangely reminiscent of the Homer of the first act.

Socrates: [calls out to one of those exercising] Apollodorus, less lusciousness, my boy. You'd stuff sausages as if you were making love. 'Tis an exercise for reason this.

He's calm and cool. The exercise continues, and no one flickers an eyelid to show that Apollodorus heard.

Socrates: [cries to another] But not a broomstick, Thoas. Your arms jerk like a puppeteer's doll. Reason's alive and elastic, boy. Court him nicely, then.

Thoas: [from the middle of the class, in a strangled voice] I'm trying, Socrates.

Socrates: [sharply] Don't try, but be! [Turns to Plato beside him.] You see, Plato, as babes all men receive from Heaven bodies of flesh. But in time they perform on

112

Socrates...   themselves a kind of transformation. So Thoas now has naught but a body of wood, and Apollodorus of melting candy. Some of the others I'm too delicate to speak about.

The exercise comes to an end, the music ceases, and the young-men break up. Some gather round Socrates and Plato, among them Thoas, an awkward stiff young man.

Socrates: [*to Thoas*] Did you ever know a woman, or a nice young boy, Thoas?

Thoas: [*overcome with embarrassment*] I . . . why . . I thought. . . .

Socrates: I knew it. You're drying up like a dead leaf, boy. When the last sap's dry, that's the end. Then they'll pound your dried-up soul, and sell the powder to scribes for blotting parchment.

Thoas: [*white*] Socrates, it isn't my fault. . . .

Socrates: We don't speak of fault. We speak of harmony, and lack of it. Do you believe your body to be harmonious?

Thoas: No, Socrates, it is not.

Socrates: Because your soul's not either. 'Tis dried up. This is the root of it.

Thoas: [*desperately*] I do my best.

Socrates: The best's not in you. Only god and harmony are best.

He gets up, and turns away as if disgusted, as he does so putting an arm about the shoulders of a plump handsome young man.

Socrates: [*gently*] And you, darling, have perfect harmony in your outward parts—'tis a pity there's nothing at all within!

The young man preens himself, obviously not finding this at all offensive. But as he turns aside, with his nose in the air, Socrates sticks out a foot, and he goes over it, head over heels.

Apollodorus: [*on the ground*] Damn!

113

Socrates: [*laughing like a schoolboy*] Where's your outward harmony now, my fake Apollo? You see, it only looks good right way up, like a bowl of porridge. If it came from within, you'd be as good a philosopher upside down or inside out.

He shoos them all out.

Socrates: Run along, my dears. That's enough for today. Be not proud; but bear me, and offend not others. [*The young men troop out, with cries of: Farewell, Socrates! Till to-morrow! Stay with the gods, master! Socrates and Plato are left alone in the empty gymnasium.*]

Plato: [*suddenly very serious and sincere*] Why do you torture young Thoas so?

Socrates: Softhearted one! He's hard as lava. We have to melt him down again, before he can grow a soul. Do you think that's done with sugared words? Suffering can melt, and for his own good I make him suffer.

Plato: Yes. I know your way. I know what's at stake. But are there no other means? It seems you drive too hard. He's desperate. The boy will do himself some harm.

Socrates: No man can grow a soul till he be desperate. Much more than Thoas.

Plato: That's for the strong. And what of the weak?

Socrates: Better they die trying to grow strong, than stew in their own weakness.

Plato: Yes, yes. but. . . . [*The words die on his lips.*]

Socrates: I never spared myself. In the army I outmarched any man: in midwinter I'd go barefoot on ice in a single shift. I do not say it to boast. But the good I gained from not sparing myself, showed me that the best service I can do others is not to spare them either.

Plato: You put me always in the wrong to argue with you, Socrates.

Socrates: Then leave it, my dear.

At this moment a cloaked figure hurries into the courtyard, throws off its covering, and reveals a middle-aged man, hot and breathless.

Crito:	Socrates, you must escape. . . immediately. . .
Socrates:	Escape from what? And whither?
Crito:	The council has given orders to take you. Tomorrow at dawn. I was at police headquarters about a slave that's lost, and heard them talking. . . . I think they let me hear, so I should warn you, and you escape, and they be saved the task. . . .
Socrates:	If it's their duty to take me, they must do so. What else?
Plato:	[*interrupting*] But what's it about? What charge?
Crito:	Corrupting Athenian youth, they say.
Plato:	It's so absurd . . . and yet. ... [*to Socrates*] You'll go?
Socrates:	Does a man leave his house when he hears that guests are coming? No, let's spend the night here, and talk, and drink a little, and so be ready for them in the morning.
Crito:	I beg you—leave now, while there's time. We'll be at Eleusis by dawn. They'd never take you there.
Socrates:	You forget yourself—and everything. Why is it the better course not to be taken? Maybe the good exactly lies in that.
Crito:	If not for yourself, for us. We need you. They want to frighten you, but if they don't succeed, I am afraid of what they'll do.
Socrates:	If you run from a fool, you convince him his foolishness is right. That's unkind to him.
Plato:	[*to Crito*] Tell us more of the charge.
Crito:	Well, it's been brewing long enough. You remember, in the old days before the Sicilian War—you were still a boy, Plato—the people and the council used to laugh at Socrates and his ways. They thought him a clown, nothing more. Though his tricks did get under some

folks' skin. Then when his friend Alcibiades began to go crazy, and there was that scandal about the burlesque of the mysteries, and A. skipped over to the Spartans, and all the rest of it, they began to put this down to the influence of Socrates. 'Destructive criticism', 'undermining morals', 'killing conscience', they used to say. And all those who had been riled by him were loudest. Finally, when Critias went the same way as Alcibiades, and he and his thirty butchered and assassinated left and right, using exactly the arguments about democracy and justice they learned from Socrates, this was too much. All those who lost wealth or relations in the troubles remembered all too well— and now they're ready. . . .

Socrates:	Well, what do you say, Plato?
Plato:	I do not know. . . . How can the teaching of wisdom leave this trail of evil and bloodshed?
Socrates:	The truth is a drastic medicine. Those who haven't good digestion it destroys.
Plato:	But before it does, they destroy thousands more.
Socrates:	Does not the sun wither as well as warm? What is already dry is burned, what moist, grows. This is the law of it.
Plato:	It sounds inevitable. . . and yet. . . .
Crito:	[*urgently*] Let's not discuss . . . come now, Socrates, I beg you. I've mules by the city gates. Let's stroll there now; wait in the park till night; and then away.
Socrates:	This is my city as well as theirs. If those less ignorant abandon it, it must get worse not better. Rather let's stay and try once more to show it reason.
Crito:	That's fatal.
Socrates:	Ill fate for body, good for soul maybe. No. I'll rest a little. Come back at midnight and we'll have a feast against tomorrow.

From higher up the Acropolis floats down the noise of a confused shouting. All this time it has been growing duskier in the courtyard, and now the glow of hidden flares begins to appear at various points upon the hill. There is a kind of muffled roar, and sometimes single voices are carried upon the rising wind:

Voices: Socrates the traitor!

Butcherboys' uncle!

He spat on the temple steps!

He's messing with our lads!

Bloody old devil!

To the cliff with him!

Socrates: [*flat and contemptuous*] The scum! [*His voice is so different—like a strange echo of the Shadow's—that Plato turns round startled.*]

Plato: [*involuntarily*] Who spoke?

Socrates: Nothing, my friend, nothing!

Plato: But. . . .

Socrates: Well?

Plato: Damn, let's go.

Socrates: I'll stay. Do thou go rest, and meet me here at midnight. Crito, bring wine. We'll have our best friends and dine together. The rest is nonsense.

The dark has leapt on apace, and now almost nothing can be seen in the gloom, but the silhouette of the Acropolis against the dark sky, and the glare of fires from there. The distant rumble mounts threateningly, drowns the Farewell! of Crito's and Plato's voices, and is all we hear as the dim figure of Socrates, sitting alone, is finally swallowed up in darkness.

ACT II SCENE TWO

L ater the same evening. A room in the house of Hellas, a hetaira —warm and welcoming, with torches burning softly against the walls, several low couches and tables, a brazier. The centre of the roof is open to the night sky, while to the left through a double row of columns, one looks down into a moonlit rose garden. On one of the couches lies Hellas, lazily plucking a guitar while a slave-girl in the shadows plays a harp.

Hellas: [*sings*]

My soul melts, when of my love I dream,
And flows to him for whom I long,
Leaving my body tenantless indeed
Empty vessel echoing empty song.
O wraith, return!
O wandering wraith, return!

Yet 'tis right that he my soul should snare,
Whose child it is, conceived in love,
For till it melted, I did not know 'twas there,
And till I lost it, I had none to lose.
O wraith, return!
O woeful wraith, return!

But now I've lost my soul, and know it gone,
And how it would be were it here.
O what great joy if I could call it back—
To give it once again unto my dear.
O wraith, return!
O tender wraith, return!

Her voice dies away, and she lays down the guitar. A man's figure comes up out of the garden, rather weary but as if coming home. It is

118

Plato. She turns her head towards him smiling, but does not rise. He throws himself down on the couch by her, kissing her hand.

Hellas: Darling!

Plato: It's soothing here—I'm a little weary.

Hellas: A cup of wine, some sweetmeats—I'll feed you, dear.

Plato: No, let me rest awhile.

Hellas: Lie still: I'll have my girls dance. They'll weave a spell upon you, and you'll sleep.

She claps her hands. The harp sounds again—a different melody, tender, haunting, reminiscent of some mood one cannot catch. As if from nowhere, half-a-dozen girls in loose white tunics and full trousers, with transparent white veils, are there in the flickering half-light of the torches, poised to begin. Liquid chords. And softly the dance unfolds— advancing, retreating, promising, withdrawing. It is very tender, very tragic, all the moods of a woman's life—dream, virginity, longing and fear, ecstasy, childbearing, motherhood, loss and loneliness—yet no more than an echo.

Plato: It is true, a spell of gentleness and sleep is woven over everything.

Hellas: You like them? They're from Lesbos.

Plato: It is beautiful, but I prefer you alone. [*Hellas claps her hands again, and the girls are gone.*

Hellas: There! as you wish! [*Plato kisses her gently. Then he draws back to his own couch soberly.*]

Plato: Tomorrow at dawn they take Socrates.

Hellas: At last! So long you feared it!

Plato: Yes, ever since I met him I knew it must be so.

Hellas: And can nothing be done?

Plato: I could, but he does not wish. Crito had good mules ready to take him by night to Eleusis. He would not go.

Hellas: What will you do?

Plato: Stay with him—what else?

Hellas:	I don't know . . . it's dangerous . . . I am afraid. . . .
Plato:	[*as if to himself*] It is strange. I feel some great drama in the making. And all the plots and betrayals are brewing, and one feels them brewing, and cannot lift a finger to prevent it. For what must be, must be. I am a man of water: if I had but to raise an arm to save him, I think I could not do it.
Hellas:	It is not like you, daring one.
Plato:	Not like. And the worst is that something in me says the mob is right. I hardly dare admit it to myself. They are blind, but they feel something that they hate, and would destroy it . . . the instruments of Nemesis. . . .
Hellas:	But you loved Socrates. . . .
Plato:	More than myself. He is the wisest Greek. Why criticise the lion when one bears with toads and wolves? Yet, being so wise, why's he not wiser? I'm full of joy to hear him, but saddened somehow.
Hellas:	What is it irks you?
Plato:	Always the indefinable. His logic's like crystal—gods' light shines through it. But sometimes he seems to use it like a small boy with a shiny potsherd, flashing sunlight into the passers' eyes.
Hellas:	'Tis very Greek.
Plato:	Exactly. But he should be more than Greek.
Hellas:	What more?
Plato:	Uncannily he knows each man's tender spot, and bears upon it till he writhes. I know the method of the school—and aim. I know 'tis to seek and overcome one's weakness with his help. And doing so gain what's far more precious than one's pain. Yet sometimes there seems more pain than necessary . . . . And tonight, coming here, I heard that Thoas fell on his own sword. . . .

120

Hellas:	[*really appalled*] Oh, horrible! How horrible! What do the others say?
Plato:	They say that Thoas was not strong enough, shouldn't have been there; that when the peasant thrashes, the grain comes clean, but the chaff's crushed.
Hellas:	[*shudders*] Ugh! 'Tis Spartan!
Plato:	Just so! We Athenians think the Spartans lacking in fineness, boorish, with a trained dog's courage. Their very virtues remind one of what's missing. And Socrates, because he has all the virtues of the Greeks, makes me seek a virtue the Greeks have not got. What's lacking in his philosophy? I can't define it.
Hellas:	[*suddenly moved, not listening to him*] I love you, Plato.
Plato:	[*slightly impatient*] Yes, but I'm thinking. . . . [*He pauses, then suddenly turns and looks at her.*] That's it! How strange!
Hellas:	What do you mean?
Plato:	He cannot love! The Greeks cannot love!
Hellas:	How?
Plato:	Once in Smyrna I saw a house afire, and a Jewish father rush in to rescue his little boy. He was weeping, crying, quite beside himself. Some Greeks were disgusted at his uncontrol. But he rushed in for love. And they could not have done so for philosophy.
Hellas:	They say love is not a manly sentiment.
Plato:	Yes, they do. Yet it made that Jewish father more than manly.
Hellas:	[*provocative, to see what he will say*] They say your Socrates loves young men.
Plato:	That too—the fashion of the Greeks! He plays the fashion shamelessly. But 'tis not love, for all they talk of it. And in old times 'twas called perversity.
Hellas:	[*still provocative*] Why not love?

121

Plato: There's something I half remember . . . but cannot quite. . . . Gods dancing . . . music of the spheres . . . Hermes and Aphrodite . . . and I . . . and you. . . .

Hellas: [*very moved*] Yes, go on. . . .

Plato: Long, long ago . . . or not yet come . . . and here . . . or somewhere else. . . . I can't remember. . . .

Hellas: A green hillside, bare under the sky beside an olive tree.

Plato: [*startled*] Why do you say that?

Hellas: I don't know . . . some dream . . . but what of love?

Plato: [*strangely, as though remembering a lesson*] The gods love because they seek perfection. From their love a new world is born. And the image of their love on earth is the love of men and women. Without knowledge of that image pursuit of the gods grows strangely hard and cold. . . . I can't express it. . . .

Hellas: And Socrates?

Plato: This Socrates does not know. Else he could not play with boys. Nor torture Thoas for wisdom's sake. Nor could his dear pupil Critias slaughter a thousand citizens in the name of order. Nor that other, Alcibiades, trick his way through life. All Greek virtues . . . lacking love.

Hellas: [*with passionate violence*] I hate your Socrates, hate him. I tell you, hate, hate, hate. . . .

Plato: [*staggered*] But Hellas. . . .

Hellas: I hate Socrates, and I hate all Greeks. They treat their wives as breed cows, make poems for boys, and amuse themselves with courtesans. And love's flown from all.

Plato: [*tenderly*] Yet I learned it from you. And you a courtesan.

Hellas: In this age, what else should I be? Once I was a shepherdess.

Plato:	[*intrigued*] You never told me.
Hellas:	[*absently*] Didn't I?
Plato:	[*suddenly feeling that she knows more than he does*] Hellas, what can I do?
Hellas:	Wake him and remake him.
Plato:	[*startled*] What did you say?
Hellas:	Dismember and remember.
Plato:	Where did I hear that? What does it mean? Socrates. . . .
Hellas:	[*coming across and kneeling by his couch, in a different voice*] About your Socrates a legend is being spun, a legend that will be stuff of the memory of Greece to all eternity. Yet there's still a drop of poison there. 'Tis this I cannot bear. That in his legend a drop of poison should eat away the hearts of men not born. My own sons perhaps. . . . I cannot bear it. . . .
Plato:	[*slowly, to himself*] Dismember and remember. . . . But what can I do? Socrates is as he is.
Hellas:	His legend will be what men believe of him. Socrates thought to make his companions souls. They too mould his.
Plato:	I do not understand.
Hellas:	There's a tale our ancestors would take common babes, and while the bone was tender, bind their heads to noble shape—which, later hardening, they became in fact. . . . Canst make your Socrates more noble than he is? Give him the shape he should have in posterity?
Plato:	[*shocked*] Lie, you mean?
Hellas:	[*turning the mood*] O dear silly simple man! Suddenly honest when he does not understand! As if he'd not lie anyway. Come, let Hellas teach thee to lie softly. . . . Lie well, lie still, then . . . lie with me, my dear. . . . *She takes his head in her arms. The curtain falls.*

Act II Scene Three

T he same gymnasium as in Scene I. Towards morning. Starry sky, faintly paler in the east. Torches burn low in their sconces, lighting a low banqueting table to the right, on which guttering candles flicker over dishes, bowls of fruit, orange-peel, scraps of food, cups and jars of wine. Half-a-dozen couches are set about the table, some dark with sleeping figures, while other figures lean on their elbows, and two or three sit up together on one couch arguing.

The central figure, on the other side of the table, half-facing the audience, is Socrates. He produces a strange impression—there is a sort of drunken abandon in him. He puts his arm in a maudlin way round Apollodorus beside him, or sticks his face close into the face of Plato on his other side; and yet beside him the others, for all their vivacity, look asleep. He is awake: he can do anything, because he knows what he is doing. There is something frightening about him.

Socrates: [*each arm about the others' shoulders*] Another hour to dawn! But whose dawn, that's the question. Mine certainly—but is it yours? [*He sticks his face searchingly first into Apollodorus' then into Plato's, as though to find an answer there.*]

Apollodorus: [*indistinctly*] Not mine, Socrates. I'm prac'lly 'sleep. Lemme lie down a li'l. Few hours' sleep, 'n I'll be fine. You look after dawn. Keep it warm for me. . . . *Socrates gives him a push, so that he collapses on to his couch and in the same instant falls asleep.*

Socrates: [*to Crito opposite*] And you?

Crito: I'll share it with thee, master.

Socrates: Pah, pretty words! Have you the price of entrance. . . Have you?

He turns and suddenly glares into Plato's eyes. A strange spasm—of distaste, longing, determination— passes over the latter's face.

Plato: [*rather coldly*] We'll see when it comes.

Socrates laughs, whether ironically or with affection is difficult to say. Then pours out more wine into the cups near him, and thrusting them into the hands of all who are able to hold them, lifts his own in a sort of toast.

Socrates: [*in half-drunken, half-nonsensical recitative*] The dawn, the dawn! The heavenly lawn, The lawn on which the sheep are shorn, And born to morn, Or torn from dawn, To mourn and mourn and mourn and mourn. . .

Figure: [*Some figure in the darkness begins clapping.*] The dawn! The dawn!

Socrates: Idiot, 'tis the sparks before thy eyes where a winejar fell on thee!

He suddenly rises, and for a moment seems to loom above them all. Then he moves round the table, pushing, kicking, dragging up the lazy figures.

Socrates: [*shouts*] Up, up! Show me what you'd do to the dances now! Have you won souls to move these drunken bodies, or were the puling nurselings dissolved in alcohol? Come, up! Rouse up!

He goes round, cracking heads, smacking bottoms, whacking the dark figures with his knobbly staff. There are cries of protest, and yelps of those suddenly woken from sleep by a painful blow. But all do try to stagger to their feet, some steadier than others.

Socrates: The polyrhythm!

A flute begins to play, and the six in rough formation try to do a strange dance or exercise to its music. This consists first of a series of rhythmic movements with the legs, backwards, forwards, sideways, then skipping, in changing time. Then the music changes a little, and they add another series of movements with one arm, also changing, but in contradictory time to the first: then a further series with the other arm, again in opposing rhythm. At the best of times the exercise would be almost impossibly difficult. Now it produces a most extraordinary impression —the lurching of tipsy bodies, combined with an almost superhuman effort of attention to make these bodies do this intricate series of movements against their very nature. Several miss the time, become confused, and find it again. Two figures sway together, get thrown off balance, and tumble in a heap. Socrates kicks them.

Socrates: Spineless worms!

But the others struggle on; and with another change in the music, add yet another rhythm—of the head—in yet another time. Each figure is now like some strange clockwork monster in which many different motions, working at different speeds, stop, start, and overlap. But no sooner is the fast motion mastered, than they begin to call out the letters of the alphabet in time to the different motions. All are making a tremendous effort to master their machines. There is an almost unbearable sense of strain. Another becomes confused, misses his step, and falls.

Socrates: Enough!

And as the others cease, he does the exercise himself, in its entirety, perfectly, harmoniously, effortlessly—a man who knows every part and member of his body, and it obeys him. Then they fall back to their couches round the table, with Socrates among them. He fills his cup again, and leaning over the still sleeping Apollodorus, pours it in his ear. Then, rocking with laughter as Apollodorus starts up spluttering, throws his arm about him.

Socrates: How much longer till dawn? How much longer till these damned dunces of the council come?

It is in fact much lighter, and only a few of the brighter stars now shine in the western sky. The torches blaze very yellow in the twilight. Plato has drawn away from the drunken group, but Socrates sees and rivets him with his gaze. Plato returns it.

Socrates: [leaning across the table with drunken concentration] Well, scribe, forget not to write it well. Make us all heroic figures, with a few touches of modest valour for yourself.

Plato: 'Tis right. I'll try.

Now Socrates and Plato are sitting across from each other on the stage, Socrates among the sprawling party at the table, Plato—wax tablet and style upon his knee—on a stool set against a column opposite. His eyes still meeting the gaze of Socrates, Plato's hand begins to write. And as he writes, slowly a change begins to come across the scene. Slowly Socrates raises himself, straightens, stands up beyond the table, the look of intense awareness not weakening, but, as it were, becoming purified as he does so. A kind of coolness and sweetness seems to flow into him, and as his figure stands erect, a new nobility fills it. The others too, like men waking from a dream, shift slowly into positions of grace and dignity, listening.

Something has happened to the scene also. A haziness passes over it; the table is now bare and rude, the couches are revealed as plain wooden benches, the statues disappear, and in the light of dawn we see that it is in reality a prisonyard in which the group is gathered.

As the figures stay motionless in the pale light, a coarse squat man with a red face, bristle black hair, and a bunch of huge keys at his leather belt, enters from the right, and walks across in a business-like way to the table.

The Jailer: [*professionally cheerful*] Morning, gents, morning everybody. Good news for Mr. Socrates, this fine morning. We'll have that chain off in a jiffy. By order of the Council. Of course, everything sweet has a sting in the tail—as the man said when he sat on a bee while stealing honey. But that's another question.

Crito: Friend, what is the sting?

The Jailer: Well, I wasn't to say really. They . . . well . . . the Council . . . that is . . . begging your pardon, gentlemen, but Mr. Socrates has to drink the poison today at sunset, Athens time.

There is complete silence. The jailer goes behind the table, and ducking down beside Socrates with a clanking of keys, rises in a moment triumphantly holding out a chain.

The Jailer: We're short of good chains like that, believe it or not. Such cheap locks they put now, you'd hardly credit. [*He walks away.*]

127

Socrates: [*still standing, still looking at Plato, with great nobility and humour*] How strange the thing called pleasure, and how close to pain—as now I know, when after the chain's ache, my leg feels downright pleasant.

The jailer turns at the door, his chin unexpectedly shaking.

The Jailer: You wouldn't be angry with me, Mr. Socrates? Would you. sir? Some of them get angry with me —though it isn't me that gives the orders. But you wouldn't, not you, sir—the best and most decent gentleman as ever stayed here. Well, good luck, sir. Good luck —and . . . and take it easy now.

He suddenly bursts into tears, and goes out. Still looking at Plato, Socrates slowly seats himself. A faint haze passes over the scene again. It is now full light. Plato still returns his gaze, but now his hand is writing.

Socrates: [*with quiet nobility*] There is a doctrine whispered in secret that man is a prisoner who has no right to open the door and run away.

Cebes: [*pleading*] Then why so anxious to leave, Socrates, leave us and the service of the gods here on earth? Does it not grieve thee?

Socrates: Grieved would I be to go indeed, were I not sure that I go to other gods who are wise and good, and to men departed, better than those I leave behind.

Cebes: Will you not leave your thoughts with those you leave?

Socrates: I'll try . . . what is it, Crito?

Crito: The Jailer says you're not to talk too much. It hinders the poison, makes one dose not enough.

Socrates: [*gently*] What a nice man! But let him mind his business . . . and make three at least.

Again a haze passes over the scene. When it clears it is midday, the sun high and bright, the shadows short. Socrates talks across the table to the others—but also beyond, as if to Plato, who still watches him and writes. The conversation is extraordinary easy, intimate.

Socrates:	The state of sleep is opposed to the state of waking. Out of sleep, waking is born; and out of waking, sleep. And the process of birth in the one case is falling asleep, and in the other waking up. Do you agree?
Cebes:	[*sitting opposite, in line between Socrates and Plato*] Certainly, I agree.
Socrates:	Then take life and death in the same way. Is not death opposed to life?
Cebes:	Yes.
Socrates:	And they are born one from the other?
Cebes:	Yes.
Socrates:	What is born from the living?
Cebes:	The dead.
Socrates:	And from the dead?
Cebes:	I can only say—the living.
Socrates:	Then the living—people and things—are born from the dead?
Cebes:	It's clear.
Socrates:	And one of these processes is visible—for surely the act of dying is visible?
Cebes:	Surely.
Socrates:	Then are we going to leave out the opposite process? Can nature walk only on one leg? Will not death have some corresponding birth?
Cebes:	Certainly.
Socrates:	And what is that process?
Cebes:	Return to life.
Socrates:	And return to life if there is such a thing, is the birth of the dead into the world of the living?
Cebes:	It looks like that.

Once more the haze draws across the stage, and once more clears again. Now it is afternoon, the shadows longer, the fight is softer and less fierce. All still sit as before.

Socrates: You and all men will depart some time or other. 'Me already the voice of fate doth call,' as the secondclass poets put it. Soon I must drink the poison. But first I'd better bathe, to save the women some washing afterwards.

Crito: Have you any orders for us, Socrates? We'll vow anything you wish.

Socrates: Nothing special, Crito. Only watch yourselves, as I always said. For so you'll help me and my work and all of us, whether you vow or no. And if you don't, all your promises won't help.

Crito: We'll do our best, Socrates. And how shall we bury you?

Socrates: [*laughing*] Anyhow you like . . . but you must catch me first. . .

Again the haze falls and is withdrawn, and it is evening - shortly before sunset. Enter the Jailer, still rather shaken. He is carrying a cup. Very gravely Socrates rises and slowly walks across to meet him.

Socrates: Well, my old friend. You have experience in these matters. You must tell me what I have to do.

The Jailer: It's like this, sir. Take it in one swig—like beer. Then you just keep walking up and down, until your legs feel heavy. Like after eating too many oysters. Then you lie down, comfortable. And it just works very easy, very simple. Nothing nasty about it nowadays.

He holds out the cup. which Socrates takes, with a little bow.

Socrates: [*making to spill a little on the ground*] What do you say about a libation to some god? Would it be right, or not?

The Jailer: [*doubtful*] Well, we only make just enough, Mr. Socrates—you see, it's rationed. sir.

Socrates: I understand: in that case I must ask the gods to give me pleasant journey—without payment. Thus. . .

Looking out at the audience, he quietly and cheerfully raises the cup to his lips, and, his eyes unblinkingly upon them, drains it. Those about the table turn away, some brushing their eyes, others weeping openly, one or two watching white-faced. Apollodorus suddenly cries out, a terrible heartbroken wail.

Socrates: What's that strange outcry? Did I not send the women away, that a man might die in peace? Quiet then, and patience.

He walks up and down a little, looking enquiringly at the jailer, who begins to sniff again. Then, very slowly and with dignity, he lies down at full length upon the bare table, the others remaining seated about it.

The Jailer: [*feeling his legs in a professional way*] Begging your pardon, do you feel that, sir?

Socrates: No, I cannot say I do. A little pause.

The Jailer: [*feeling higher up*] Nor there either?

Socrates: No. . . . [*He feels himself in the upper leg, and groin; and adds, half-apologetically*] When the poison reaches the heart, that's the end.

He looks round at them very sweetly, and then with deliberation, draws the sheet up over his face and head. There is a half-minute of complete silence and stillness. Then he carefully draws down the sheet, and turning his head towards Crito and towards Plato, who still sits beyond:

Socrates: Crito, I owe a cock to Asclepius: will you remember to pay the debt? Then quietly he draws the sheet over his head again.

Crito: The debt shall be paid, master. Is there anything else?

But there is no answer. The figures about the sheeted body grow as still as it. Slowly the light fades—the last glow lingering upon Plato, who still sits motionless, his style listless in his lap. He is weeping. The curtain falls.

Act III Prologue

The amphitheatre of heaven. The planetary gods in a semi-circle on the flight of stairs, their folded wings rising against the starry sky beyond. A silver radiance picks them from the dusk. At the highest point, Apollo shines golden and alone. All is immense, radiant and still.

Below, in the forefront of the stage, one small dark prostrate figure.

Apollo: [*in a voice which vibrates through heaven*] Greek, thou shalt learn of time. For time is the greatest mystery, containing all other mysteries. Men—like eyeless fish—swim in the deeps of time. The gods—like dolphins at play upon your winedark sea—bask in and out at once, gambolling 'twixt time and the sunlight of eternity. Wholly beyond time only the Nameless dwells.

The Greek: [*still prostrate*] I am but man, my lord.

Apollo: Emerging from time, men grow like gods.

The Greek: Show me, my lord.

Apollo: Behold the first secret—there are many times.

A strange melody begins to play, which contains within it many different rhythms— a slow bass beat, which reverberates through the floor of heaven; another, its octave echo, vibrating on another level; and yet another, and another, and many others, quicker and quicker, higher and higher—one within the other—a counterpoint of times.

Suddenly the gods raise their right arms before them, as though to evoke life from the void. A pause. Stillness. Then left arms, summoning, are raised—and in the same instant their right arms outstretched begin to tap, in quick oscillation, the heartbeat of animals and things. The two times interweave. Another beat, and

132

heads too turn right, then left, commanding east and west. And the three times interpenetrate, beat together, like the complete ticking of a clock.

Till suddenly, at the deep slowest beat of time, all the gods leap to life. Their feet, planted apart, shake the very earth as they descend. The melody repeats. Again the great chord, the feet of the gods change place, earth rocks, and all begins anew.

Then, as though to evoke from the still vibrating earth some new form of life, left arms rise once more. And now, in quicker time, heads turn right, then left, to summon east and west; and quicker again, right arms tap the heartbeat of animals and things. And once more the thunder.

So that, from the very gods themselves, from their feet, arms, heads and hands, many motions, many speeds and rhythms are imparted to the quarters of the universe. And all is governed as by some immense and cosmic metronome.

And with each successive thunder of their feet, the gods cry out in turn:

Chronos: The time of my footstep an epoch:

Hera: The time of my glance an age:

Hermes: The time of my bidding a lifetime:

Ares: The time of my pulse one page.

Aphrodite: The time of my breath germination:

Selene: The time of my motion a tide:

Apollo: [*motionless*] The time of my love transformation, Where now has forever inside.

Suddenly the gods cease their rhythms, shaking one arm up and the other down, as though to scatter their creative force above and below. Then they drop to their knees, and with their left arms bent to one side, revolve their outstretched right arms in wide circles, alternately gazing at the audience and away. It is the same combination of many times in another manifestation. But the circling arms are strangely reminiscent of the turning of planets in their orbits, and the changing regard of some cosmic alternation of day and night.

While with each greater chord, the gods again cry out, but in different tone:

Selene: I revolve—the egg has changed to worm:

Hermes: I spin—and movement starts to rule:

Aphrodite: I gently shine—the child breathes, is born:

Ares: My course complete—he's passion's fool:

Hera: Slowly I turn—the human being mates:

Chronos: With my full circle; half his life is o'er: He weeps, and fearful prays the Fates . . .

Apollo: [*motionless*] Until I swallow him once more.

The kneeling gods also fall motionless, their arms crossed upon their breasts.

The Greek: [*still prostrate, with reverence and longing*] Swallow me, swallow me utterly, my lord.

Apollo: All men but one or two beg that I eat them not. Thou dost better. For when a man prays with his whole heart for what must be, then what must be is not what he fears.

The Greek: Devour me and show me, lord.

Apollo: Since thou beg the first, the second lies open to thee. Behold the second secret! Time is change: change return: and return the way out from time.

Now the six gods and goddesses are standing. Immobility and silence lie upon them, and they are clothed in dusk. Behind, Apollo burns.

A rose glow falls upon the first. Very slowly Selene steps forward, and rocks, as if some strange rhythm possesses her, hand high and pointing to some unknown aim. A rhythm goes by; and the same motion passes with its glow to the next in line—while Selene stands still, one arm held high, intently listening. Another rhythm, and the pointing gesture passes to the third, listening to the second, and a new gesture, green-glowing, clothes Selene. So the intricate figures pass from god to goddess. goddess to god, until the whole line is in separate motion—vari-coloured, yet with one rhythm, one rock and dip, as though some sea-swell animates them all.

And now it is seen that the gods are but instruments of the moods, colours, symbols that pass through them: that a whole pattern moves together, its figures rippling from end to end, like light upon dancing waters and that these figures go in pairs, coupling now these, now those of the gods in combination. But all changes, all moves, all shifts, and all remains the same. Each gesture passes, to return elsewhere; vanishes into nothing, to be reborn at the beginning.

Apollo: Look, then, how the harmony of heaven brings all things to all men. And takes all away again. Be brave, and look: for thou hast said the word that can unlock the universe.

Very slowly, the Greek raises himself from his prostration, shielding his eyes, and then kneeling, he slowly draws away his hands.

The Greek: [*awed*] I behold, and it is wonderful!

The dance continues, the gestures, figures, colours, passing from god to god, from place to place, till all glitters and shines with magical illusion. Then, almost unnoticeably, Selene falls still, and the last light dies from her. And her companion next; and is enveloped too in dusk. And so, as at the beginning motion and light entered the quiet line, so now they retreat from it, and dusk and silence recapture one by one the gods.

Apollo: So time brings all. Light and dark, youth and age, all colours, forms, influences, music, and all history—of worlds and men. Time brings the very marriage of the gods, brings offspring to them, then dissolves their bond, and brings other unions, pregnant with other possibilities. Of one such conjunction, thou and thy race were born. Were born in time—gods' time indeed—yet being in time, already the sands run low for thee and thine. Thy task achieved or not achieved, a greater presses.

The Greek: Tell me, my lord.

135

Apollo: Time brings all. Life, death—and even miracles. This is the greatest mystery, most difficult to fathom —most marvellous and terrible both for gods and men.

The Greek: If I should be destroyed, still tell me, lord.

Apollo: I will tell thee. Beyond time, where alone exists the Nameless, all is miracle—wholly and forever miracle. Time, like a moving curtain, hides miracle from men—lest they be destroyed before they long for it. But time's not seamless. And from age to distant age, when the cycles which thou hast seen pause in their perpetuity, a crack may appear in time. Its very motion brings the fault within its fabric. And through this fault divine, this chink, the eternal miracle shines through to men, descends to earth—infinity incarnate, eternity in time.

As Apollo speaks, all the light on the stage is gathered into him; the rest fades into dusk, into darkness, from which the voices of the gods soar suddenly, in paean on paean, each mounting above the last, higher and higher, in one great fountain of rejoicing.

> Rejoice for a fault in time!
> Rejoice that men now may climb!
> Rejoice that hell's pains can end!
> Rejoice that the gods descend!
> Rejoice that by Nameless grace
> God yet may show his face,
> And through a fault in time
> The light divine
> May shine
> Shine . . .
> Shine . . .
> Shine . . .
> Shine . . .

Each repetition is taken up by another voice, higher and more soaring than the last. And with each, the light on Apollo seems to gather brilliance, grow more dazzling, till nothing else is visible, and of him naught but light itself. Slowly this radiant Apollo comes forward. The prostrate figure of the Greek, caught in his flame, seems

136

suddenly to catch fire and vanish. And still he advances, to the height of the front steps, every second growing in glory, until as he dazzlingly descends . . . . the curtain falls.

Act III Scene One A.D. 33

On board an *Egyptian ship off the Greek coast. In the foreground is the main deck. On the left the stairs up to the forecastle, on the right the main mast and mast-works. Beyond the rail can be seen a shining expanse of sea, and in the distance the rocky shoreline of Corfu, honeycoloured in the sun, with here and there a green valley coming down to the sea. Over everything lies the stillness of noon.*

By the mast, in the shadow of the soil, a man is sitting on a coil of rope. He bears a strange resemblance to the Homer and Plato of the previous acts, but is older—about 40—bearded and in the prime of life. Close by him squats a sailor, splicing rope. Up in the forecastle, to the right, very much in the background, and hardly noticeable at first, is an old Hindu fakir, crosslegged on his mat, one arm upraised and the other outstretched—completely motionless.

Apollonius of Tyana:	[*looking out towards the shore, half to himself*] How strange! This was the very place. Thirty-three years ago. And the ship, the sea, the sky, the shore —all exactly as it was!
The Old Sailor:	Thirty-three years! Isis, some water's flowed down the Nile since then. That time I was working a dirty dhow with goatskins. The Roman census lads came on at Alexandria, but they couldn't stand the stink, so I never got counted. . . . What made you think of it?
Apollonius:	I was a boy, sailing back from Rome to Athens with my parents. All was wonderful—as it sometimes is in childhood. Early morning. The sunshine, sea, creaking of ropes, the voyage, the unknown future—I stood alone on the deck, drunk with it all, and looked out to just that shore. Then suddenly—I can't describe it — time seemed to stop. Utter stillness fell, and swallowed us. All motion died in air and sea. Earth seemed

138

Apollonius... turned to glass, and my heart with it. How long it lasted, I could never tell. Then—in the stillness—rose from the shore an immense and timeless moan. Such sadness, as though nature's heart would break. And from the land of Greece came tens of thousands of faint voices—water and wood spirits, animals, it seemed, godlings and sylphs—like a great mist of wailing. One could not bear the sadness of it. For like a single voice, 'Pan is dead!' they cried. And again, 'Great Pan is dead!'—till I longed to throw myself into the sea for very sorrow.

The Old Sailor: Ay, I heard the story. One Greek chap I knew was on a boat what heard it, and several did chuck themselves over like crazy, so he said. Luckily he was tight, and could hardly stand, so he just sat and stuffed his ears. Turned him fair inside out, he claimed. 'Great Pan is dead!' [*He shivers.*]

Apollonius: Yes, only a Greek could understand, I think. 'Twas as though you heard your motherland die beneath your feet. And I—who was born in Cappadocia and reared in Rome—knew in every nerve that I was Greek and always would be, and that in that day some incalculable sorrow came to me. Afterwards I said, like all the rest, 'Why, Pan is superstition, a pious story, no one believes in him nowadays'. And later I said, too, that Pan—if there was a Pan—was god of the age 'fore ours, god of pre-Homeric Greece, and all the rest. It did not help. Something had been taken from us Greeks, something had gone forever.

The Old Sailor: And that was all to it?

Apollonius: No—as the wailing died, I heard, high and far off, a choir of different voices. But as the others seemed to rise from earth, these spun down from heaven, high and thin and clear as bells across the sea. Almost inaudible. 'To us this day a child is born,' they sang. But so far off they could not touch me or my sorrow. As

Apollonius: ... though, one"s own wife dead, one heard a wedding song across the fields. . . . All this I remember as though it were yesterday.

As he has been speaking a young woman has entered from the right, and paused behind the mast, listening, without his being aware of her presence.

The Old Sailor: What's your business now?

Apollonius: [*with changed voice, very matter-of-fact*] I trade in wisdom, buying some here, selling at profit there.

The Old Sailor: Who sells?

Apollonius: A few old men—one in Baghdad, another in Alexandria. It's a small business, but worldwide.

The Old Sailor: Who buys?

Apollonius: A few who are tired of cheaper wares. A Roman circus owner, grown tired of circuses: an Egyptian scientist who finds science dull—and so on.

The Old Sailor: And it pays?

Apollonius: Too soon to say—one has to pay in advance, then give long credit. We'll see.

The Old Sailor: Sounds worse than goatskins—they charge spot cash upstream, then the leather sellers down in the city won't pay till it's made up in saddles and sold again. No profit in that—so I quit. What d'you expect?

Apollonius: Ah, that's the devil of it. One can buy the theory of the universe, the explanation of everything—and sell it, too. And that's the best business that there is so far. Certainly it changes men. Much falls away. They see bigger worlds, invent, discover—yet something's missing. And since that day that Pan died, I cannot find it. As though all's stuck, waiting for something. . .

Hellas: [*quietly, from behind him*] Will you teach me?

Apollonius: [*turning sharply*] You! . . . [*But almost in the same moment it occurs to him that he does not know her after all. He stops, puzzled.*] I'm sorry. I thought. . . .

Hellas: [*coming forward*] When I heard you speak of that day, I felt I had been asleep for thirty years, and had not known it. For an instant I seemed to remember some time before . . . Pan still alive, and I. . . .

Apollonius: But who are you?

Hellas: Hellas my parents named me. Some call me Maria— that's Roman fashion.

Apollonius: You've been in Rome?

Hellas: Like every other Greek. I gave music lessons, taught singing and dancing there—and heard your reputation.

Apollonius: You know me?

Hellas: Stories only. The Sphinx, they call you.

Apollonius: Seven years I spent under the Pythagorean vow of silence. And speechless, began to see.

Hellas: Magician, wizard, too.

Apollonius: [*wryly, with a touch of sadness*] 'Tis they who long to mystify, not I. With every image, every sound and smell and sight, a drop of divine energy enters us. Ordinary men, in talk and careless action, spill out these drops again as soon as they're received. In care and silence they accumulate—giving the power to withstand what's mechanical. This is your wizardry.

Hellas: And what did you see in silence?

Apollonius: [*suddenly speaking to her, as he has spoken to no one else*] Many things. But chiefly this, that Greece droops, like a girl grown listless, awaiting too long her lover. She goes about her tasks, does what she must—but with neither heart nor knowledge in it all. Everywhere offerings are made, statues carved—by habit: the temples tended—but none remembers why. . . .

Hellas: [*slowly*] Yes. this listlessness I know . . . but how to escape it I know not. . . .

Apollonius: Nor I yet. And not to know sends me demondriven, from city to city, land to land. looking for something. . . .

Hellas: And what do you find?

Apollonius: Everything and nothing. In Egypt, Persia, everywhere I see wisdom buried. Great wisdom. Like coal beneath the ground. But how to fire it and kindle Greece. I do not see.

Hellas: Why look abroad?

Apollonius: How to say? The lover comes, and the listless girl awakes. Some new force must come from another land, another line, to wake Greece from her sleep. The fire of another life, not hers, must rouse her. . . .

Hellas: [*deeply strangely*] Yes, so it is. For it seems to me I've been sleeping too, as my homeland has. I thought to go back. But perhaps I too must go beyond, to seek. And later return perhaps . . . and we wake together.

The Old Sailor: [*absently*] When I ferried those goatskins down the Nile, we used to pass a kind of lion with a woman's face, all made of rock. Big as a mountain. The people there say she's been sleeping for five thousand years. . . .

Hellas: Five thousand years! [*shivers*] It's cold suddenly. . . .

The Old Sailor: Ay, they say she'll not wake till the sun himself comes down from heaven. . . .

Apollonius: [*reverently*] Phoebus Apollo. . . .

The Hindu Fakir: [*as though part of some continuous prayer grew audible*] . . . Om Brahma Om. . . .

The Old Sailor: [*catching sight of him*] Ra save us!

As this goes on, a strange change has been taking place in the light. The whole sky above the shore has been growing darker and darker blue, almost indigo, while at the same time the vertical light shining down on the boat has been growing brighter and brighter and more blinding. The three men look up one by one, Apollonius in longing, the Hindu Fakir slowly and deliberately as though he already knows what he will see, the Old Sailor suddenly startled out of his wits. Hellas sinks on her knees and hides her face.

Gradually, the same ringing that was heard in the first prologue begins to sound, at first very faint and distant, then as if filling more and more of the air, louder and louder, wider and wider, till one feels something must burst within one's very head. Now the sky is almost black, the boat as if white-hot. The ringing grows unbearable—and splits in a single thunderclap.

In the same blinding instant, the incandescent disk of the sun shoots vertically down the black distant sky and vanishes below the horizon, plunging all in darkness.

There is utter silence, save for infinitely faint voices, an echo of an echo, endlessly far away:

> The King of the Jews!
> Crucify him! Crucify him!
> Verily this man is the Son of God!
> This day shall ye be with me in paradise!

Then utter silence and blackness for a whole minute. And as suddenly and terribly as before, the blazing sun shoots vertically up through the black sky, filling the boat with the same lurid glare.

The three men are revealed prostrate, their faces on the deck, their arms in horror or adoration above their heads. And the air is full of innumerable voices, above, below, near, far, in all the heights of heaven, crying:

> Risen! Risen! Risen! Risen! Born! Born!
> Born! Born! Saved! Saved! Saved! Saved!
> Risen! Born! Risen! Born! Risen! Saved!
> Risen! Saved! Risen and born and saved and risen!
> Risen and born and saved and risen!
> Risen and born and saved and risen!

143

Endlessly, as the curtain falls upon the motionless boat and the motionless figures bathed in light.

ACT III SCENE TWO

A year later. The throne-room of some eastern caliph. Slender columns, arches and niches rising to a gilt and fretted dome. Gorgeous curtains of velvet and damask to break the light, deep carpets of silk upon the floor; and in the rear centre of the hall marble steps mounting to a golden throne, beyond which can be seen—most delicately framed—a pleasure-garden with cedars, orange and lemon trees, and a fountain sparkling in the sun.

The room is thronged with men magnificently dressed— some in long Persian gowns, others in dragon-painted mandarin robes, yet others sashed, trousered and with jewelled turbans on. Ambassadors, ministers, generals, councillors move gravely amid the crowd of slaves wielding fans, of soldiers with scimitars drawn before their bearded faces, of huddling and hopeless petitioners.

To the right in the foreground kneel Apollonius and his companion, the old Hindu Fakir, still half naked and still with one arm held above his head.

Apollonius: [reading from a small illuminated scroll which he holds in his hand] 'Thy task achieved or not achieved, a greater presses.' [He turns to the Hindu] So it is written in the Caliph's summons—and rings familiar somehow. The phrase comes pat to my mind, as though I heard it once. But what could it mean? Or rather, what to him? To me indeed, 'tis pregnant.

The Hindu Fakir: What does it mean to you?

Apollonius: That day we were stricken to the deck by light from heaven, I knew my task. Something within me spoke. 'Redeem the land of Hellas; redeem thy land from the slavery in which she's sold,' it said. . . . 'As another this

Apollonius... day prepares to redeem thee and all mankind,' the same voice added. That I did not fully understand. But the first was clear enough.

The Hindu Fakir: What slavery is your country subject to?

Apollonius: To Rome and superstition. . . . There's hardly a Greek but barters his birthright for Roman patronage. All the art, wisdom, skill and culture that our fathers left us, is now for export. Our most hallowed customs, sacred rituals, made shows for Roman tourists. And in this whoring of our heritage, the very true grows false, beauty's a bawd, and wisdom but the tout for her.

The Hindu Fakir: And how will you redeem her?

Apollonius: [with eager memory] It seemed my task to make all new again. Gather all knowledge, skill, magic and holiness from the whole world round, and giving it sense again, redeem her with this gift of all that human beings have. This ransom won, I'd bring to Athens— and buy her free again. . . . So seemed my task. . . . [polite] And yours?

The Hindu Fakir: [his arm still raised to heaven] To point.

There is a swirl of movement on the far side of the hall: a fanfare of trumpets, and the crowd parts to let through a guard of soldiers— tremendously tall, with scarlet uniforms, golden breastplates, plumed helmets and drawn scimitars. Far off a herald cries:

Herald: Hear all peoples!
The Great Caliph comes!
The Son of Sky,
and Lord of all the Earth approaches!
Obeisance! Homage!—
upon pain of death!

All prostrate themselves and hide their faces, except Apollonius and the fakir, who draw a little behind a curtain.

146

And over the sea of backs, in the space behind the soldiers, a nervous little man in tight blue trousers and a skimpy blue jacket, can be seen hurrying painfully. His jewelled turban is disarranged and rather too big, and he keeps adjusting his spectacles as he comes—so hurriedly that the fat vizier who is trying to keep a small blue umbrella held over his head, is in danger of tripping.

The Caliph mounts the marble steps to the golden throne, straightens his turban and spectacles.

The Caliph: [*impatiently*] Well, what are we waiting for? Let them get up, for heaven's sake. Always wasting time. What's first today? [*The gorgeous throng gets rather painfully to its feet.*]

The Vizier: [*trying to regain his breath*] Sire, the Lord of Battles craves your counsel.

The Caliph: Still can't keep order, eh? Damnable inefficiency. Well, what nonsensical story this time?

The Minister of War: Sire, a rout of beggars is forcing their miserable presence on your Serenity's inviolable frontier.

The Caliph: [*irritably*] Well, why don't you mobilize the garrisons?

The Minister of War: In consequence, Sire, of a most intricate chain of cause and effect, your garrisons are now reaping the just reward of their loyalty in the third circle of paradise.

The Caliph: [*exploding*] What! Well, send up more at once!

The Minister of War: Sire, the troops in the capital have made it known that they would die rather than exchange the sacred task of guarding your august presence for worthless duties upon the border.

The Caliph: Well, what the devil do you expect from me? Why are you minister, eh? Do something about it, man!

The minister of war withdraws backwards down the stairs, as gracefully as he can.

The Caliph: Well, what next?

The Vizier: The Master of the Harem offers a dance of maidens, newly brought from the West, for your judgement. Sire. [*discreetly*] Now—or later perhaps?

The Caliph: [*suddenly efficient*] Why not now? No time like the present. [*severely*] Remember that!

The Vizier bows. The master of the harem mounts part-way up the marble steps, and making a signal towards the distant archway, a path is cleared through the crowd. A dozen girls—in filmy robes of blue and gold, and veiled to the eyes—come running to the throne.

Music begins. Some play, some dance; and between them something inexpressibly delicate is woven amid the pretentious magnificence. The music weaves, weaves in the hush, like a spider spinning—and to it the girls weave their movements, their bodies, their filmy draperies of blue and gold. One of them, in a long arabesque, sweeps by the pillar where Apollonius and the Fakir are sitting.

In the instant recognition flies. It is Hellas. Her eyes above her veil ask Apollonius some question. He starts up. But she has danced away, and the weaving group of girls—like blue butterflies—comes gracefully to rest upon the lowest steps of the throne as the music dies.

The Caliph: [*briskly*] Very instructive, very. Pity I'm so busy nowadays. Great pressure of work. Very little time for cultural matters—most unfortunate. . . . [*regretfully, to the Vizier*] Well, we must get on, I suppose?

The Vizier: A delegation from the Royal Astrological Observatory, Sire.

The Caliph: [*yawns*] Well? [*The Chief Astrologer, an old man in a long blue-black robe and tall conical hat, approaches nervously.*]

The Chief Astrologer: [*much too fast*] Sire, as we reported last year, a comet was observed which, in relation to the then aspect of your august horoscope, boded most unfavourable personal conditions for yourself. In the hope of discovering other neutralizing influences in the heavens, we built a new telescope which—the claim is

148

The Chief Astrologer...	conservative—revealed twice as many celestial bodies as were previously known. Unfortunately, this telescope showed the presence of four more comets, all hostile. The Royal Observatory therefore petitions for a small increase in its subsidy to permit the construction of a further telescope to my own design which—at a modest estimate—will bring in view ten times....
The Caliph:	Idiot, have the first telescope destroyed at once? ... Next!

The tempo has been getting quicker. All the time different officials have been pulling at The Vizier's sleeve, inventors pushing exhibits through the crowd, petitioners squeezing forward. Now one ragged man breaks through, and throws himself upon the steps.

The Ragged Man:	[*urgently*] Sire, in my province they are starving. Men fall in the fields from hunger. Children die in the gutters, their mothers too weak to bury them....
The Minister of Supply:	[*angrily, from the other side*] It is a lie, Serenity. Statistics show that last season's crops were the best for forty years. If the Lord of Battles didn't make money by having his troops live off the land....
The Minister of War:	[*shouting*] Sire, it's most unfair. In the name of economy, logistics and common sense, we send the army to the food instead of the food to the army....

Other voices make themselves heard, other figures press forward to the throne.

Sire, a scheme for compulsory procrastination...

Sire, the post of UnderSecretary ... my nephew's brother...

Sire, an invention to make ice from dewdrops... There is complete babel. The Caliph thumps on his throne-arm with his fist.

The Caliph:	Stop this racket, for heaven's sake. I can't hear myself think.

There is a moment's lull. But things have got beyond the Vizier's control, and the next minute the clamour rises again, worse than before:

Voices: *Sire, the national emergency. . .*

                  Free turbans for all. . .

                  My cousin, Sire. . .

All this time Apollonius and Hellas have been gazing at each other, as though transfixed. The crowd surges between them; neither can move; no word can pass. But their eyes tell everything.

The Vizier: [*shouting at the top of his voice, tries to regain command of the situation*] Sire, a magician from Athens is here. The best in the West, they say.

The Caliph: [*also shouting against the hubbub*] Then what the devil's he waiting for?

The Vizier makes a sign over the heads of the crowd, and suddenly those around Apollonius and the fakir begin to push them through to the front. At last they emerge, and stand before the throne.

The Caliph: Pleased to meet you, very pleased to meet you. Terribly busy. Never a quiet moment. Always like good tricks though. Well, what can you do?

Apollonius: Give you a quiet moment.

The Caliph: Splendid, splendid. Let's have it.

Apollonius raises both arms slowly to heaven. There is a long roll like thunder, a cloud seems to pass over the scene—and suddenly the stage is empty except for the Caliph, Apollonius, the Hindu Fakir, and Hellas hiding behind a pillar.

The Caliph: [*blinking*] Why . . . what? Where. . .? [*Then he notices what has happened. He seems to stretch, expand.*] By Jove, deuced good trick that. Never seen it before. Why, I feel better already. . . . [*He stands up and stretches in the new found space. He seems to grow larger, taller, the worry goes out of his face, and he takes his glasses off.*] Wonderful. . . how do you do it?

Apollonius:	It's the psychological method of magic, sir. All those people were different sides of yourself. You couldn't choose between them. Then for one lucky moment you called on me, the magician. Lucky, because I am the only one who can make the rest vanish for a while. For of course I am a side of you as well.
The Caliph:	Very glad to hear it. I'm sure.
Apollonius:	You wanted time to think?
The Caliph:	[*a little startled*] Yes, to be sure—time to think, certainly, certainly.
Apollonius:	Well, what will you think, now you have the time?
The Caliph:	H'm, yes, now what was I going to think about? Let me see. . . . [*There is a pause. The Caliph rubs his nose thoughtfully.*] It was very important too. Annoying, very. . . . [*Then he suddenly remembers something.*] By the way, we didn't mention your fee. The usual thing for a successful disappearance is three wishes. Of course there are several hundred wishes on the prohibited list nowadays. So it isn't what it used to be. Still. . . .
Apollonius:	I must warn you that they will all return as soon as you let me go.
The Caliph:	Well, well, it can't be helped. What do you wish?
Apollonius:	I wish your help to gather all the true knowledge in your kingdom.
The Caliph:	Simplest thing in the world. A letter to the Minister of Culture, the Royal Societies. . . . And your second wish?

Hellas runs forward from behind her pillar, and throws herself down by Apollonius, clinging to his leg. Apollonius places his hand protectively on her head.

The Caliph:	[*with reserve, inspecting Hellas*] Yes, of course it's the usual thing for a second wish. . . [*notices Apollonius*]

151

The Caliph: Well, if you insist. Not my style, of course. . . . [*A pause*] And the third?

Apollonius: [*slowly*] I wish to know what you were going to think of when you had the time.

The Caliph slumps back into his throne thoughtfully, and his head drops slowly in his hands. Apollonius stands upright before him, Hellas kneeling at his side. The Hindu fakir squats, his arm still pointing impassively to heaven. A very long silence. There is still silence as the curtain falls.

ACT III SCENE THREE

A halt in the Syrian desert. Sand and sandy scrub, stretching flat under a green evening sky to a line of mountains on the horizon. Negro bearers are unloading cases to the right, muleteers preparing fodder for donkeys and camels tethered in the background. Under the shelter of a heap of baggage, rugs are laid out for the evening rest. Apollonius and The Captain of the Caravan are busy with a list; Hellas lies watching them.

Apollonius: [checking the piles] . . . Four cases of astronomical instruments, two cases alchemical furnace and retorts, three rolls of maps, six cases manuscripts . . . yes, it all seems there. [He wipes the sweat from his face with his burnous.]

The Captain of the Caravan: It's a terrible load for such a journey, sir—here we've been on the move for thirty-five days without a break, and the men are getting restive.

Apollonius: No, they must hold out. The worst is over. How long to Palmyra now?

The Captain of the Caravan: Maybe a week. But Palmyra's not much of a place to rest up, sir. The men are saying that Baghdad's only two days south. Now that's something like a city— bazaars, girls, everything you want.

Apollonius: They must wait a little longer. A week to Palmyra, you say. Another to Antioch, and if we can find ship quickly—but a third to Athens. One month more, and we'll stand on Grecian soil. [He turns triumphant] To found the greatest academy of pure science in the world!

Hellas smiles without speaking, perhaps agreeing, perhaps humouring him.

153

The Captain: You don't quite understand, sir. The desert's not like a city. You have to humour the men a bit. Because—when all's said and done—you're in their power. . . .

Apollonius: [*incredulously*] I . . . and this wealth of knowledge. . . in the power of slaves?

The Captain: It's said, 'Wealth makes the caliph shine the beggar's shoes'.

Apollonius: [*suddenly angry*] They must go on.

The Captain: [*under his breath, touching his forehead with his palm*] Only Allah can say 'must'. . . .

The light is dimming a little. The bearers and cameleers have made all ready for the night. And now there comes a high haunting sound of music in the silence. Thin wailing cries echo the rise and fall of a flute; grow nearer, eerier. And suddenly a crowd of the bearers breaks in from the right, and ignoring Apollonius and the Captain, form a lamp-lit circle round the flute-player who squats, still fluting, in the sand.

The music becomes restless, vibrating: and the circle, holding out their arms towards the centre, begins a kind of shaking dance, tapping now with left hand and foot, now with right. Gradually the shaking seems to take possession of them, as though some kind of energy and urgency were being generated. The motion changes irregularly, violently from one side to the other. The rise and fall of the tune grows more forceful, more commanding. And the dancers begin to cry out, in long high ejaculations which chill the blood.

Suddenly, at a change in pitch, the circle flies apart, and the men stream off to the right, shaking, leaping and wailing in a wild abandon of energy.

Hellas, Apollonius and the Captain are left alone, a dim group sitting upon the rugs. It is dusk. The cries continue in the distance.

The Captain: I don't like that at all. It's a dance they do when they want to work themselves up to something desperate.

Apollonius: [*sobered*] Offer them more money.

The Captain:	It may be too late. They know that all this stuff would fetch good money in Baghdad. If it occurs to them. . . .
Apollonius:	[*appalled*] But our instruments, our books—it's the whole knowledge of the world assembled here. . . .
The Captain:	[*grimly*] With some drink inside them, they won't see it quite like that. After all, that's only your idea. . . .
Apollonius:	Only my idea! . . . But it would take ten fortunes and twenty years to gather this again. There's work for three centuries to develop the wisdom that lies cradled there. Why, it's the whole future of Hellas that's at stake.
Hellas:	[*quietly*] Nay, 'tis brass and paper.
Apollonius:	[*excited*] It's knowledge. In times of fatness, men no longer value knowledge. It's grown too cheap. They throw it away, or use it to play marbles with—like children who come unaware upon a hoard of pearls. 'Tis then the wise man, like a scavenger, collects what the rest despise . . . and makes all new. . . .
Hellas:	'Tis renewed only in his heart.
Apollonius:	Knowledge can change anything, even men.
Hellas:	Only if they be changed already: and then they have it anyway.
Apollonius:	[*desperate*] It's my life's task.
The Captain:	[*speculatively*] Might fetch a hundred thousand dinars . . . in Baghdad. . . .
Hellas:	[*softly*] Thy task achieved or not achieved, a greater presses.

Apollonius buries his head in his hands.

Apollonius:	[*in a whisper*] Must all be swallowed up?

The cries and wails in the distance begin to change tone, grow more aggressive, gain in volume. The flute acquires an exciting, maddening quality. The bearers are coming back. Suddenly they stream on to the stage, cradling camel-whips. The flute-player is joined by a drummer:

they squat in the centre, the others forming a V about them. A sudden alarm comes into the music. The dancers begin to flex their knees in quick time with the urgent pulse of the drum. And all at once they throw themselves into a pure war-dance. Their camel-whips are transformed into swords, the slash and double-slash of their taut arms into the swing of heavy blades. And as heads dart left, right, up and down, on guard against every side, swords flash and flash again, attacking on every quarter.

Apollonius, Hellas and the Captain of the Caravan crouch in the shadow. Apollonius draws his scimitar. The war-dance reaches a peak of frenzy; till suddenly the men break from formation again, and leaping and slashing upon all sides, tear down a dozen bundles from the pile, then yelling and wailing in triumph, bear them off into the darkness.

Apollonius is about to leap after them with drawn sword, but the others hold him back. It is dark, save for the glow of camp-fires where they went.

Apollonius: *[breaking loose]* Quick, we must rescue what's left ourselves, load what mules we can, and off while they're occupied!

He frantically begins to pull down the baggage-pile, select cases, harness the mules, tighten straps. In the glow of fires off, his shadow lurches fantastically, furiously about the scene. The captain of the caravan, a smaller shadow, echoes his. Hellas very quietly rises, gathers her cloak about her.

And unnoticed in the turmoil, an old man in a long rough robe, with cord and scrip about his waist, staff in his hand, enters gravely from the left, from the dark desert. He is carrying a lantern. When he is in the middle of the stage, Apollonius turns suddenly with a bundle, and with a start finds himself face to face.

Apollonius: *[caught in full flood]* Well, what can I do for you, my man?

Very slowly the old man raises his lantern until it lights their two faces, and gazes piercingly into his eyes.

The Christian Apostle: Love the Lord thy God with all thy heart, and with all thy soul, and with all thy strength, and with all thy mind; and thy neighbour as thyself.

The pair are frozen, looking at each other. Then the old man slowly lets down his lantern, and slowly, slowly, leaning on his staff, goes off into the east and darkness.

Apollonius is left standing motionless in the middle of the stage, lit only by distant fires off. All excitement, all activity has left him. He turns gravely to the captain of the caravan.

Apollonius: Take what you need. Divide the rest among the men—and let them sell it in Baghdad. We go alone.

The Captain: [*aghast*] Alone?

Apollonius: No longer quite.

He takes Hellas' arm, and throwing his bag over his shoulder, they walk off slowly, into the darkness—westwards.

The curtain falls.

Act IV Prologue

T he amphitheatre of heaven. Stillness and peace.

A great calm lies over all - as the vast blue vault lies over the radiant centre of the stage.

But this time another music plays. It is simpler, a soft pulse and double-beat, like the faint beating of some enormous heart.

And the gods no longer weave their circle, but stand in line on the lower step of the amphitheatre, tall, noble and silent, with Apollo in his radiance behind and a little above them.

Gradually the music grows louder, the throb of the heart ever deeper and more compelling. And suddenly, silently, the gods who stand alternate step backwards with the beat; pause motionless; with the next beat take a step behind the rest; pause motionless again; and with the third beat are hidden from our sight. Chronos, Aphrodite and Hermes stand alone, Apollo revealed in radiance between them.

For one measure Hera, Ares and Selene remain eclipsed; then with the next they step aside, with the third forward, and with the fourth the line of the gods is again unbroken.

Slowly the throb and double-beat take possession of the heavens. Calm and unmoved, as though their movement were itself the pulse which drove some heart-blood through the universe, the other three gods step back, step sideways, are hidden from us: step sideways, step forwards, and form a line again. So the alternation of the gods follows the pulsation of the beat and as each trio is hidden, Apollo shines between the rest and, as all reappear, so he in turn is hidden.

A new note enters the music. And this time, as Hera, Ares and Selene retreat, they throw their left arms up; as they move to the side, left falls and right swings up; as they pause hidden, their arms are behind their heads. Then as they move to the side again, right arms rise, forward—left arms again, and in line once more their arms are before them, touching finger-tips.

The second trio follows suit. The first repeats. And again a new rhythm enters. As they step back their heads turn right, sideways left, and motionless their heads are raised to heaven. For a long time so, and then yet another note. Not only do the gods step, but as they step, they dance in place, a play of twinkling feet: and their arms rise and fall, their heads turn and drop, in an interlacing of alternate motions, an ever renewed pairing and parting to the slow, all-pervading pulse.

And now, beside the arms, the head, the dance, as the first trio retreats, they cry—with each beat a word:

Brooding!
Joy!
Love!
Struggle!
Wisdom!
Peace!

They are in line again, and the second trio begin as the first continue, joyously, pealingly:

Conception!
Embryo!
Birth!
Youth!
Manhood!
Death!

And as they move, turn, dance, the two sets of cries mingle and merge; and as the second trio take up the second chorus, the first cry out a third:

Growth!
Ascent!
Decay!
Crime!
Healing!
Rebirth!

And now all the motions are flashing and weaving together like some living whole, and the words break together in great chords of sound with every beat:

Brooding! Conception! Growth!
Embryo! Joy! Ascent!
Love! Birth! Decay!
Youth! Struggle! Crime!
Manhood! Wisdom! Healing!
Death! Peace! Rebirth!

As the motion, the throbbing, the chords of song are at their height, the small dark figure of the Greek may be seen climbing the stairs of heaven from below. And at the same moment, in his tremendous voice, comes Apollo's thunder-clap:

T-i-i-ime, STOP!

In the instant, the kaleidoscope congeals, the godlike figures stand frozen in mid-dance. Hera, Ares and Selene alone are seen, the rest eclipsed, with Apollo shining in glorious radiance between. The lights shining on them are mauve, red and green; they deepen and grow fearful.

The Greek: [*in panic*] Where are my mother and my lord? Hermes! Aphrodite! . . . fled from heaven itself! Woe, woe is me! He falls on his knees, beating his breast.

Apollo: Poor foolish mortal!

The Greek: [*wildly, to himself*] I knew it. They are angry. Not for nothing have the years grown more terrible on earth. Our wickedness offends the gods themselves. And now the most fearful's come. They've fled. There's no hope. . . No mother, lord for Greece. . . Nothing now. . .

Apollo: Blind child! How short of sight? How short of time!

The Greek: [*throwing himself down before Apollo*] O mighty lord, forgive me, forgive us Greeks. I failed in all my enterprises. E'en with thy help, I failed. In every task attempted, wickedness crept in. With every year more rottenness, more crime. The more I struggled, the more it seemed that darkness hemmed us in. . . And now our very gods are gone away from us. . .

Apollo:	[*in gentle majesty*] How to explain? How to confine our immortality to thine? Thou too wert made immortal. Yet what little immortality, how small!
The Greek:	Tell us, great sire!
Apollo:	How to explain that all the toil and tedium of thy years, the growing terror of the centuries, are but a breath for us? My children, Hermes and Aphrodite, looked in each other's eyes. And there was an age of paradise on earth. They barely drew apart. It seemed that desolation came. . . Yet 'twas but a moment—one glance, one breath, no fault of thine. . . Canst thou transcend thy humanity enough to comprehend?
The Greek:	I see suffering all about me. It is difficult.
Apollo:	Yea, it is difficult for thee. For one moment thy godlike parents are eclipsed—as in heaven's majestic course, so too am I. To thee it seems all's lost. Yet 'tis but an instant. Look then . . . and rejoice!

And with the same tremendous voice, he cries:

T-i-i-ime, ROLL ON!

And suddenly, the whole motion, the chords, the heavenly cries and dancing colour live again. All is movement. All is living, breathing; all dependent on some hidden play, some deep disturbing heart-beat of the universe.

And Hermes and Aphrodite have emerged; alive with their warm and tender colours, noble, magnificent and young. The Greek falls in obeisance before them.

Apollo:	What little faith ye have! What terrors spring from thy weak perception, so short of sight!
The Greek:	[*still obeisant*] Forgive me, lord.
Apollo:	Think ye that this can be tainted by all your wickedness on earth?
The Greek:	[*cries out*] NO, no, no. . . .

Apollo: Yet is the gap between us too great for thee to bear, too vast for understanding as thou art. 'Twixt our time and thine the gulf's unfathomable. So must I temper our time to weakness of thy intellect. Watch then, and try to understand—that thy decay may not be what it seems.

And slowly something strange begins to happen. The music, the dance begin to slow down. More slowly weave the figures, turn heads. arms uplift. The cries grow more drawn out, the intervals more long. And the very motions of the gods from one posture to another, slow down, expand, grow long and lazy—like some tremendous clockwork running down.

Imperceptibly the tempo dies. From slow to slower the figures interweave. And what was joy and twinkling gaiety before is now, by elongation of its time, grown ominous. Some strange threat seems bound up with the slow deliberate turning of a head, the long slow lifting of an arm. Some terrible intention masters all the gods. And what was light as air. easy as breath at speed, becomes by pressure of time a tedious and overpowering task.

Now the music has grown so slow that it is no longer harmony. It draws out into a groan and dies. And the movements continue their inexorable running down in silence. Like a quickmoving tinkling brook that is slowly overcome by frost, the group gradually congeals. Now a single step back is a long minute's effort; the eye can no longer follow the invisible uplifting of an arm. And as movement becomes unseen, fear grows.

At first, as the gods grew slower, a strange fever seemed to possess the Greek. His small mean figure darted feverish about them, head and arms jerking in contrast with their immense deliberation. And in measure as they slowed, so he grew quicker and more afraid.

But now, in awe and terror he draws back before the unseen motion, which yet brings change, some fearful change.

For the lights are slowly changing too.

Now Ares stands in the midpoint of the front line, and the red glow deepens on him, spreads, fades all the other lights. And Aphrodite, who stood next to him, slowly, inevitably withdraws, her backward step drawn out intolerably. At last one foot rejoins the other; the warm light upon her slowly fades. Her other foot begins its sideways movement to eclipse. Slower and slower she moves, but moves inexorably. Unseen by watching sight, the hem of her robe, one arm, one shoulder move behind Ares' scarlet silhouette. Her warm light pales, dies. Now her breast, her neck, a half of her figure are eclipsed.

There is no light upon the stage but waxing crimson glare, soft waning glow. And with each second the first grows fiercer, and the last more faint.

Now but Aphrodite's profile—infinitely sweet, infinitely compassionate—one arm, the outline of her robe remain. Slowly, slowly she moves into eclipse.

And the little figure of the Greek, frozen too, one hand in horror to his open mouth, is silhouetted against the crimson glare which now possesses all the stage. The curtain falls.

ACT IV SCENE ONE A.D. 268

A rocky shore near Cape Sunium. Dark, stormy and windy. The sound of the sea beating against the cliffs. Ruins of a temple upon a headland left. Huddled under the rocks an old man—perhaps 65—with a white beard, evidently exhausted and in pain, sheltered by a young woman wrapped in a dark cloak. The man is Homer-Plato-Apollonius in extreme old age.

Hellas: This is where Porphyry's message said to set us ashore. There's the ruined temple to Athene that was to be the meeting place. Lucky the boatman knew it.

Plotinus: [*gently*] Why could we not come to Athens? 'Tis a little fantastic, this.

Hellas: Porphyry said that one could not know from one week to the next in whose hands would Athens be. The barbarians are pouring in from the North, riding twenty miles a day, and looting and burning in the bargain. And not a single regiment to hold them. . .

Plotinus: Not a Roman legion in Attica! 'Tis like the end—or the beginning. . .

Hellas: The beginning?

Plotinus: When Greece was young, there were no legions.

Hellas: So long ago! Yet almost I remember. When the little boat was carrying us in against the tide, I thought: 'This water never knew baths, nor Roman aqueducts. 'Tis Greek Poseidon bears us up—terrible, godlike, the deep of life and death.'

Plotinus: [*slowly*] Yes, to our land. Twenty long years in Rome—yet we were strangers there; ambassadors, now coming home.

Hellas: But you were born in Egypt. . . .

Plotinus: [*terribly weak, but smiles to himself*] Nearing home then.

Hellas: [*with a gesture of love and pity, wraps her cloak around him*] My father! Doubly dear father!

Plotinus strokes her hand, looking at her with great affection. The storm beats up in gales of wind and rain, tearing their capes and drowning their voices in the roar of the sea and bursting breakers.

Hellas: [*shouting above the storm*] Poseidon . . . Poseidon . . . is angry!

The lash and beat of the water breaks over her shout and bursts thunderously wave after wave, till its rhythm can be heard as a wild bass song, filling the whole scene.

What shall men do when the waters rise—Poseidon!
When the crashing waves wash down the skies? Poseidon!
What but rock can bear the shock
When the floods are loose and gods' dams burst?
Who shall survive when the oceans thirst?— Poseidon!
. . . Poseidon! . . . Poseidon! . . .
[*dying away, each 'Poseidon' the bursting of a wave.*]

When swirling seas shall swallow the shore— Poseidon!
When cities and ships go down their maw—Poseidon!
Sea alone when land is gone,
When the whole earth is a flooded vault,
And heaven itself is soaked and salt—Poseidon!
. . . Poseidon! . . . Poseidon! . . .

Once the end came in heavenly flame—Poseidon!
And once in blizzard and hurricane—Poseidon!
Fire and air left some to spare,
But when crashing waves wash down the skies,
What shall men do when the waters rise?—Poseidon!
. . . Poseidon! . . . Poseidon! . . .

A cloaked figure can be seen against the skyline, struggling head down against the wind. It slips into a gully and comes scrambling down the cliff to the shore—a sturdy man of about 35.

Hellas: [*rushes forward and throws herself in his arms*] Porphyry!

Porphyry: You came . . . after all.

Hellas: We did not wish, he came. [*she indicates Plotinus*] He had us give out that he was dead—and amid the mourning, came.

Porphyry: [*kneeling before him*] Father and master!

Plotinus: [*kindly*] Well?

Porphyry: [*earnest*] Why did you come? This is no place. . .

Plotinus: I have a journey to make . . . from here.

Porphyry: To Egypt?

Plotinus: Perhaps. We'll see. How are the brethren? How is Athens?

Porphyry: Our people are well, but very ill with Athens. There's but one day left, they say. The barbarians came through Thermopylae three nights ago, shaggy ponies as far as the eye could see, we heard. They're massing at Thebes—all there's in flames, the temples looted, butchery. . . . Come not to Athens, father!

Plotinus: Flames would be warmer than this shore. Besides, 'tis too late to go back now. After so many years . . . I'd like to see my friends.

Hellas: What shall you tell them?

Plotinus: [*strangely*] Tell, I don't know. What will they see—'s the question. [*He struggles to his feet.*] Well, when can we go?

Porphyry: There are mules and a litter waiting beyond the cliff. They will carry us to Athens in three or four hours. Time to see the brethren and get away before the

Porphyry... Gothic scouts ride in. Though there's panic everywhere. . . .

Plotinus: Then let us go up. [*With an immense effort he straightens himself, and makes to clamber up the rocky face of the cliff, just able to lift one foot at a time to the next hold.*]

Porphyry: [*in horror*] You cannot go up there!

Plotinus: [*panting*] We must all go up. . . . There is no other way. . . . It is too wet and cold down here.

Hellas: [*runs to him*] No, no, you are sick, too weak. Wait. Let help come!

Plotinus: [*to Porphyry*] Help me then!

Porphyry, coming below, helps to place his foot in a crevice in the rock, then half helps, half heaves him further. It is a tremendous struggle. After gaining a few feet, Plotinus almost collapses, falling across a ledge of rock to rest. The wind and storm beat up, tearing about them, deafening. But Plotinus, with a great effort, raises himself, stretches up his hands, feels with his feet, hauls himself further. From below, Porphyry helps as best he can. There is nothing but the roaring of wind and rain, and in a pause the terrible panting of the old man. For what seems an immense time they struggle there, no word spoken, gaining a foot at a time. Hellas is kneeling below, her eyes lifted towards them, as if praying. One still more violent gust and scream of wind—and in the moment's lull that follows:

Plotinus: [*panting terribly*] Only thus one climbs. Dost thou understand?

Porphyry: [*in an agonized voice*] Not fully, father.

Without saying anything, Plotinus makes another supreme effort, gains one more foot. So it goes on—for perhaps five minutes. At last Plotinus heaves himself on to the top of the cliff, and half sits, half lies there, as Porphyry scrambles up beside him. A single rift of light opens in the low leaden cloud behind them.

Plotinus: [*faintly*] You see?

Hellas: [*shouts up from below*] Are you safe?

Plotinus: Nearly safe.

Porphyry: [*peering into the gloom*] Mules and men—they are coming to take you on. It is safe now. Let me stay with Hellas.

Plotinus: So be it.

Hellas: [*entreating from below*] Go now, father, I beg you go— but do not leave me quite.

Plotinus: I will come down to you again—later.

And struggling to his feet, he gathers his staff, his cloak about him, and step by step hobbles along the skyline to the ruined temple left, alone. Porphyry crouching at the top of the gully, and Hellas standing below with arms outstretched, watch him go.

But he does not turn back. The storm rises again, the roaring of the wind grows, the beating of the breakers upon the cliffs surges ever more terrible and insistent. And as the turmoil swells, once more the deep bass song begins to surge through the elements:

> *What shall men do when the waters rise—Poseidon!*
> *When the crashing waves wash down the skies? Poseidon!*
> *What but rock can bear the shock*
> *When the floods are loose and gods' dams burst?*
> *Who shall survive when the oceans thirst?— Poseidon!*
> *. . . Poseidon! . . . Poseidon! . . .*
>
> *When swirling seas shall swallow the shore—Poseidon!*
> *When cities and ships go down their maw—Poseidon!*
> *Sea alone when land is gone,*
> *When the whole earth is a flooded vault,*
> *And heaven itself is soaked and salt—Poseidon!*
> *. . . Poseidon! . . . Poseidon! . . .*
>
> *Once the end came in heavenly flame—Poseidon!*
> *And once in blizzard and hurricane—Poseidon!*
> *Fire and air left some to spare,*
> *But when crashing waves wash down the skies,*
> *What shall men do when the waters rise?—Poseidon!*

HELLAS

. . . Poseidon! . . . Poseidon! . . .
The curtain falls slowly upon the storm.

Act IV Scene Two

An open hillside with a road leading down into Athens. It might be the same scene as Act 1, Scene I, except for an ancient statue of Hermes at the cross-roads, the head and one arm missing, and an abandoned booth for food or drink upon the right. The tree too, if it is the same tree, is now bare and some branches have been torn off, apparently to kindle the burnt-out fire which lies below. The whole scene is grey and bleak, save for a flickering red glow down to the left, as though from a fire far away.

Up from the direction of this glow comes trudging a nondescript little man pushing a handcart, in which are a baby, two jars, a sack, and some odd bundles. Two dirty unkempt children are hanging on the sides, and a ragged woman enveloped in a shawl follows a little way behind. At the same moment Porphyry and Hellas, cloaked, enter from the right, so that the two parties meet in the centre of the stage.

Porphyry: Where to, citizen?

The Man with the handcart: [*dully*] Don' know. This way like.

Porphyry: Why, what happened?

The Man with the handcart: The bloody Goths'll be in town by night, they say. Everyone gets 'is throat slit, they say, and the women somethink else first. Better get out while the going's good, I thought. Not much to lose. So 'ere we are.

Hellas:

Porphyry: [*gathers the tired children to her cloak*] Poor dears!

[*catching sight of something in the cart*] What's this? [*He leans forward quickly to pick it up. The man makes a feeble move to stop him, and then stands there sheepishly, too tired to trouble.*]

170

Porphyry:	[*unwrapping a bundle*] Great gods! The Holy Mother in pure gold! [*in horror*] Athena . . . from the temple treasury!
The Man with the handcart:	[*protesting weakly*] 'Tweren't me as took it, sir. There was a crowd of 'em. Said if the Goths were going to get it all, Greeks might as well 'ave some first.
Porphyry:	They sacked the temple treasury? Greeks did that?
The Man with the handcart:	Well, it sort of 'appened like. One moment they was out in the street, calling for the defence of the city. Then someone shouted: 'There's gold in there!' And the next minute they was swarmin' through the sanctuary, and the stuff was all over the place. I just picked this off the street, straight I did. Might as well me as the next man, I says to meself.
Porphyry:	So low Athens fell! [*He stares at the statuette in his hand, awe and bafflement mixed upon his face, for it has no meaning any more. Then he notices the wrapping*] And this? Why, it's a papyrus from the academy. . . .
The Man with the handcart:	Sure, they were blowing down the street like beech leaves—so I picked one up to keep the figure decent-like.
Porphyry:	[*not hearing, reads softly from the fragment*] 'And the Stranger said: "Listen now. During a certain period God himself guides each cosmic being in its course. But when at last the circle of its allotted time is done, he lets it go. And it of its own accord runs back the other way—a living creature endowed with intelligence returning to him who fashioned it in the beginning." [*The paper falls from his hand, a groan comes from him, and his whole body seems to wilt.*] O Attica! Attica! [*His voice breaks and he buries his head in his hands.*]
The Man with the handcart:	Well, I'll be getting along, I guess; though where to, Pallas only knows. . . . [*He takes the statuette, smears some dirt off with the back of his hand, wraps it in the*

The Man: *papyrus, and puts it back into his cart. Then he jerks his head at the woman]* 'Ere, let's go!

Without a word, she drags herself up, and shuffles off after him, still unknown in her shawl. Hellas comes over to Porphyry, kneels, and takes his bowed head into her lap. He does not resist.

Hellas: My dear! My very dear!

Porphyry holds her without lifting his head or speaking. And all at once one notices that they have fallen into an echo of the attitude of Homer and Hellas in Act I, Scene I. The same hillside, but unkempt and grey; the same tree above them, but bare and jagged; and Hellas poised above Porphyry who has let himself slip wearily to the ground. But now it is he who has forgotten, and she who understands.

Hellas: [*stroking his hair, tenderly*] Suppose I were to be with child by you . . . a little chubby one, with your curls, your voice. . . . [*With sudden force she lifts up his head and looks deep into his eyes.*] You would not let them kill it, Porphyry? You would protect it with your own life? You promise me that? Promise? [*She speaks with passionate demand—a new Hellas.*]

Porphyry: [*deeply moved and troubled*] Hellas with child by me? Now, at this time. . . in ruin and bloodshed. . . . O gods, what have you done?

Hellas: [*with deep fervour*] Yes, what did they to us, Porphyry? That time you came to Rome, that marvellous terrible time . . . did I conceive, or Aphrodite? Something was fashioned there, as god and goddess wheeled together, in a blaze of blinding light. Some new cosmos, some godling gotten. And in that moment you were in my arms. . . .

Porphyry: [*holding her close to him*] What else did you see, Hellas?

Hellas: I saw time open, and in its womb lay all of Hellas long since buried. The ruins rose again, stone upon stone, grew fresh and gleaming; fallen columns stood; marble glistened and whitened newly in the sun. The sadness

Hellas...   of this last age fell away, and the great marble palaces, exquisite temples, bazaars and brothels on the hill turned gay as 'twere high summer. Then figures swarmed like ants upon them, and roughening the bright Stone, bore it away and back into the quarries. Over the place grass grew, fresh flowers bloomed. Men sang, quarrelled, cheated, fought, loved and tortured each other. . . and seemed each moment younger and braver in the doing. Slim ships like needles flew back from every coast on earth, made fast in harbour, where singing lads took them apart and carting the beams out into the hills, there set them up . . . and straightway they were trees. And thus the forests spread upon the land, all filled with scent of pine, flower-carpeted, gay with birdsong, so that the hearts of men were glad again. And in that dawn I walked upon this very hill, and by this very tree met a blind minstrel boy . . . and stopped, and lay down . . . and you, and he . . . and all was blinding light. . . gods dancing . . . utter wonder. . .

As she has been speaking the light has changed slowly, so that for a little the sky seems blue, the grass green, and the tree clad in blossoms—a hint, a memory. Then it turns back again, and once more all is bleak, grey, save where in the distance the red glow ominously flickers. From the right the little man with the handcart, one unkempt child, and the weary invisible woman in the shawl, trudge back again.

Hellas...   [*hushed*] And yet—most glorious and terrible, nothing grew nor passed: but all was there. Those babes who played with young lambs in the first innocence of time, laughed forever in the grass: and in the same moment others fell screaming under the Gothic hooves—but all eternally. And I was there in every scene, that dawn, the hot high noon, the bloody sunset . . . with some task laid on me. Ah, what weight of knowledge!

Too much to bear. . . . Hellas and Porphyry cling together.

The Man with [*sniffling*] They got the kid. Trampled 'er down. Just
the Handcart: like that. Wivout a thought. Then one leans down from 'is 'orse and grabs the statue. 'Gold!' 'e says. 'For that

you can 'ave a chance on yer bleedin' life. Ten minutes to get the 'ell from 'ere!' 'e says. And we runs for it, leaving the kid. Not even a decent coffin. Poor kid! [*He wipes his nose and eyes with his sleeve, sniffling. The woman does not move or make a sign.*]

Hellas: O gods. . . .

The Man with [*turning to them*] You'd better push on. The 'orses went the Handcart: the other way. But there's a party'll be 'ere in 'arf a minute. Excuse me, lady. [*He pushes the little cart, the one child hanging on, the silent beshawled woman following, and they trudge off left, back towards the red glow.*]

Hellas: We must find father, and the brethren . . . Now, while there's time.

Porphyry: [*galvanized into action*] Yes, take them away somewhere. One still might buy a boat, and make for Italy . . . your father. . .

Hellas: [*very quietly*] . . . has a journey to make from here. Come, let us go.

They take hands, and go off down the hill left, towards the ever-brightening glare. The red creeps slowly up the western sky, begins to touch with blood the broken Hermes. Far away one can imagine a low crackling.

Then suddenly shouts, orders, war-cries, clatter and beat of hooves. Near pandemonium. A single horseman bent low over a shaggy pony gallops at top speed across the stage from right to left. A moment's pause. Then, with an ear-splitting yell, a second, spinning his javelin. Half the sky is crimson now. And when a party of foot-soldiers, in belted skins and wadded leggings, bursts like a torrent across the stage, their weapons and shields, antler and lion-muzzle crests seem bathed in blood itself from the reflected light. Each man carries a dagger and a wavy two-edged sword, with which he plays tricks, spinning them from hand to hand, tossing them in the air, balancing one across the other, with roars, war-yells, and shouts of laughter. From the round skin shields, strapped to each forearm, animal faces grin.

There is some kind of an order above the din, and with an answering shout, sixteen men run forward into a · V-shaped formation, while the rest squat round in a half-circle behind them. Three potdrums and two harsh flutes begin to beat a strange exciting rhythm, and in sudden unison the circle of men begin to shout, on two rising notes, rocking as they do so:

Ya Hu! Ya HAQQ! Ya HAIY!

Ya HUKM! Ya HAMD! Ya HAL!

As they rock forward, the second syllable, in a strange high tone, seems to shoot from the tops of their bowed heads with intoxicating force. Suddenly the sixteen men begin a fierce dance to the same rhythm, swinging half right, stamping first with one foot, then the other, and in the same moment cutting the air with their swords and jabbing with their daggers. Then in unison they all swing forward, stamp, stamp, swords up and then straight ahead, daggers jabbing, and at each rhythm shouting with the others:

Ya Hu! Ya HAQQ! Ya HAIY!

Ya HUKM! Ya HAMD! Ya HAL!

The whole air begins to vibrate with the double shout and double stamp, as the warriors swing half left, cutting and jabbing; then forward again, then in a single whirl threatening and cutting at the circle of shouters behind them. But the shouters only roar the louder, more overpoweringly:

Ya HAKIM! Ya HALIM! Ya HAFIZ!

Ya HASIB! Ya HAKIM! Ya HAMID!

The rhythm grows fiercer and fiercer. The warriors, swinging now right, now left, now back, now forward, seem to become a single whole, fighting on all sides, against all comers simultaneously, invulnerable, irresistible. Now the whole scene is bloodred, the whirling swords and daggers flash scarlet, as though fresh used, in the glare from the left. The stamping, drumming and shouting grow to a crescendo, as if generating a single irresistible whirlwind of violence. Then, at a sign, the shouters leap to their feet, and with one great roar, all surge together off the stage to the left, down towards the glare of burning Athens.

ACT IV SCENE THREE

T he same open-air gymnasium in Athens as in Act II, Scene I, but
under a dark and livid sky. The same courtyard, surrounded by a
pillared colonnade, statues and stone seats. But ivy and moss grow up
the columns, some statues are broken; and the Acropolis beyond has
become overgrown with slums, so that only confused glimpses of the
ancient splendour are visible.

Moreover, here and there upon the hill, fires glow redly, an echo of
the fires on the night of Socrates' condemnation— but redder and
more ominous. A huge blaze near the Parthenon lights the whole sky
with crimson. Ugly shouting in the distance.

Round about the courtyard, upon the steps and seats, sit twenty or
thirty men and women, both in loose white trousers, Eastern-
fashion, and loose white tunics, which the women wear longer and
sashed with coloured scarves. There is a strange calm among those in
the courtyard, yet charged with deep emotion, and contrasting
strangely with the wildness and turmoil one feels abroad in the city
beyond.

On a stone seat to the right sits Plotinus. Musicians—men and
women—with guitars and flutes, sit upon the steps around him, but
at ease, as if waiting for something. A sacrificial fire, with calm white
flame, burns near by.

Suddenly from the left two cloaked figures appear. A gust of the
violence beyond seems to enter with them. They cross to where
Plotinus sits, and throw themselves wearily before him. It is
Porphyry and Hellas.

Hellas takes Plotinus' hand, and lays her head upon his knee
without a word, as if coming home.

Porphyry: [*full of emotion and excitement*] Master, thank God
you reached here safely!

176

Plotinus: [*calmly*] Why not? It was arranged.

Porphyry: [*still breathless*] The Goths are a mile from the city gates. One can see the dust of their hooves on the road from Marathon. We were but minutes ahead of them.

Plotinus: [*still calm*] Well, good that you were.

Porphyry: It's still clear by the Sacred Western Gate: we could get away to Eleusis, if you're quick. Go back to. . . .

Plotinus: [*as if quietening a small boy*] Nay, be more calm. It is too late for that. Stay here. Make yourself at ease.

He strokes Hellas' head upon his knee affectionately. The excitement seems to die out of Porphyry at his words, and he too relaxes at Plotinus' feet.

Porphyry: [*under his breath*] Pardon, master. . . .

Plotinus: I came to be with you at the end of all our days. Think you I would go away again so soon?

An Eager Young Man: Will you not save yourself for us?

Plotinus: [*gently*] Better, I think, if we all go together.

Eager Young Man: To your land of Egypt?

Plotinus: [*strangely*] Perhaps you could come there.

Hellas: [*raises her head*] Tell me rather of Greece, my father.

Plotinus: [*stroking her hair still*] A thousand years ago the blessing of the gods fell upon this place. The soul of Hellas was flung down from heaven upon this very hill. How beautiful it grew! Clothed itself in temples, music and philosophy, spread to the very ends of earth and taught truth there. And in each age new men made themselves messengers between her and the gods who sired her— Homer and Plato, Apollonius— so that she never could forget her origin. But souls of civilizations too grow old, their bodies weary, duties done—and turn them at last with longing to another

177

time, not this: some other dwelling where the years flow differently from ours. . . .

A Stranger at the Door: [*cries out suddenly in a loud voice*] Beware the wrath to come!

Plotinus: [*quietly*] Welcome, stranger! We would beware that which was also.

Hellas: [*shudders*] Who is it? He frightens me.

Porphyry: [*stands*] Declare your business, stranger!

The Stranger: [*in a loud violent voice*] I am a chosen Christian! Come to warn thee! For ye are good men, and may yet be saved from your damnable superstitions. It is the eleventh hour—repent then in time! I, in the name of Christ, command thee!

Plotinus: [*softly*] In time, or in eternity? . . .[*more aloud*] Stay with us, stranger, you are very welcome.

The Stranger: The Goths are at the gates! God's ire incarnate! All rottenness, all that's ancient and decayed must go down before them! Let them burn, destroy! Upon your ruins grows our New Jerusalem!

Hellas: [*her shudder turning to deep terrible sobbing*] O Athens! Athens! [*Far away there is a new burst of shouting, war-cries, oaths.*]

The Stranger: [*fiercely*] The very devils work for us. They destroy but to make room for what we have to do. A few years more, and Christ will reign openly—new Emperor, new Empire! Ours, ours is the future!

Plotinus: [*soothing Hellas, softly*] And thine the sweet past. Go back and be refreshed. . . .

With blazing eyes the stranger strides among the waiting men and women, staring into their faces, pauses before a statue of Aphrodite, and, with a sudden tremendous blow, knocks it from its pedestal. The marble figure falls and breaks in two.

The Stranger: Whore of Babylon!

There is a sudden sigh of horror from those looking on, and two or three men leap up to throw themselves upon the Stranger. But Plotinus, raising his hand, by some inner force arrests them without a word.

Plotinus: [*gently*] 'Tis but a figure of stone. Learn to bear all. [*For a moment angry murmurs, a movement of indignation, a woman's wail—then silence again, silence charged with intense emotion. The Stranger turns; and with blazing eyes, stands in the middle of the stage, as if challenging them to deny him anything. Yet something in the strange hush makes him pause.*]

The Stranger: What do you wait for, O unhappy ones?

Plotinus: [*calmly*] The beginning, friend.

The Stranger: And where, deceiver, shall you find it?

Plotinus: In the end.

Far away, the shouting has grown to an immense roar. Rattle of hooves, cries, crackling of fire. The glares in different parts of the city seem to be joining. All in the distance is black smoke, red fire. Yet still in the courtyard calm and silence.

Plotinus: Our deliverers draw near. May they share the goodness that their act makes possible.

Eager Young Man: I have a sword, master. Place me in the entrance to keep them off!

Plotinus: [*quietly*] Remember to do as thou must. [*The Young Man goes off eagerly. Plotinus turns to Porphyry beside him*] But a little while ago, and those would have been your words.

Now Plotinus, Hellas and Porphyry are very close together. Hellas has her head upon Plotinus' lap, her hand in Porphyry's, who kneels with his other arm about her, staring fixedly into his master's eyes. The three in some way form one whole, apart.

Porphyry: [*under his breath*] How quick to act! How hard to bear!

Plotinus: Bear all, for all to bear thee.

Hellas:	I will bear thee.
Porphyry:	Bear me!
The Stranger:	[*his back to them, cries aloud to the audience*] Whither?
Hellas:	Inwards.
Porphyry:	Backwards.
Plotinus:	Upwards.
The Stranger:	[*with blazing eyes, urgently*] What shall be born, O wicked ones?
Hellas:	A hero.
Porphyry:	A soul.
Plotinus:	A world.
The Stranger:	[*in a terrible voice*] Devils, tell me whence?
	From the womb.
	From the heart.
	From the head.
	[*all his violence upon the audience*] By magic, by wicked magic?
	By woman.
	By man.
	By god.
	[*bitterly*] Can whore and harlot bear?
	If she but love and dare.
	Can pagan live again?
	At both ends of the chain.
	And shall magician pray?
	After his fashion, yea.

A pool of light has begun to glow about the group of three, and the stranger is silhouetted darkly against them. Voices from those around echo Plotinus' words.

Pray in our fashion! The great, the holy prayer, Pallas, attend us! Hermes and Aphrodite! The prayer, the prayer!

All sink upon their knees in a great semicircle about the trio, their heads bent and their arms crossed upon their breasts. The stranger, too, in the centre front of the stage, eclipsing the group of three, falls on his knees facing the audience and with head back, hands together, remains motionless in Christian prayer.

The musicians begin a strange solemn melody of strings and flutes, and a wave of inner concentration passes through the kneeling figures. There is a long waiting count, and then slowly, all together, the men and women lift their heads and raise their arms, palms forward in adoration. Then they cross them again, and counting always, go through a long strange ritual of invocation and prostration, bowings and turnings, lunges to left and right, beating of breast and head, as though in some prayer of motion not words, some deep, exact and emotional language of the body.

The light on the trio has grown stronger. And now Plotinus rises slowly, wonderfully. He is no longer weak and old, but nobly straight. Slowly he moves among the praying figures, and as he passes each, lays his hand lightly on their crown. Each one he touches, and, as he does, each seems as if filled with the light that follows him. Calm falls upon them, and their movements become pure and perfect.

When he has finished, slowly, gravely, Plotinus begins to turn, left hand raised, as if to receive some gift from heaven, right extended as if to pass it down to earth. His revolving is calm like the slow spinning of the sun, making a centre and focus to the ecstatic gestures of the prayer.

The flutes and guitars play. The white-clad figures turn this way and that, bow, bend and abase themselves, lift their heads, raise their arms in longing skywards. And behind it all one now feels a strange inner pattern, some inner time of attention, some knowledge of deep and hidden things. With hands crossed devoutly, they bow to the East, South, West and North, prostrate themselves again, then with their own hands lift themselves by the neck once more. With gesture of rejection they fling themselves away, abandon themselves, throw themselves down, beat foreheads on the ground in gratitude and longing. This, as the sky darkens, the red glow sways and flares, is true prayer, the only prayer, prayer of body, mind and soul in unison, prayer of those who have given all, who can no longer turn back, who must pass beyond the end.

181

Now the white figures have rolled upon their backs, beaten their heads again in self-abandon on the stones; and then, as if in sudden vision, shielded their eyes from the blinding white light that flares for a minute across the sky.

The music throbs more nobly, more longingly, more majestically, as the clamour of the mob and army comes closer down the hill. The praying men and women lift themselves, up, up in gratitude and adoration. They know, they have seen, they have naught to give but thanks. An extraordinary calm hangs over and protects them, an extraordinary confidence and certainty shine from each face.

For now the mob is at the door. There is a babel of shouts, clash of weapons, flare of pine torches. The eager young man has put up his sword, been driven back, tripped, and the torrent of savage soldiers pours shouting over him—to burst, screaming, swords flashing, hot with blood and sweat, among the still kneeling figures. Frenzy of war-dance drowns the rhythm of the prayer. Those in white vanish beneath the rush, swords strike, daggers plunge—soft groans, limp figures sprawling beneath the throng. The stranger kneels, as he has knelt throughout the prayer, motionless, hands uplifted, untouchable.

Behind him the trio of Plotinus, Hellas and Porphyry are linked together in the same strange concentration, a glow of light focussed upon them. Plotinus stands straight and motionless, after the turning. Hellas kneels with her head buried in his robe, Porphyry beside her, gazing up at his master. The slaughter swirls about them, in a rising passion of blood and violence. The sky is black, the torches sway drunkenly about the stage, peals of thunder roll.

And gradually, behind the pandemonium, grows faintly audible the strange ringing with which the opera began. At first one cannot be sure that it is there. Then imperceptibly it penetrates the clamour, pervades it, masters it. The scene now is hell, scarlet and black shadows battling with animal cries over shapeless figures amid ruins crashing and crumbling into darkness. Ever deeper darkness—save for the pool of light that bathes the one still group.

And now the ringing grows unbearable, penetrates all, shatters the ears, seems as if it would disintegrate hell itself. Out of the pitch black a huge barbarian rears suddenly behind the group, scarlet, sweating, *swinging bloody sword. The three do not move, Plotinus' gaze is fixed unflickeringly in Porphyry's, his in the other's. A life-line lies between them. For a fraction of a second all is still, the ringing utterly unendurable. Then the sword plunges in Plotinus' back, and, with eyes wide open as if in consciousness, the old man topples towards gazing Porphyry.*

There is a terrible sound as his forehead crashes upon the other's upturned face, then utter darkness, ringing, ringing, ringing. . . .

Epilogue

A nd suddenly the amphitheatre of heaven is there, and the gods dancing, music of the spheres, and the whole kaleidoscope of heaven turning in radiant aura of motion, music, love and coloured light. Nor does the ringing pause, but unimaginably swells, till it and the blinding radiance are one—and in this ringing radiance Hermes and Aphrodite move to each other's arms, while in the foreground the small straight figure of the Greek, arms uplifted in adoration, mounts once more towards them.

The curtain falls.

THE END

Hellas

The Mirror of Light and Other Works

THE MYSTERIES OF THE SEED

The Mirror of Light and Other Works

Foreword to
The Mysteries of The Seed

If *The Theory of Celestial Influence* is Rodney Collin's cathedral of ideas, and *Hellas* is his grand historical pageant, then *The Mysteries of the Seed* is his intimate chapel—a quiet, candlelit space where the central secret of the Work is whispered rather than shouted.

In this short, lyrical drama, Collin strips away the vast complexities of cosmology to focus on the single, essential atom of spiritual life: the seed.

To the modern mind, the Eleusinian Mysteries are often little more than a footnote in a history book, a curious agrarian cult of ancient Greece. But to Collin, who viewed history not as a linear record of events but as a living genealogy of wisdom, Eleusis was a "School." It was a laboratory of the soul where the science of regeneration was preserved and transmitted.

In this text, he takes us back to 800 B.C., a twilight era where the Achaean kingdoms have faded and the distinct form of the Attic state is emerging. But the setting is secondary; the real location is the human heart, and the time is always now.

The play dramatizes the myth of Demeter and her daughter Kore (Persephone)—her abduction by the underworld, the mourning of the mother, and the cyclical return. However, in Collin's hands, this is not merely a fertility myth about the seasons. It is a precise allegory for the Fourth Way idea of conscious evolution.

The "seed" is the human essence. It must fall into the dark, cold furrow of the earth—the body, the material world, the realm of mechanical habits—and it must "die." This death is not physical cessation, but the death of the false personality, the shedding of the husk of vanity and imagination. Only through this voluntary darkness can the green shoot of the "new man" emerge.

What is fascinating here is how Collin weaves the agricultural and the spiritual into a seamless garment. He reminds us that the laws of nature are the laws of God. The same force that splits the acorn to release the oak is the force that breaks the human ego to release the soul.

"A grain fell in the furrow, died, and was reborn," the chorus intones.

It is the universal formula for immortality, echoing from the wheat fields of Attica to the parables of the Gospels. The character of Triptolemus represents the initiate—the one who learns that bread is not just food for the body, but a symbol of the "holy loaf" of shared understanding and union with the Divine.

Collin is suggesting that we are all, in a sense, seeds waiting for the courage to fall. We cling to our safe, dry existence in the granary of ordinary life, terrified of the burial that precedes germination.

The Mysteries of the Seed is a delicate, poetic work, less demanding perhaps than his dense theoretical writings, but no less profound. It asks us to trust the dark. It invites us to look at the "fruitful dark, o stillness, silent wait" not as an end, but as a beginning.

For anyone who has ever felt buried by circumstance or suffering, Collin offers this gentle, potent reminder: you are not in a grave; you are in a furrow.

Triptolemus between Demeter, Persephone and the priestess of Eleusis.

THE MIRROR OF LIGHT AND OTHER WORKS

The Time and Place

T HE LESSER and Greater Eleusinian Mysteries, in the form that became famous all over the ancient world as from Pisistratus, were founded sometime around the 13th Century B. C. The tradition is that Orpheus and his followers instituted them. According to other sources they are older still, and were given to the Pelasgian women by the Danaids, initiates from Egypt, subsequently destroyed by the Dorian invaders, and reformed by Orpheus.

The account of the Myth of Demeter and Kore follows a sixth century Homeric hymn.

The following dialogues and scenes take place about 800 B. C. The Achaean kingdoms have vanished. Athens has ceased to be a kingdom: it is an aristocratic Republic. Eleusis has made a treaty with a late king or early archontes of Athens, and has been merged into the Attic state.

The Mirror of Light and Other Works

The Eleusinian Myth of Demeter and The Rape of Kore[1]

A LL-MOTHER Demeter whose hair is blown wherever winds carry the wheat and chaff from swinging swingle to the sound of threshing, whose gold-red cloak unrolls its border by the summer path, wide-breasted, crowned with the holy diadem of wall and towers, Demeter dwelt at peace amongst the gods.

One day her daughter Kore descended to earth to meet the Okeanides in the plain of Nysa where they used to play.[2] While they danced and sang Zeus watched them and with cunning lie sprinkled the deep grass with flowers, violets and the wild orchid in the green shade, saffron and blue irises behind large boulders, the briar rose on the forest wall.[3]

The young girls began to pick flowers; Kore, her arms already filled, went far afield, and now she saw a golden daffodil with its multiple bells on a straight stem.[4] One, ten, a hundred more. The plant exhaled a sweet hypnotic scent. The Maid knelt down; joy turned to breathless desire and wonder to obsession.

---

[1] No doubt an oral tradition existed previous to the hymn, and also earlier writings that have been lost. The Homeric hymn was preserved for a long time on mount Athos. An Orphic hymn tells of Demeter's arrival at Eleusis as the guest of Dysaules, the ill-housed, and his wife Baubo, the Anatolian goddess. Demeter taught their son Eubuleus, the swine herd, and Triptolemus. Other traditions speak of Musaion and Eumolpus, son and grandson, or else disciples of Orpheus. Eumolpus founded the priestly dynasty of Eleusis. On accession the Hierophant laid down name and assumed the name of Musaion or Eumolpus alternatively. Orphic hymns are short and compressed, Homeric hymns are long and descriptive.
The Homeric hymn falls into four sections: the Rape of Kore; the tale of failure over Demophoon; the Institution of the Mysteries; the ascent of Persephone, and the Myth of the Chariot elaborated by Plato in the Phaidros.
The Eleusinian theory of the soul can be considered the inspiration of Greek transcendental philosophy.
[2] Legendary Nysa, birthplace of Dionysos, here thought to be in Caria.
[3] On a blue and white frieze of Knossos the young god is depicted picking saffron. The Titans have lured him out of bounds.
[4] Narcissus Orientalis of Asia Minor grows on the shores of the Bosphorus, in Ionia, Anatolia and Syria. A tall stem breaks into multiple blossoms. Though they are small the scent is very strong.

Intent on the flower of death, she was seen by the Cronide, Lord of many Names, the Dark One, Spirit of Gravity and Ruler of the Deep. A child of heaven, through forgetfulness, had come too near the radius of his power.

The ocean swelled, the earth was rent, infamous vapours veiled the light of day. The ground split open; on his chariot drawn by two immortal steeds Aidoneus halted, framed in smoke and flames. He ravished Kore and carried her away in a fast flight. She cried out loudly to her father Zeus but neither god nor men heeded her voice. She struggled hard and lost not hope as long as she could see the mountain chains and the veiled violet sea gyrate below during the infernal journey.

Hecate heard her cry, and great Apollo, but he was busy in his cave receiving the allotted sacrifices. The chariot went down and with it went the sole witness of the scene, the swineherd Eubuleus and his beasts. Swallowed by a crevasse Kore saw the light of day no more.

DEMETER heard her child's last desperate cry. She started from her lion-footed bed. She knew her daughter had met with a bad fate; she held her temples in distraction, she tore her head band and she wailed. She wrapped herself in seven darkening veils and descended to earth.

Carrying a lighted torch, she wandered for nine days in earthly gloom until she met Hecate who told her that she had heard the cry but did not know who had ravished Kore. Together the goddesses visited all-seeing Apollo, who alone knew that Zeus had promised Kore to Aidoneus, who was Demeter's own brother, for a wife.

When Demeter heard this she was angered with the gods. She left her home amongst them and took her cruel sorrow to the cities of men. And no one, for a period, recognized her for she hid her divine beauty well.

DURING HER wanderings Demeter came to fragrant Eleusis by the sea, ruled by Celeus from his walled city. On a hot day tasting of dust, cicadas marking endless time, she came within view of the acropolis on the ancient hill. Sadly she sat down to rest by a clear-flowing spring, for she was weary indeed.

196

The townspeople came that far to draw sweet tasting water.[1] Demeter leaned in the cool shade of an olive tree, the trembling leaves marked her veil and gown with mottled pattern. She might be taken for a peasant or a palace nurse.

Presently came three young girls with copper pitchers;[2] they were the king's daughters. Neither of them recognized the stranger. While they drew water they looked curiously at her and one of them spoke to her, surprised to find such an old woman outside the city walls and all alone on a hot day:

"Why are you not in the town, good lady, in a cool shady house where younger women can take care of you?"

While thus addressing her the princess wondered, for she could not make out Demeter's station. She seemed poor and humble enough yet there was something grand about her as of royal breeding. It was difficult to know how to address her.

Demeter told her story:

"Good day, dear children, may the gods grant you kind husbands and the blessing of children. I am a stranger in this country, maidens, and my name is Dos. I come from Crete. We have been carried off by pirates and with many others I was brought to these shores, as far as Thoricos. We anchored there, for many more women were to be brought on board. That evening a feast was held on the shore, near our landing place. During the revelling I fled, hiding in the dark woods. I have been wandering since in search of a home. I do not know your country or your people. Dear children, have pity on me; help me find some work; a house in need of one who knows how to nurse a baby, make the master's couch, look after things and supervise the women".

Hearing this sad tale they felt pity for the aged stranger and one of them replied:

"Good lady, life is often harsh and painful; we must bear what the gods ordain".[3]

The three princesses conferred what to do, and decided to speak to their father. There were the large households of Triptolemus, Diocles,

---

[1] *Callirhoe, the traditional well of Eleusis with a dancing ground for women nearby.*
[2] *Pausanias gives them names reminiscent of Thracian tribes.*
[3] *This saying occurs many times in Greek literature.*

Polyxenus and Eumolpus, also their own, the royal household of Queen Metaneire to consider; one would have to see. They returned to the palace and told Celeus what they had seen and heard. The king listened attentively and at once despatched his daughters back to fetch the stranger, offering her a post as nurse to his small son, the late-born Demophoon, with generous pay.

So now Demeter followed the three princesses heading for the palace, walking behind them who were fair as flowers, clad in her black veil. They entered the gate of the royal palace. It was there that Metaneire awaited them, seated on a hunch of the solid slope, holding the baby to her breast.

Now Demeter's manner proved in no wise that of a suppliant stranger. As she touched the threshold, surrounded by the curious women of the royal household, the portal and vast hall were flooded with divine clarity. The queen grew pale with fear and, filled with respect, offered her throne to the stranger. But Demeter declined and remained silent, with downcast eyes, until Iambe had placed in front of her an ordinary massive seat of stone, covered with a white fleece.[1] On this Demeter seated herself and covered her head with her veil.

For a long time she remained in silent dolour, refusing food and drink, without taking notice of anyone, until the moment when Iambe, who was later to become her favourite, began to dance for her; she danced a pantomime of plants and animals and men coming together in the mating season and of the comeliness of sex.

As Iambe swayed and lifted up her skirt, Demeter smiled, and then laughed out aloud. Now Metaneire offered her sweet wine but she declined, saying that it was forbidden her, but asked instead for a mixture to be prepared of flour and water, and a kind of mint. This the honourable Dos accepted in order to found the holy rites. While she drank of it, the women pressed around her and the queen addressed her thus:

"Hail, woman, I believe indeed that you were not born of common parents, they surely were of noble birth, for your features betray a dignity and grace such as do those of our just kings. Alas, in spite of our griefs we must bear what the gods ordain; we are mere mortals and their yoke weighs heavy on us. But now that you have come, all

---

[1] The following ritual action was included in the Dromena. The sacred drink was called the Cyceon. The plant a kind of fern or mint.

I own is at your disposal. Please consent to bring up this child of mine given me by the immortals, this late-born son, unhoped for, object of all my prayers. If you raise him to reach the age of manhood I will reward you generously".

Crowned Demeter replied, "May the gods accord their gifts to you. I will gladly undertake to nurse your son. I do not think his nurses' imprudence will cause him to suffer a bad fate or corroding ill. I know of an antidote to evil, stronger by far than pierced wood, and of a goodly remedy that drives away the evil fates".

With these words Demeter took the child to her immortal breast and held it close. His mother was glad to see this happen.

And Demeter nursed and raised the boy, fine son of prudent Celeus. He grew like a divine being, without taking the human breast and indeed without any sort of ordinary food. Demeter rubbed him with ambrosia and fed him with her divine breath. It was her design to make a god out of the mortal child.

It was a marvel to everyone how he grew, resembling a god; and Demeter would have freed him from old age and death but for the folly of Metaneire.

I T HAPPENED in this manner: During the night Demeter stirred a fire in the hearth and placed the infant in it, skilfully increasing the heat and duration of this secret treatment. But Metaneire suspected something and hid one night to see what was happening.

When she saw her child laid in the glowing hearth, she shrieked aloud with horror:

"My son, the stranger hides you in a great fire and makes me cry and suffer bitterly!"

And the barbarous queen moaned, her knees gave way and she sat down, rocking to and fro, beating her thighs. Demeter turned and faced her with royal wrath. Angry, she took the child out of the fire and placed him away from her, on the stone floor. And she called out:

"I swear by the river Styx by which all the gods swear that I would have made your son into a god! Folly has made you commit the grossest error. I would have given him imperishable privilege. Now he cannot escape the fate of death. After the cycle of years is closed, the sons of Eleusis will fight each other forever, and the only immortality granted him will be that of fame!"

The palace became illuminated with Demeter's presence. Old age left her and she appeared in her true form, scented with summer and exuding light. She passed from room to room.

For a long time Metaneire remained speechless without even a thought for her cherished son. His sisters, attracted by his lamentable cries, appeared. One of them took him in her arms, another revived the fire, yet another raised his mother to her feet and led her away. Pressed round the child they bathed him who kicked and howled, used to different hands.

Demeter returned and spoke once more: "Let the people of Eleusis build me a temple at the foot of the Acropolis, above the clear-flowing spring, on the summit of the hill. There I will found my mysteries. There you shall pray to me and celebrate them reverently".

A T DAWN, after a night passed in sleepless vigil, Queen Metaneire and her attendants hastened to the king and recounted all that had come to pass. He in turn summoned his people, and a temple was planned and erected according to divine request. Demeter dwelt there, and continued to mourn for her lost child.

The years were barren. Oxen ploughed dry ground. Corn would not sprout and barley came up dry and pale like madmen's hair.

T HIS ZEUS saw and he reflected on the matter. He sent down winged Iris and other gods to placate Demeter, but she refused his gifts and would not listen to their pleadings. Finally Zeus despatched Hermes to Erebos; Argeiphontes of the golden wand. Him he instructed to exhort Hades with gentle speech, and to bring back holy Persephoneia from dark mists into the light, to dwell amongst the gods.

And Hermes delayed not; rapidly he plunged from Olympus into deep Borboros. Hermes found Pluto reclining by his listless wife. "Dark-haired Aidoneus, return Persephoneia or Demeter will destroy mankind; she will not leave her temple on the rocks. Have mercy on the race of men".

Hades looked at his queen, reflecting gravely upon the matter. Finally he acquiesced:

"Go Persephatta, go to your black-veiled mother. But remember that the husband you have in me is not unworthy amongst the immortals. When here with me you will ever reign over all beings that live and move;[1] you will be privileged amongst the gods".

When Persephone saw him thus relent she was glad; she changed under his eyes, life came back into her gaze, joy flooded her limbs and she began to dance. But before she departed with Hermes, Pluto gave her the seed of a pomegranate to eat.[2] This he did secretly, while glancing furtively about him, his object being to charm Persephone, and bring her back for part of the year, preventing her from staying forever with her mother in the upper region.

Then Hermes himself attached the steeds to his golden chariot. Persephone mounted it and at her side, holding the reins and whip with powerful grip. Argeiphontes traversed the subterranean palace. The horses flew obedient to his touch. They drove through sounding caverns and emerged from a grotto by the shore filled with transparent water and with rings and sheaves of reflected light. Neither the sea nor rivers nor grassy vales arrested their immortal flight. Fast they ascended to the hills, cutting through dense white clouds.

HERMES STOPPED in front of the fragrant temple where Demeter dwelt. When she perceived her child, Demeter, like a maenad, leaped for joy. They ran towards each other, but even amidst the joy of mutual greetings Demeter thought of something and she enquired anxiously:

"My child, tell me the truth. Have you accepted food or drink before leaving Hades? If you have not, you could live henceforth with me and your immortal Father".

---

[1] Not over ghosts but over the living on earth.
[2] The pomegranate, a symbol of forgetfulness. It grew on the spot where Orestes had slain his brother and on the tomb of suicides.

"Mother", replied Kore, "by using a ruse and force my husband made me eat the ripe seed of a pomegranate. I am his willing wife and he has power over me".

And she related to her mother the story of her rape and of the life below, and how she had parted from her dark-haired husband.

"Since you have eaten of the cursed seed", said Demeter, "you must annually return to the Land of Shades, but for two parts of the year you shall be with me and the other immortals. When the earth turns green and fragrant with flowers, you shall ascend from the dark mists, a marvel to both gods and men".

Mother and daughter passed the rest of the day in each other's company, united in heart and mind, giving and receiving a thousand tokens of mutual love, and now at last their hearts ceased to ache.

Later Hecate joined them; she who precedes and follows Persephone in the mysteries, and she gave to the goddess many signs of her attachment. The storm god gave his assent to Persephone's annual return. He sent down Rhea to summon Demeter to heaven, and the shining goddess descended to the plain of Rharia to meet her daughter there.

Demeter obeyed the decrees of the highest god. Now in the barren plain she made the corn sprout, made leaves and blossoms grow, and soon fat furrows filled with greeneared corn.

She instructed the just kings, Triptolemus, Diocles, the Master of the Carriage, powerful Eumolpus and Celeus, chief of the people. She taught them the accomplishment of her sacred mysteries, and revealed to them the lovely rites, the royal rites impossible to divulge, to penetrate or to transgress. Blessed those amongst mortal men who have been initiated in these mysteries! Those who have not taken part in the holy rites do not have the same fate, not even in Hades.

As an expression and an outer symbol, and as the basis for her work she gave the Greeks knowledge of the culture of the soil.

Soon noble-ordered grain swelled the plain of Rharia like gentle breath, the ears of corn moved in measure like a choir of dancers, rare poppy flashed, like grace, in the wide field. The hills of Attica were terraced and planted with vine, and in the orchards ripened heavy fruit.

After having established these mysteries, the goddess joined the other gods in high Olympus. There the two deities remained with Zeus of the thunderbolt.

Blessed by him whom they deign to love: to his mansion they send Pluto, giver of true wealth.

NOBLE DEO of fragrant Eleusis, and Paros girded by the waves, and rocky Antron, you who bestows the gifts of the seasons, and you, beauteous Persephone, grant me a life according to my heart's desire. Let me remember you with other songs.

THE LESSER MYSTERIES I

D ISCOURSE *of a mystagogue on the eve of the Small Eleusinian Festival held at Agra on the Ilisus, outside Athens. End of February. He is addressing older mustai and young neophytes at Athens.*

FRIENDS new and old, we have come together this day so as to clear our minds, and see the meaning of tomorrow's rites.

Those amongst you who have been initiated in previous years will know what is meant, but will do well to recollect themselves tonight, and to refresh their memories. Those who are here for the first time should try and reflect in their own minds:

What is it that you want?

How does your aim and the experiences that brought you here to our sacred telete relate to the rites of spring?

Did not, while you unquestioningly belonged to the circle of again-becoming, the coming of the deity mean plentiful crops, the fertile heifer in your stable, a god glowing in the grape, in the lust, too, that tightens limbs like sails, known with your husband, lover, wife or slave, and only that?

You may have known these things, and they are good; good as the cloudy blossoms, spawning fish, the nesting birds. And yet, the earth is full of ills, and ills the sea.[1] You have found life wanting, you have come.

Could not your feelings and your intimations, different from each to each, yet be likened to a breath of spring?

You have been dead; and now new life has begun to stir.

The god in you was absent. We herald his coming.

---

[1] *A line from a Boeotian poet.*

You were asleep like seed in wintry soil; obscure longing born of divine discontent has come to your dreams.

Like Kore you had fallen into generation.

Like Persephone of the lulled eyes you lived below, in bondage, amongst your herds and houses, children, goods.

Like Demeter great Love has mourned for you.

Now Light is kindled in the darkness.

The Wisdom of the gods, like Hermes of the golden wand, has come to rescue, and conducts you during our ascent.

Does the past life lie behind you like a barren dream?

Or have you always known, and loved, and waited in the dark?

Have you come here for grief and loss, satiety, a questing mind, for expiation of a burdening wrong? From the passion of hot youth or the disillusion of age, fear of death or any of the gnawing hungers? Has the god claimed you as his own; do you, like Ariadne, wait for the true Love? Or have you, like Semele, known the fertilizing flash of divine lightning, death rehearsed?[1] There are these and other motives for return.

You have begun to die, and we teach you to die and be reborn.

Tomorrow, by the banks of the Ilisus, take in the beauty of the world, the detail and the Whole; remember, try to apprehend how behind nature of the seven veils Mind remains stable, ancient and unchanged.

In generation, Chronos' realm, place is always and only place, and time is always and only time. This and individuation is the cause of ill.

The universe, the world in time and place are the imperfect image of the One.

The God whose garment is the sensible world is free of time and its conditions. Him we shall celebrate with our epoptic hymns.

Each blade of grass, each furry beast, the sprouting shoot upon the tree, to seeing eyes shines with the fulgent light of Dionysos.

---

[1] *Divine lightning kills and thus bestows eternal life.*

Those manifold changes that he suffers into winds and water and earth and stars and the birth of plants and animals are called Disappearances and New Births and the song sung to him is full of sufferings and wanderings, but also of great joy in another Birth.[1]

Now I want you to understand that near the Metroon of Demeter, during the festival of spring, we abstain from mourning;[2] we do not mourn our losses nor bewail our infirmities. Come to the holy place without your woes and your desires. You then may feed on Greater Life; you may perceive the way we lead.

After the festival is over, on the last day of Anthesterion, we meet again at this same place.

I shall begin the initiation to our sacred telete.

---

[1] Plutarch. On the Ei of Delphes.
[2] Abstention from mourning was part of the Pythagorean purification. Diogenes Laertius VIII 317.

THE LESSER MYSTERIES II

AND THEN WILL ALL THE MUSES SING
OF MAGNUS ANNUS BY THE SPRING
AS THOUGH GOD'S DEATH WERE BUT A PLAY[1]

A GRA. *A kurotrophos—one who teaches the young—is talking to a visiting priestess of the bearded Aphrodite of Perga. She is a short muscular woman with fleshy features and a neck that juts forward from rounded shoulders. She has an air of concentrated vitality and alertness. Doric Pamphilia, of which Perga is the capital, is her home. That part of southern Asia Minor is still cut off from the other Greek colonies, and Perga a stronghold of Asian religious tradition. The priestess is of Hittite race; she knows the dialect of Pamphilia and has learnt Greek; she has become discontented with the formalized traditions of a crumbling empire. She has sailed down the Cestus, and, passing through Cyprus, has come to Greece.*

Kurotr: What you have told me, noble Mezulla, of your cities and sanctuaries south of the Taurus ridge is of great import. The founders of the Mysteries had much contact with Egypt and Phoenicia, especially in the past, but our knowledge of the Eastern empire, in spite of Phrygian conquests, has been restricted. It will be pleasing to the gods that you have mastered Greek, and that the winds and Fates have brought you here. Let me now, since this is your earnest desire, speak of the Mysteries of Agra.

                They are most venerable, like your own, though not as ancient. Therefore the sap of life still courses in them lustily.

---

[1] *W. B. Yeats. Two Songs from a Play.*

Orpheus founded them, the Thracian Bard, in order to effect purification from a bloody deed. Of our hero Hercules you know.[1]

Mezulla: By Tesup, the pyres with his effigies burn annually on our coast. The peoples of the south call him Baal, or Sandon, and it is said in our land that he gained initiation from our priests. Near the Pontic confines of our empire he won the double-headed axe from them.[2]

Kurotr: The emblem of the Heraclydae. And what it signifies we know.

Now, as you saw, the sanctuaries on the Ilisus; founded to purify Heracles, who was not Greek and could not be admitted to Eleusis, belong to Kore and the Mother, to Artemis Agrotera, the Huntress; chaste Artemis who hunts down the wild beast out in the hills and in the breast, who delivers from mad passions, who purifies and hits the mark, she who directs the choir of the Muses, the same that you and past generations of Melissai have served.[3] At Agra she shares honours with another: Telepinu, if I remember rightly, you have called him.

Mezulla: The Divine Son of Tesup.

Kurotr: Zeus. We call him Dionysos; Zagreus is his Asian name with us, and it signifies great Hunter—of darkness and barbarous ignorance. The Divine Incarnation of immortal creed. Together the great gods ensure fertility.

Mezulla: And so with us, in the heroic past.

Kurotr: Now in the month of Anthesterion we celebrate the annual preliminary initiation here. The visitors, our neophytes and the Athenian people, come down from Athens and pitch their tents in the sacred grounds. This to remind

---

[1] *The Murder of the Centaur Nessus by Hercules. Diodorus of Sicily IV 14.*

[2] *From the Amazon queen Hippolyta. Some scholars believe that the Amazons were Hittite consecrated warriors.*

[3] *These various functions and attributes of Artemis are given by several ancient authors. Artemis is another aspect of the Mother deity. She is Asiatic. Artimus Ibismus in Lydia. A cone-shaped idol with a female bearded head in Perga, that seems a triangle or mountain to the eye, the same as the bi-sexual Aphrodite of Cyprus and the great Mother of vanished Pessinunt. The cone-shaped goddess is also Aegean.*

them of a barbarous state before the goddess gave us agriculture. We take the throng down to the river and there asperse them with the sacred water. Public lustrations are for all to see, and are a rite. The inner meaning is expounded to the neophytes, and are, for them, a preparation.[1] They then receive instruction on the meaning of true poverty, and are sworn into lifelong silence. Our mystagogues perform the sacred dance with clashing bronze,[2] like the great planetary gods revolving round the human soul from birth.

The immortals themselves initiate the mystae, in truth revolving round him day and night, as sun and stars. And God supreme, is he not the great coryphaeus of the universe?[3]

[*He is not telling anything. This is philosophy.*]

Orpheus brought us these from Thracian Samos, and there, if you were initiated, is a choregie and play.[4]

Mezulla: The dances have been known in our cult.

Kurotr: And to the Phrygians after you. Have they not come from Media and Baktria, and beyond?—so Dionysos said, the roaring god whose servitude is sweet.[5]

[*A pause. The two remain in deep thought.*]

Kurotr: With these and similar ceremonies we speak to the new neophytes, Athenians mostly,[6] seldom strangers who have come to settle here, or who inhabit other parts of Greece. And speech we use but sparingly at our Mysteries of Spring. But it so happens that people who have never

---

[1] *The difference between exoteric and esoteric teaching is noted by Clement of Alexandria, among others.*

[2] *The "Thronismos", part of the purification ceremony. The mystagogues dance round the candidate seated in a chair, beating bronze instruments.*

[3] *Dion Chrysostomos XII 387 (202)*

[4] *Plato. Euthydemus 277 c.*

[5] *Euripides. Bacchae.*

[6] *Every inhabitant of united Attica was called an Athenian. Barbarians were admitted if they spoke Greek and settled in the country. But all through antiquity thoughtful individuals travelled in order to study at the various schools.*

heard of truth and have reflected little, find their minds are opened; such is the action of the Divine on the sleeping soul.

[*A pause.*]

Kurotr: Sometimes, within the sacred precinct, the god comes in a dream. We use the juice of poppy and essence of mint.

Mezulla: Across our northern ranges, so I learnt, lie fields of a black poppy on a tableland. The Idaean priests distil the juice from them.[1] The poppy is the sacred flower of the Mother.

Kurotr: Only Demeter knows of its right use.

Mezulla: Most true, I have seen it abused in Eastern ports.

Kurotr: Well, you will understand that what we show with rite and song, is a first introduction into a cycle of ideas. We chose our people, and during the six months that divide from the Great Eleusinians, we give oral instruction to our neophytes—here for artists at the temple of the Ilissidian Muses—at Athens, and in Eleusis. We teach the knowledge of the self, gnome, the power of right decision, cosmology, arithmetic, astronomy, the sciences, medicine and the crafts and their right use in daily life; other things too according to the needs that rise from year to year. For nothing, in the mysteries, must fossilize; for they are ever young."

Mezulla: [*moved, for she has seen great connections*]

Telepinu descends, and is reborn with every year. . .[2]

---

[1] *This is conjectural. Some schools used drugs. But the fields of the black poppy are first heard of in the Osmanli period. Karahissar, the "Fort of the Black Poppy", now stands in ruins above the modern town. The corybantes of the Phrygian Cybele were known for their orgiastic dances.*

[2] *Mezulla refers to the myth of Telepinu recorded in cuneiform writing on clay tablets, published in translation by Gotze and other Hittite scholars. It is a fertility myth similar to those of Sumer, Egypt, and to that of Kore. Telepinu descends and drought ensues. The great goddess sends the bees to find him.*

THE LESSER MYSTERIES III

SPRING is the time of birth and death,
For the dumb ache to move the buried root,
The snake spreads terror in the tender vein.[1]
Ghosts crowd around, avid for the new womb
Demons crowd inner space, feed on the coursing blood.
Beware of the polluted air, the clammy moon.

Spring is the time to exorcize the house
With branch of buckthorne,[2] blood and tar,
With clashing bronze; foot on the ancient fleece.[3]
We signal the catharsis of the inner man.
We show you the reversal of the signs,[4]
And how to tame and use the swift, bright power.

---

[1] *Here emblem of the fertility demon; of the energy, sexual power.*
[2] *R. Cathartica. Purging Buckthorne. Used with tar to remove unclean spirits during the Anthesteria.*
[3] *The fleece of a Ram, Zeus Codion. The golden fleece. We meet with it in the Dromena; in the spring festival the initiate places his left foot on it to symbolize participation in the everlasting sacrifice of the dying god. Bronze purifies, the noise keeps evil influences at bay.*
[4] *Of birth and death.*

The Major Mysteries I

D IALOGUE *between a Kerykes and a Mystagogue.*[1] *Eleusis. One day in early summer.*

Kerykes: I have asked you, Poimander, to come and visit us so soon in the year in order to discuss the coming Dromena. Have you thought about it yet? Have you begun to work on it?

Poimander: I have thought much, Hermippus, but have written nothing. We spoke about it at Lysander's house. We agreed that the myth has a triple meaning: that the Descent of Kore symbolizes the fall of the soul into generation and multiplicity, descent into a netherworld at physical death, and the way as taught in the Mysteries: the craft of dying practised in this life. We have not decided which, if any one, of these meanings we should stress in the coming Dromena.

Kerykes: Good. Whichever you choose—unless you wish simply to represent the Rape of Kore as laid down in the sacred hymns—abide by it and do not mix the lines of thought. One interpretation, if rightly put, implies the others. It will be pleasing to the goddess if you do something different from the Dromena four years ago, when we enacted Her myth, with dances.

           [*A pause.*]

           Do you think you could divide the chorus to show the parallel between bodily death and death in initiation?

Poimander: [*reflects*]
           It could be done, but not by me. Two choruses are difficult to handle and have never been tried.

---

[1] *Kerykes: descendant of Keryx, son of Hermes, initiate who lives at Eleusis.*

Kerykes: Do as you deem best.

Poimander: I have some notes on the theme of Royal Initiation. It is very high, very far from where I am; these are only thoughts on what we have heard.

Concentrates, quotes from memory:

On the Royal Initiation that is rarely spoken of.[1] The highest degree of initiation demands superior qualities of being, an unceasing watchfulness, also a final stage of admission to the Royal Rites.

The initiate suffers great trials.

He renounces his self-will completely, he renounces even Beauty.

He sheds all that holds him back.

He passes the statues of the Soul and of Thought.

He casts off his garments.

He remains alone.

He advances, revolving round the Centre.

His feet are immersed in water, his body and head are dry.

He enters the sanctuary; there, by divine Grace and Love he experiences Union. He becomes a God.

He leaves the sanctuary. On emerging he beholds the statues of the Beautiful and the God.

It is difficult to cleave to divine Union.

The many fail, though some have seen and known with Memory.

He who has been made whole, and known the flight of the alone to the Alone, can still fall back, then reascend.[2]

Things recorded of the Royal Initiate, of his Birth and Growth and the true doctrine, and greater magistrature;

[1] *Les Mysteres d'Eleusis. V Magnien. Payot Paris. P 353.*
[2] *Plotinus.*

how, gods and divine men having chosen Him, He acceded to great commandment, and how He established Himself, and how a conjuration arose against Him and until what point it succeeded, though not finally; these things are worthy of being remembered and have been told.

They have been told of holy Osiris;[1] we could tell a similar tale.

Kerykes: [*reflects*]
Very beautiful. But not this year. There are many new neophytes, from Boeotia too, and the islands. Give them something more immediate and practical, nearer their own stage of development. It will be best to compose a Dromena about the secret doctrine showing the stages of the journey of the soul, with our ceremonies and symbols which you know. This, in a wider circle, includes the elements of Royal Initiation and refers to the myth of Demeter. Do you think you could do that?

Poimander: I can try.

Kerykes: Lysander can assist you. But remember that we want you to compose from your own understanding of our teaching, from your experience and divination.

Be very strict with self-purification. You know, but need to bear in mind that euphrosyne is a necessity for this creative work. To lead the good life, one of piety, gaiety and humility, to write from that inner gladness which is also good sense and from a healthy soul; that is right. Be careful, practice sophrosyne; that quality which supports moderation, balance.[2]

Do not leak. And never work from memory of mere words. Reach out for the incorporeal idea, and what it has wrought in your soul; then you shall have atopia, the freshness and originality that comes from living faith.[3]

[*A pause.*]

---

[1] Synesius. De providentia II 4.
[2] Definitions given by ancient authors.
[3] Plato. Phaidros 229 b.

Kerykes: It is our aim to keep the holy truth alive by our active understanding. For this reason the Eumolpides have decreed of old that we should ever recreate the Dromena.

[*A pause.*]

Pray to the Muses to inspire you. See Parysatis about music and the postures. Begin soon, and when you are ready, come down together to discuss the parts and the beginning of rehearsals.

And now tell me about yourself . . .

THE MAJOR MYSTERIES II

T HE MIDDLE of September. After a few days of festive preparation in Athens the procession of mustai start for Eleusis in the forenoon. The sacrificial pigs and travelling bags have been sent ahead. The statue of Iacchos is to follow. The pilgrims carry as yet no sacred objects, but bread and goat cheese for the day. They leave the city along the paved sacred road that crosses the Cephisus bridge, the plain and wooded outskirts of Athens and climb the height to the Aigaelaos pass flanked on both sides by ancestral graves.

Early in the day the procession reaches the bridge that spans the Cephisus. It is here that, following an ancient custom, the participants make fun of each other's weaknesses and bad features, and this they do with gusto, giving full scope to their quick Attic wit. The theory has been put forward that Athenian comedy had its origin here.

The people approach the bridge with mirthful expectation, some apprehension too. As they draw near jibes and laughter begin to fly about and loosen the ranks.

The wife of a senior Kerykes, who has been in Athens to visit a friend and is returning this way, mounted on a mule, leaves the procession and stations herself near the bridge head. She is well known for her caustic gift of observation and quick tongue. A Thracian by birth, she has the high cheekbones and pale grey eyes of the North, a homely figure and a commanding presence. Her deep-set eyes wander with amusement over the known faces. They come to rest on the wife of an Athenian aristocrat, a wealthy member of the Areopagus, a tall slim woman with hooded eyes and a proud mouth. She walks near the head of the procession.

The Priestess: Room, room for Galaxoroe!" [*She cries, giving her mule a spur so that it starts.*]

216

Slaves, where is her barge, eh, clear the landing place.

[*Pushing and laughing the people round Galaxoroe clear the ground before her and bow down in the oriental manner. Two men rip off branches from a wayside bush and walk behind her, fanning like Egyptian slaves.*]

Alcmene, Leda, fortunate Europa, [*The priestess mimics Europa caressing the neck of the divine bull.*]

Those were the days, what, Galaxoroe? [*The great lady cannot help laughing though a trifle uneasily.*]

She has come to Eleusis for several years and already knows that her caste pride is her worst side. The oligarchs of Athens are still rich and powerful though a new merchant class is slowly coming up. She has been brought up on her father's estate and there has known her equals only, and the humble farmers that worked the fields for him. She has married a steady, unexciting noble. Citizens of every rank come to Eleusis, and she had not liked mixing with them when she first came. Occasionally she is still visited by dreams and aspirations of mythical grandeur and eminence that find no scope in small Athens, and certainly none in the strict discipline of Eleusis.

But now the priestess has spotted a fine girl with the tight glowing skin of youth and a big, graceful body. With her almond shaped dark eyes and secret smile she is the living image of the Maid. She does not look her best today, sweating and with untidy hair bound at the top of her head. Always looking for appraisal she knows what is coming to her and tries to behave unconcerned.

With an exaggerated gesture the priestess throws up her arms, places one elbow in a cupped hand and her chin in the other; a frequent attitude of the girl who tries to hide a slightly receding chin in this manner.

The	Kallimache! [*She mimics her*]
Priestess:	Help with the washing?
Kallimache:	But there is my dancing lesson to attend, and I want to go to the beach. Oriander says I have improved my carriage, every one looked at me as I crossed the agora yesterday, like a caryatid he says. I must have that

Kallimache: Tyrian linen; father really might give it me, instead of buying another dreary piece of land".

[Kallimache reddens under her tan, the neighbours giggle and a young man shouts.]

Young Man: Better be noticed, beauteous Kallimache, than to be ignored. That never happens to you, eh?

[*He makes his way to her side with protective male arrogance. He has Ionian blood, and looks, and is a promiscuous young man, attracted to the girl and to many others. The priestess knows his cockiness but for the moment leaves him alone, since an impulse mixed of sex and kindness brought him to the girl's side; she rides to the end of the line where shouts and laughter soon betray her presence.*]

Kallimache: O Hernander, stiff in the buttocks, turkey-cock! [*And she blows herself up and hollers like a turkey. The youth flashes ungry dark eyes at her but she laughs good-naturedly and taps a passing youth on the shoulder.*]

Come on you, carry on now, go on, do it.

But he is too shy. Instead a short stocky man with blunt features leaves the ranks. He whisks out a tear jar and steals up behind a young woman who tends to make up situations. Just now she fancies herself in love with the husband of a friend. The man, who looks like, and is called Silenus in jest, silently thrusts the jar under her nose and saunters off. She looks startled. But already he has spotted another victim. He snatches off his pointed travel hat with a wide brim that shades the eyes and is turned up at the back and, bowing abjectly, like a beggar, he runs alongside a citizen who is known to be tight-fisted.

Silenus: A coin for Hermes, one coin only. [He chants in a whining voice. And in his ordinary manner]

Can you bear it, does it pain you badly?"

[*The others, entering the game, clutch at their satchels with a pained expression; and...*]

Come, act it.

The Citizen: But I always...

A Chorus: Give plenty at the temple and for the poor.

The citizen decides then and there to increase his donation to Eleusis. What he does not know is that it will not be accepted, since it will be done to be seen of men. He has a lot to learn, but he will.

Silenus has spotted a small corpulent woman with a pitiful expression. "No, I am not enjoying myself, how could I enjoy myself like other people. I feel miserable, things are different for me". After some more of this, instead of laughing, the woman's face puckers and she begins to cry. She is hard of hearing and in poor health. The teachers try to wean her from self-pity. Instantly the others surround her and Silenus hugs her: he has given her more than she can take. Another older woman gets off her mule, and they seat her on it. Silenus pats it on the buttocks:

Silenus: There, there. [*The kindness and attention has restored her and she is glad to ride. Trot, trot, the animal takes her along the paved road. Silenus looks along the ranks once more.*]

Ah, there he is, and she right beside him. [*He reaches into his pocket and makes for a couple. He sidles up to the man.*]

How about a visit to the slave market, Colonus. Too busy, eh, with the warehouses and affairs of State. [*And in a stage whisper, with hunched shoulders he mimics a Phoenician merchant*]

Leetle Nubian girls, only twelve years old. [*He brandishes some tablets with satirical drawings but quickly hides them. The girls round the two look away, people laugh and the man, who tends to pomposity, looks interested. Now Silenus brings out a phallic amulet and dangles it before his eyes, then gallops off, laughing like a goat.*]

This scene was aimed at the wife of Colonus, who has eyed it with dark suspicious eyes. Her nose is too long and she is gaunt, with fine eyes. She has followed her husband, seeking initiation more out of a somewhat mean sexual jealousy than other reasons. This the teachers know, but they also know that underneath her sharp nosed irritation is genuine affection for her husband and a sensitive emotional nature.

An elderly neighbour who knows her jealousy better than she does herself, chaffs her:

"Look out, august Hera of the snowy arms, do not let them get away with it".

She is about to reply sharply when she thinks the better of it; one must not show anger at Cephisus. "Just wait, I will give her a piece of my mind back in Athens".

But now the bridge has been left behind. Hilarity subsides, Silenus is seen talking earnestly to a man at the end of the line who has not been ragged.

The procession crosses the plain which is partly wooded and partly cultivated, and from the farms situated in the fields come husbandmen, their women and their children with offerings of grapes and figs, and with gourds of water mixed with wine or honey. At midday the procession halts where the road begins to rise, to rest and feed under some ancient pines that exude freshness even in the midday heat. Fern and heather grow beside the mastic bushes.

The animals are left to graze and drink from a wayside trough. After a rest and sleep of some of the older people, the pilgrims set out again, for the pass is still well ahead of them.

The hillside resounds with solemn hymns and prayers. Silenus plays a flute, and distant shepherds answer his in a dialogue of question and answer, and these are old Arcadian melodies. Some girls have made garlands of flowers, vine leaves and grapes plucked from the wayside.

Now Silenus discards his hat and staff, his cloak and peplum. Almost naked, hairy and shining like red glazed clay, he really looks like a satyr emerged from the woods. A cymbal starts the rhythm for a slow dance. Silenus passes his flute to a youth who takes up the tune and he begins to dance ahead of the procession. He seems a sylvan disciple of Bacchus, carrying out some simple steps with intricate variations, expressing reverence, a search, and joy. The people watch him quietly.

Later, the olive trees cast marked shadows east, the bees are fewer, freshness meets them from the heights. And as the shadows overtake them, the pilgrims reach the pass, and on the other side lies Eleusis across the bay of Salamis.

As they descend a slow winding road a mild still night begins to fall. When they finally reach the shore at the foot of the hill, the procession stops for a last rest; many people discard their clothes and are wading into the shallow water. At some distance from the shore where it is still shallow enough to stand, deep enough to swim:

Kallimache: It is good that it should be dark. So many men.

Older woman: Better for me than for you, my dear.

Third woman: Never too tired or too dirty to be thinking of them, eh?

Fourth woman: We should remember the meaning of this rite.

Older woman: Come, come Melissa, we do remember, no need to be preaching. Besides the day of purification is tomorrow.[1]

A silent girl swims out with fast strokes. Lies on her back and looks at the immense and starry sky oned with the dark diaphanous sea which is deep green, almost black; on the curving beach she has seen how it unrolls a fine border of foam, as from a woman's garment. The girl feels the water on her naked skin. She is a conscious part of the Whole, and it is infinite, and beyond speech or thought. This is ecstasy. Wrapped in the living cloak of the Divinity she prays:

The Silent Girl: Heavenly Aphrodite, great Urania, whose spangled cloak unfurls a gleaming hem with gentle rhythm, unfold me . . .

---

[1] *"Halade mustai" ("Into the sea, ye initiates!") was the call to the ritual bath.*

THE MAJOR MYSTERIES III

FOR FOUR *days the mustai have stayed at Eleusis, have bathed and fasted, offered their sacrificial pigs and played strenuous competitive games. Now they are gathered after nightfall to await the coming of Iacchos.[1] He is on his way from the Iaccheion of Athens, carried by a group of epheboi.*

Melissa: Should we not light our torches?

Kerykes: Not yet. The dusk of Salamis awaits another light. Let us go down the sacred way and meet the god.

The mustai fall into rows of two and two and, always watching the pass, slowly descend to the shore. The mediterranean sky deepens and now, over the mountain ridge appears a pinpoint of light. The epheboi with the statue have come within sight of Eleusis. Their distant chant is faintly heard. The light is that of a single torch carried ahead of the god. Absorbed, the mustai watch the light advance.

Melissa: The first-born Star of Night. [*In a flash she sees many things together.*]

Kerykes: Star from the East. Hail Iacchos! Hail the Light! Now let us sing.

And the hills resound with hymns that celebrate the giving and receiving. One by one the torches of the mustai are lit; reflected in still waters, they move to meet the god.

---

[1] *Iacchos is Phanes, and Phanes is Dionysos. The symbol here of divine consciousness.*

The Dromena I

T HE TELESTERION is built of brick and wood in an early Doric style.[1] It is oblong with four columns at the front and a few steps descending there and at the back, and is surrounded by a wide enclosure and a wall of rough hewn stone. Laurel, bay and stone oak grow there, and the wild flowers of the season. It faces south-west; at the back of this temple is a space reserved for the Dromena. Except for a short run along the steps that descend from the back wall which is paved, it is covered with short thick grass where flowers grow: crocus and anemone in early spring, poppy and camomile and the mint used in the mysteries later in the year. It ends in a semi-circle of terraced seats cut into a hillside; during the festival these are covered with wooden planks. It is partitioned off from the rest of the grounds by wooden walls, and is reached by two slightly sloping corridors built into the sides of the Telesterion, and from a small aperture leading down from the altar. It has no other access. The grounds are closely guarded by fierce dogs. It is severely prohibited to enter unbidden.

---

[1] *Of the original Telesterion no trace has been found.*

The Dromena II

PRE-DAWN *at the Telesterion of Eleusis. It is quite dark with an autumnal tang in the air and distant stars. The chosen mustai, a hundred people or more, file in through one of the side entrances and take their seats. They are wearing their usual clothes and over them the skins of animals, mostly of fawn or goat to protect them from the cold.[1] Each carries a small cushion to sit on.*

The people are in a state of deep religious emotion and mental alertness induced by the impressions and experiences of the past few days; by a catharsis of mind, feeling and the bodily system, and by a drug used at Eleusis. A housewife, shivering a little, in a low voice to her neighbour:

Housewife: Did they give you the mixture to drink?

A Physician: Yes, as soon as we awoke, it was stronger than on previous days.

Housewife: It does not taste good but it feels good after the long fast.

Physician: It contains everything the body needs—and more: water, flour, honey and the juice of the sacred mint. [*Gravely*] Demeter herself invented it.

Housewife: Is it true that fasting without games is bad for you?

Physician: That is so.

A Poet: We should not talk. Soon it will begin.

A Girl: What will it be? A spectacle?

Poet: So I believe.

---

[1] The obvious garment to wear during nocturnal orgies and during the ceremonial dances in honour of the dying god that were sometimes held on the snowy summit of a mountain. Participants of religious ceremonies are seen wearing them on early seals of Asia Minor. The mustai are the descendants of a long line of "satyrs".

A few people only talk in whispers.

Girl: How well one sleeps in Eleusis.

Poet: By Zeus, yes. I had a dream...

Girl: [*eagerly*]
Me too; a winged horse sprang from a rocky shore as of
living pentelic marble in the rising sun...

Others: Silence now, silence.

*There is a movement in front of the temple wall. All sit in silence.
Reverent concentration gathers force. The eye gets used to the dark
and distinguishes moving shapes entering and taking their stand: the
chorus of the Kerykes; the hymnodes. An ephebe pyrophoros enters
carrying a lighted torch with which he kindles torches held aloft by
two epheboi dressed in black and white peplums respectively, facing
each other across the scene of action. The light reveals the following
scene:*

*In the centre of the paved space which fronts the steps and temple
wall, on what seems a couch or bier covered with furs and linen
clothes lies a woman in a posture of sleep or death. She wears festive
clothes and elaborate gold jewels; her hair is curled and banded; at
her head are placed a bowl and a jug of clay.*

*The action of the Dromena is played in a highly stylized manner.
The protagonists move as figures on a frieze or in a sacred dance. The
chorus alternatively speaks or chants for them, as the text requires.*

Chorus: Mountainous homeland, veined great-breasted sea; the
coast, a shining sodden floor where Thetis' stallions race
with unbound manes.

Islands that draw our pentecosters of the curved prow.[1]
The hamlet in the wood, white smoke rising in a straight
line from homely hearth.

The cool, serrated panoply of shade, ripe gourd out in the
field.

And bees intent on the erect corolla.

---

[1] The usual type of early Greek warship was the pentecoster, or 'fiftyoar', a long narrow galley with
23 benches with two oarsmen at each. It came into use about the 8th century, and in Homeric
poems appears as something wonderful.

225

The winds of Greece on the warm stone fashioned by Gaea, or made noble by man.

Stem rocky home of kings, ringed round with lake and marsh,

Or girded city, work of Erechtheus:

Agora, temple, alcove, laughter, tears.

Exchange of gold and ware, caress and thrust of sword, and death.

A carcass in the asphodels, a festive bier.

Beyond, barbarous shores, Herculean Gates and pathless waterways.

And to the West, the Island of the Blessed.

Fish, insect, fowl and beast.

The race of men.

This Cosmos: earth and moon, sun, planets, fixed stars, galaxies.

[*A pause and change of key*]

It is a dream, dreamt in a dark cave.

While the chorus continues the woman, with her eyes still closed, stirs lightly, rouses herself on one elbow and lifts her closed face as if listening to voices coming from far away, above herself.

Chorus: This world of multiplicity, these myriad forms.

Like a deep-scented flower of death burst into many blooms.

It roused desire, Psyche, lured you from heavenly life.

From being one, your self is broken in the prism of time.

For twenty centuries of stony sleep you dreamt a dream.[1]

Often you stirred, and listlessly sank back, fed by unholy pomegranate and dark caress.

---

[1] Paraphrase from W. B. Yeats. *The Second Coming.*

But now your hour has come.

Rise up, entrust yourself.

To divine guidance of the holy creed,

And follow Hermes of the golden wand.

Arise, of the water of forgetfulness. Drink.

Of the water of remembrance. Drink!

The woman slowly opens her eyes and sits up. She picks up the jug and empties it to the left. She picks up the bowl and, turning her head to the right, she drinks of it. She looks around her as if trying to make out where she is. She tries to rise to her feet but fails, and sinks halfway back.

Chorus: As yet you dream that you have wakened Demons and vengeful shades lurk in the gloom. The low dream holds you in its grip.[1]

Resist it.

The two epheboi lower their torches one after the other. It grows dark. Enter three daemoniac masked apparitions with dim glowing torches. They dance round Psyche while the chorus speaks.

Chorus: Face the dread apparitions born of your own mind;

Empusa of the triple face; dog, ass, and woman,[2]

Your own multiplicity. Know her for what she is.

A creature of the low imagination.

Distrust, believe her not, be mindful.

And invoke great Hermes. Distrust the mortal mind,

It fills a false Elysium and Borboros with fancy shapes.

During the last lines the ritual dance led by the female mask, which expresses exaggerated vanity and is decked out with vulgar

---

[1] On the low and the high dream: T. S. Eliot, Essay on Dante. Also: Proclus MS. Commentary of the first Alcibiades of Plato: ". . .in the most holy of the mysteries (i.e. the Mysteries) prior to the manifest presence of the god certain terrene daemons present themselves to the view, disturbing those that are initiates, divulging them from the undefiled good, and exciting them to matter. .". I believe he speaks of imagination in the spiritual life.

[2] Suidas. Aristophanes. Frogs.

ostentation, is joined by more figures of demons and of genii who are slight caricatures of real ones.

Chorus: Pray to the gods, awake, lend them no force.

Psyche stirs with an effort to awaken from the nightmare. She lifts an arm, passes it over her eyes; it sinks back. The demons fade.

Enters Triptolemus with a lighted torch. He is played by the Hierophant of Eleusis and wears the purple Asiatic cloak with narrow sleeves. Silently he stands over the sleeper, and his being expresses calm, infinite compassion, stern, conscious love. This is the Good Shepherd. He touches her on the forehead but she cannot see him, except in her dream.

He lowers his torch. Simultaneously the Erinyes appear in the background; a close knit group with masks and live snakes coiled round their heads and necks. They advance as one, taking short leaps and shaking their torches at the sleeping figure.

She turns away as if in anguish and hides her head in her arm. While the Chorus speaks she turns as if giving them half a backward glance, but quickly hides her head again.

Chorus: Do not look back or the erynies will get you

And cast you back into the pit, and this is second death.

There is no going back, only a going forward or a going under.

The sacred precinct shields you from their wrath,

Enter, remain therein; it is in you.

Cast down the burden of past folly and enchantment,

The dreaded sisters thrive on false remorse and the wrong memory.

Give up your suffering, lend it no force.

Remember who you were from the beginning,

A child of starry heaven, pure, unspoilt,[1]

Freed from obsession with past wrong and old desire

---

[1] Suidas. Lexicon: Pneumaticon Soma: "luminous vehicle which is of the nature of the stars, is eternal and is nevertheless imprisoned in the body".

Chorus...   You shall face Triptolemus, Judge of Dead and Living.

Psyche moves and slowly rises to her feet. She opens her eyes. While the erynies stay in the background she moves slowly about as if looking for an exit. When she cannot discover one her movements register disquietude and anguish.

Chorus: Winged Hermes travels light, and so must you. Divest yourself of wishing, willing and imagining, Know that nothing is yours, nothing is needed on this journey save the eidolon.

Psyche takes off her necklace, armbands and tunic. She remains in a short white peplum, symbol of the eidolon or vehicle, the body; or what is essential in contrast to what is inessential and acquired. The erynies fade. It is dark.

A pause.

When it grows light Psyche is not there. Enters Demeter, holding aloft her torch, clad in her seven dark veils. The part is played by the Hierophantess of Eleusis who moves with impressive dignity. She seeks her daughter.

Chorus: [*this is a dirge*]
Kore, my child! I have scanned earth and sky

Asia and Europe, the blind, cruel sea,

The hidden mountain caves ever shrouded in mist

The crowded cities of the East. In vain!

Forgetting and forgotten, my Beloved, by gods and men

You are yet present in a Mother's heart and

I shall wait, and never rest from toil until

My deathless eyes behold you once again.

But who can show a way?

Demeter sits down and veils herself. Enter Hecate from the other entrance. Growling and alert, three powerful dogs strain a chain she firmly holds. They are the fierce trained animals that guard the temple precinct which it is forbidden to enter without permission. In the Dromena they symbolize the three-headed dog of Hecate, which stands for right attention in the Eleusinian teaching. Hecate is the goddess who guards this teaching and keeps it alive in the home, in everyday life. She guards the mysteries, she guards the family.

Hecate: Revered Deo, you have called and here I am.

Come with the speed of wind from my cavernous home[1]

For it is I who heard Persephone

And I can show a way; for did you not

Entrust me with the sacred fire of the earth, the hearth?

I watch in the deep gloom, my triple-headed guardian

Well knows the way of Love, the secret path.

Prescribing and recording I precede and follow.

Demeter has risen and has greeted Hecate with a gesture of joy and hope. The goddesses meet in the centre and embrace. Then Demeter comes forward and raises her arms as if addressing heaven:

Chorus: Cronide, brother, you who are the Power

Hear me who am Love. By your dark thunderclouds

I swear: I shall not rest from toil nor wear

Immortal youth, nor dwell in my true home until

I find and bring to you our child, the human soul.

She turns and faces Hecate. With a gesture she beckons to her to lead the way. Hecate bows to her, the goddesses leave.

Follows an interval of perfect starlit silence. The mustai become aware how still it has become; even the distant sea is sleeping, and this hour animal life is hushed. But now, from the hillside some distance away, comes the sound of flutes, a slow dirge which gathers momentum, then breaks off and starts again on a livelier note. This is no coincidence but part of the Dromena. Some hieraules, consecrated musicians, have been waiting in the hills for a light signal from the Telesterion, and are now playing parts of an ancient

---

[1] *The cave of Hecate was shown at Eleusis. Legend places Hecate at crossroads, i.e., the soul meets her at moments of decision, of birth and death, and there she is either terrible or benevolent. The initiate learns gnome, the power of right decision. At times Hecate is close to Artemis: both are representations of esoteric work.*

Phrygian shepherd's song recorded by Orpheus and his followers. They symbolize the 'Satyrs' or thyrsos-bearers, the voice of the mysteries reaching the soul engrossed and lost in sense-based life, and we imagine them moving with lighted torches through the dense woods, espied from afar.

Perhaps wakened by the sound, the cocks of Eleusis begin to crow on nearby and distant farms[1].

It grows imperceptibly lighter. Dew has begun to fall.

Psyche has come in and, as if seeing the thyrsos bearers in the distance, above the heads of the spectators, has slowly raised her arms in a gesture of hope and humble greeting.

Chorus: Psyche, Beloved of the gods, rejoice!

The flutes of Pan, the cocks of Eleusis mark the end of night.

Enter in a single file, Triptolemus the Torch-Bearer, and three epopts carrying a seat, a white folded fleece, and a torch. They place the seat next to what seemed a couch, and is now being uncovered. It is the sacred cist of Demeter made of wood and carved in relief.

The following action closely corresponds to the one in the myth of Demeter.

One epopt places the fleece on the seat. Another leads Psyche to it and beckons to her to sit down which she does, with her back to the audience. The third places the lighted torch in her hand. The first opens the cist and extracts the objects of the cult one by one. The figurantes stay in a row, as on a vase-painting or frieze and pass the objects from hand to hand.

Triptolemus stands in front of Psyche. First, a veil is taken from the cist and placed over Psyche's head.

Chorus: Initiation is death.

Initiation is a marriage.

Be seated on the fleece of the slain god.

Receive the veil of ignorance;

Mystae, veiled one I declare you.

---

[1] *Fowl was not eaten at Eleusis, but was an article of export from the bay of Salamis.*

Chorus: To know that you know nought is the new knowledge,

    Dwell in it fast and sealed, speak not.

    Humbly, remain unseen of men.

    Before you would go up, you must go down.

    Put out your torch, unlearn your human thoughts.

Psyche lowers her torch.

Chorus: Unlearn your love and face your solitude,

    Let Pluto's darkness come upon you fully.

    Relight your torch, kindled of divine truth,

    Follow the Guide whom you love.

Triptolemus kindles her torch on his own. The Cyceon is taken from the cist and handed to Triptolemus. Psyche removes her veil from her face and receives the drink.

Chorus: I offer you the body of the god mixed

    With the holy plant that bestows unity.

    Now, distant, hardly known, hardly believed

    The voice of Eleusis sounds for you.

A branch of laurel, or of pine topped with a cone is taken from the cist and held aloft. Psyche, still with her back to the audience, looks at it over her shoulder.

Chorus: Behold the golden bough; a branch

    Of the vast, ever growing universe.

    Green thyrsos, ever green! locked up

    In it the great Fertility Wand,

    Too, of the awakened will, new Life.

    It shall be yours.

The thyrsos is handed to Psyche.

Chorus: Now face the Judge, the Master of the Carriage.

Psyche turns and faces Triptolemus for the first time.

Chorus: Face him with a heart light as summer winds

For now ascent begins, if you are ready.

At this moment the flutes accompanied by cymbals are heard again much nearer, perhaps within the enclosure of the Telesterion, and their tune is urgent and joyful. A sigh, a shiver of deep feeling and enthusiasm runs through the rows of mustai. When the tune has been played the instruments fade with the exception of a single flute. It accompanies the following words.

Chorus: Broken the troubled silence of a sleeping world

Forget dark Erebos, blind Night, shed the low dream,

And meet the dawn, the hope, new Birth of man.

The flute stops. The sea, stirred by the morning winds that blow towards the shore, sounds in the distance, like the sea heard in a shell. It is dawn. A formation of early birds, storks or wild geese on their way south pass overhead and their cry cleaves the air. Slowly the dawn colours.

Chorus: Ascend, and heed the Master of your Chariot,[1]

Divine Guide, lest you fall down, and fall again,

Hurled back into the slimy mud of Tartaros.

Control the body, rein the dual passions,

Stay watchful in the centre, harmonized

By greater Mind of godlike Knowledge.

Press forward, join our throng, do not delay

Pass on the light you have received in sacred orgy

Enter and see the Light, be freed from evil.

Before the light of day our torches pale.

Triptolemus extinguishes his torch and with him the others. The single flute begins again, and to its rhythm, as in a bridal procession, he leads Psyche off the scene, the epopts follow. A clear golden September day announces itself, a faint mist rises from the grass.

---

[1] *"Plato was not the first to take the chariot and the horses but before him those poets who were divinely inspired, Homer, Orpheus, Parmenides". Hermias. On the Phaidros of Plato.*

Chorus: They have departed, they are lost from sight.

Ascend, ascend, unfettered, free of bondage!

Forward each steed is straining to the light.[1]

Winged the chariot and the charioteer

Winged the loving soul, and crowned like a bride.[2]

Just then the first rays of a rising sun fall into the Telesterion. They fall on the Hierophantess who emerges from behind the altar. She is dressed in Demeter's red-golden cloak. With both hands she raises a sheaf of freshly cut corn heavy with ripeness, and she lifts it towards the sun.

The single voice of the Hierophant of Eleusis rings out like a clarion, decisive and with solemn emphasis.

Hierophant: Unless a grain fall into the ground and die

It cannot grow into an ear of corn.

Before you could be born, you had to die

Before you died, you had to be awakened.

This is the mystery of Eleusis.

The Hierophantess lowers her arms and bows over the corn. She sees Demeter who has found what has long been lost.

Hierophant: It has been done

It will be done

It is done.

Chorus, on a low deep note, spontaneously joined by the audience:

Hierophant: It is done.[3]

A destiny has found a perfect end.[4]

---

[1] *Paraphrase of a line from Sophocles.*

[2] *Eros has wings.*

[3] *The meaning of drama evolved from seasonal rites is correctly translated as "The thing done". (Christ on the cross had said: "It is finished"). Again, Aristotle gave as the etymology of the word "drama" a Dorian term "dran", to act, with a significance of religious character which its synonym "prattein" does not have. Encyclopedia Britannica.*

[4] *Sophocles. Oedipus at Colonos.*

All intone a hymn. While it is sung two epheboi bring in the plemochai, ritual vessels filled with water mixed with wine; holding them aloft, they empty them to the east and west as an emblem of the blessing of Eleusinian teaching flowing into Greece. When the hymn is ended the chorus speaks:

EPILOGUE

GUARD golden mysteries of holy fear

To nourish mortal souls

Whose voice the seal of silent awe controls

Imprinted by the priest of Eleusis.[1]

---

[1] *Sophocles. Oedipus at Colonos.*

The Haloa

DECEMBER at *Eleusis*. *A Festival in honour of the great Principle of Fertility. Poseidon,[1] Pluto, Zeus, and Dionysos. Mainly celebrated by women, who have come to Eleusis with gifts of corn and sea food. This is the season when they perform on the dancing grounds near Demeter's well. A priestess of Eleusis speaks to them.*

THE YEAR draws to its close.

Let us look back, my friends, as a ploughman looks back along the narrowing furrow. What have we sown, what reaped in the past year? What taken in, applied and understood?

Do you now know, in parts, what we began to teach before the Festival of Spring?

Have you begun to die? Have you begun to die to your titanic nature? Have you begun to see your inner gloom, and violence and evil, fear? Your vanity and greed and sorry pride?

Have you begun to grasp that to be mystae does not mean to be a being apart, and better than barbarian or slave, or ordinary citizen of Pallas' home, but merely one who sees, and who begins to know himself in humble silence?

Recall to mind the teaching of the year and see if you have changed.

The seed you planted last year in your field, has it begun to sprout?[2]

And there are those that ever learn yet never know. They are like one who ever ploughs yet never sows.[3]

---

[1] Poseidon was not originally a sea-god only, he merges with Zeus Chtonion, and Erechtheus, and is another form of the great fertility demon of antiquity. The snake is his sacred animal.
[2] Paraphrase from the "Waste Land".
[3] Inscription in a British School in Argentina.

At all times it is true that many are the bearers of the narthex, few the disciples of Iacchos.[1]

Many have here received instruction, but only those who strive can grow through their decline.

To be an epopt or a true bacchante is to know union with Iacchos. If you have Iacchos in the heart, he will be in your mind and limb.

You have brought corn and wine; offer yourselves in a like manner, hold not back. As you offer your womb to the male seed and bear your sons in pain, open your selves to the great fertilizing Powers. To be born woman is to know that we must labour to be beautiful.[2]

Make your new life, and feed it tenderly. Receive the Light and it shall fill your being.

Then, in great Harvesting you shall not be cast out, you will not be found wanting.

The life that you have fed, the Kouros, Son, shall be a part of a great cosmic dance.

---

[1] Plato. Phedon.
[2] W. B. Yeats. Adam's Curse.

THE ELEUSINIAN YEAR

I

THE DAYS grow longer. Pluto yields his riches,
Kore returns, the blossom-bringer, Power in the Tree.[1]
She comes to Demeter at Agrai on the Ilisus.
Low golden willows dust the whirling brook.
Pan in his cave, withdrawn, is All in all.
Artemis leads the choir of the Muses
And we have come together for a hymn of praise;
The young and old, the happy and bereaved,
Joy, joy, o joy and adoration!
Released from self we revel in great Being
O life in death, Dionysos, golden breath.
The goddess leads, like maenads let us leap with gladness,
Of horned Iacchos, Kore, and the Mother let us chant together.

---

[1] *Epithets of Dionysos, Bacchae, Euripides.*

II

The deer lies panting in the mountain cave.
Lulled by the sapless plaint of Tithoneus[1]
A pregnant hamadryad by the brook combs straight green hair,
The fibre thickens in the leaf and skin,
The fruit swells in the womb and on the bough,
Falling, it marks the hour in the silent orchard.
Gone the fine frenzy of the early hope:
We live with our love, and bear and work,
Like Delian bees we seek, now find, now lose.[2]
Dusk brings relief. Above the darkening hall
The Hunter and his Dog stalk the black Night.
We watch his fulgent rise, we hail the harvest-bringer.[3]

---

[1] Tithoneus, the cicada. The mortal husband of Aurora. She asked Zeus to grant him immortality, but the request was wrongly formulated. Tithoneus received eternal life in time, and he grew old but cannot die.

[2] The bee-women or prophetesses of Thriess who taught the art of mantic to Apollo. They were represented with their heads covered with golden pollen. In the ancient and mediaeval Near Orient the bee symbolized the Lover of God. See Hittite and Sufi literature. Greek hierophantesses and the priestesses of the Ephesian Artemis were called Melissai.

[3] Orion and Arctophonos or Sirius. These are the dog days. Canicula in Rome.

III

Reflected in the molten silver of swift flowing rivers
The island poplars darken once again.[1]
The Pleiades are sinking; bare the plain, the threshing floor
The hallowed dancing ground.[2]
Fruit scents nocturnal orchards, gift of great Eumolpus.[3]
The deepening blood of Zagreus streaks cold hills
Beneath the golden leaf and tendril swells the purple grape.
We honour our Dead.[4]
We break the boat shaped bread in memory of a journey
And a flowering mast.[5]
A grain fell in the furrow, died, and was reborn
As an ear of corn.
The ripened corn was threshed for the holy loaf.
The bread is shared and
Shall become the joyful ecstasy of union with God.

---

[1] These lines were inspired by a hauntingly beautiful passage in Cyril Connolly's "The Unquiet Grave".

[2] In Crete and prehistoric Greece the fates of Dionysos were sung and dances after the harvest on "therae", consecrated threshing floors.

[3] Eumolpus is recorded to have introduced horticulture to Attica.

[4] The dead ancestors. The dead teachers is the inner meaning; whose "communication is tongued with fire beyond the language of the living".

[5] Homeric hymn of Dionysos. Ravished by Tyrrhenian pirates he changed them into dolphins and himself into a lion. The mast began to flower and bear grapes.

IV

Winter has come, the Forces are withdrawn.
Low drift the clouds across a vast, blind sea.
The Tritons hiss and bellow in the caves.
We scan the sea and sky. We hunt in the lone marsh,
The hills scented with thyme and rain, the
Rotting acorn, pine, the furtive boar.
We sit around the hearth, we spin and weave the cloth,
We offer our tripod to Hecate;
Daily we learn to bear our imperfections.
O fruitful dark, o stillness, silent wait, infolding,
O life in death, the rightness of all things.

LESSONS IN RELIGION FOR
A SKEPTICAL WORLD

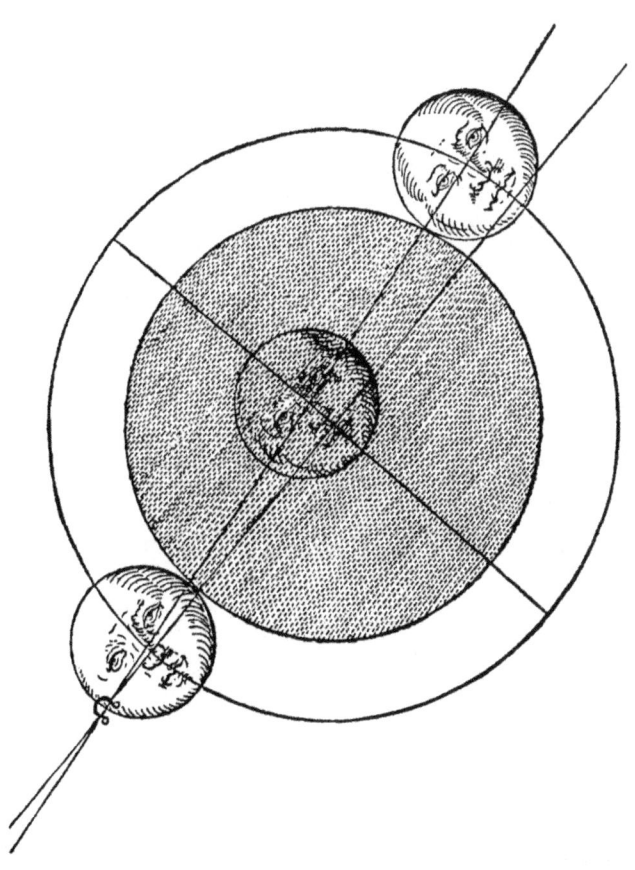

The Mirror of Light and Other Works

FOREWORD TO
LESSONS IN RELIGION FOR A SKEPTICAL WORLD

In the landscape of modern spirituality, where "faith" is often reduced to a tepid intellectual assent or a comforting social ritual, one occasionally stumbles upon a text that doesn't just invite contemplation, but demands an ontological surrender. *Lessons in Religion for a Skeptical World* (1956) is exactly such a document. Written with the blunt force of a "coarse millstone" turning in "clear water," this work—emerging from the enigmatic circles of Lima— serves as a bracing corrective to the vanity of the cultured mind.

The author begins with a premise that is as inclusive as it is terrifying: truth is not a proposition to be believed, but a reality to be made "flesh, bones and cross". In a world that hoards learning like a dragon hoards gold, these lessons act as "rods" intended to break the jars of our idle, unprofitable knowledge. We are told that honesty, sincerity, and truth are the "soap, water and towel" of the spirit. Without these, the intellect is merely a "severed head" speaking into a hollow echo.

The core of the work struggles with the paradox of human agency. It presents a world where we are, for the most part, "slaves bound to the wheel of destiny". Our steps are predetermined; our "moral quality" today is a mere mechanical echo of yesterday. Yet, within this rigid machinery, the author reveals the "riddle of the moral sphinx": the possibility of the Miracle of Love. While we move along the circumference of a circle, God occasionally offers the opportunity to change the "position of the wheel's axis". This change is not achieved through thinking, but through the creation of will.

The text's treatment of the "person" is where it reaches its most radical pitch. It dismantles the scientific and idealistic definitions of personality, labeling the un-awakened state as "false personality"—a shell that binds us to the "cellular material" of our organism. A human being, it argues, is not a "person" by default. We are "thinking bundles of rags" or "weeds destined to be burnt" until we undertake the "serious and conscientious work" of building an immortal soul. The soul is described as the "caulking" of the spiritual well; without it, the light of the spirit is simply wasted in the desert of existence.

Furthermore, the work reconciles the seemingly irreconcilable: the doctrines of Creationism and Emanationism. It suggests that these are not conflicting theories, but different "vital experiences". The Creationist is "drunk with the act of offering", while the Emanationist is "drunk with contemplation". Both are true if they come from the "heart and the bowels" rather than the intellect alone.

This is a text for the "skeptical world" not because it offers easy proof, but because it challenges the skeptic to a practical test. It asserts that God is not an "exterior object" to be demonstrated, but the "Being Who is inside the inside".

To read this is to be "shaken". It is an invitation to die to the old, mechanical self so that a "vigorous soul" might be born—a soul capable of recognizing that the "heaven of the saved" is not a distant sky, but a present reality hidden only by our own lethargy.

Introduction

H ONESTY, sincerity and truth are the soap, water and towel of the soul.

It is the message of Christ washing the feet of the apostles.

Christ and His love are great; as great as the whole sphere. It is the message of Mary of Magdala, washing the feet of Christ.

What you are going to read is an explanation of this in many words. They are all directed to the heart: do not read them with the intellect.

There are too many words for a simple truth. Why are there so many? Because they were ground by a very coarse millstone. But the water which turned the millstone was very clear and fell with great force.

We want to tell you not to believe that the love of God is so small that it can only be measured out to those who hold a determinate faith. We tell you that Christ and His love are in every faith.

It is not important what religion you embrace. It is important to be religious and to practise an authentic religion.

It is not enough to say: "I am religious". It is not enough to consider yourself religious. You must be it. And to be it, you must do it, practise it.

Vanity makes us say: "I am religious, but I do not practise any acknowledged religion". Then we feel different from the rest, from the common people, from the uncultured mobs that embrace recognized religions. We feel cultured and superior.

We believe that culture sets us apart from definite and recognized religion.

Another touch of vanity makes us say: "My religion is the only real one".

Every religion known as such is true, and only vanity and ignorance stand between us and that which we once professed.

Are there exceptions to this rule? Undoubtedly there are, but so few that as yet we have not found a single one.

What you are going to read teaches that every religious dogma is true. This is the reverse of that which was taught by the philosopher of Magdeburg[1]. Even those dogmas that contain apparently contradictory affirmations, of religions that are apparently irreconcilable, contain truth.

Are you surprised? Do you ask how this can be possible? Read without prejudice and you will find the answer.

Do you see? A dogma which seemed trivial, or even false and useless, has a profound meaning that you did not suspect. And another, apparently contradictory to the first, also has a profound and no less true meaning. You were blind and thought that you could see.

But you will remain blind until you put religion into practice.

And you must practise your religion, that which from time to time you call yours, because at one time it was yours.

With honesty, sincerity and truth; with soap, water and towel.

It will be useless only to say: "Certainly, that which I thought trivial and false is true and important". If you only say this, you will not have reached the truth. To reach it, you must live it, practise it and make it flesh.

Only when truth is made flesh, bones and cross, is it really truth.

"Take up your daily cross and follow Me". This is the call of Him Who is the truth, the way and the life.

You will ask if the truth of Christ can also be in Islam, in Buddhism and in Brahminism. We answer that the truth of the love of Christ is present everywhere.

We have been told: "Tell everyone that the love of God is everything". Now we communicate this to you.

We have learned that love is harmony.

---

[1] Kant

Find it first within yourselves by the way of truthfulness, honesty and sincerity. Then communicate it to others.

What follows are words, but they are meant as rods.

With them we would break the jars in which you thought to hoard your learning.

If you are jealous of your learning prepare to protect yourselves.

But do you not feel an inner desire to be destroyed?

To be born it is necessary to die.

Are you not bored with idle and unprofitable learning? With a learning which demands nothing of you? Which only tells you: "Listen and enjoy. You are intelligent because you know"?

The rods of our words are meant to break your jars. Set them out and experience the enjoyment of having them broken.

And you will discover a truth you did not know before. A jealous and demanding truth which will require efforts and impose responsibilities.

You will discover the source of morality.

You will know why we demand of you a cross: to be balanced, and stable. To project harmony.

You who are timorous will be shaken by these words. You should know that the dogma is true which says that only in such a religion is truth. Calm yourselves: it is very true. But do you know in what sense? Be humble, submit, bow under the yoke of religious practice; and learn with the help of our Lord.

Lima—Peru, 1956.

The Mirror of Light and Other Works

I BELIEVE IN GOD THE FATHER

D o you believe?

There is no need.

If you have will there is no need for belief in God the Father.

But do you know what is will? And do you really possess it?

Because if you knew what is will and fully possessed it, you would constantly feel the urges of your Divine Father. And he who feels has no need for belief.

We who speak to you do not believe in God except in our moments of blindness. When we are awake and vigilant we meet Him, we feel Him, we love Him and we see Him.

And when we *feel His guidance* we recognize Him as our Father.

They deny, or do not know God, who have never had will. They believe in Him who have felt His presence in an act of will in the past. Those who possess will neither deny nor believe; they recognize His divine power.

Those who take the statement "I believe in God the Father" as merely a literary affirmation are stupid.

Many sciolists are ignorant of the meaning of the expression "I believe in God the Father" and think that they are not answerable for it.

We say to you: You are answerable for everything that you do not understand in your religion.

If you do not understand the meaning of belief in God the Father it is only because you have no will and yours is the responsibility of acquiring it.

Is it your opinion that we all have will, or perhaps that no one possesses it?

Let us shake that unsound opinion.

No one has will unless he makes it for himself, and when he has made it, recognizes that he has done so with the help of God and that without Him he could not possess it.

This is the first encounter with God.

We recognize the struggle between our body and our spirit. We glimpse the light of the spirit, and we feel the yearning of the body. We create the will that unites them and introduces balance and stability.

Then we discover, by the will and not by the intellect, that God is leading us by the hand and that our part consists only in allowing ourselves to be led with honour and dignity.

This is how we recognize God our Father.

But to approach the Divine Creator it is necessary to respond to the yearning, and to have will.

ALMIGHTY

To return to the intuitive source of knowledge is indispensable. Religion is drowning in a sea of dialectics. For most men who consider themselves cultured it died a long time ago. Its only salvation lies in a return to the security of essential intellection, of contemplative reason, of love, and of honest and sincere action.

When by discursive reasoning we reduce the furniture on which we rest to particles separated by empty space, its reality and effectiveness disappear; in the same way God and the Spirit disappear— precisely because they are real and effective—when we try to seize them in the net of inductive conceptualism.

Reality cannot be demonstrated by means of discursive reasoning. Precisely only the purely ideal, in the sense of the abstract disconnected with reality —that is, the unreal, that which lacks effectiveness— is all that can be demonstrated by knowledge derived from inference and conclusion. For this reason it is possible to demonstrate the theorem of Pythagoras because the ideal triangles and angles of that theorem are pure abstractions of the mind and have no existence or reality for us. One paradoxical demonstration of the unreality of an entity is precisely its demonstrability.

To try to demonstrate the reality of God is to reduce Him to a mere intellectual possibility, that is, to non-existence. And if apart from this one tries to demonstrate His *existence*, it is as if one were trying to reduce Him to double non-existence. It is well to remember that God does not exist in the sense of an exterior object that establishes or maintains itself outwardly. God is the Being Who is inside the inside, and 'to be', refers to being "one, eternal and indivisible".

The murderers of God have been His false defenders. Let us rise against false intellectual pride.

Reality and effectiveness are degrees of endeavour and not of understanding[1]. The presence of a wall is not demonstrated by the mind but by the calamity overtaking him who tries to deny it.

The sculptor knows of the presence of his marble because of the help it gives him and the resistance it offers to his desire to realize the idea of the statue.

Man knows of the presence of his Divine Maker because of the help He bestows on him when he searches for good, and because of the resistance with which he is opposed when he wanders in search of evil.

And do you know how we know that God is almighty?

By simply recognizing, once we have acquired control of will, that we have never been forsaken by Him; not even in those moments when we most resembled mineral stone. The factual—not dialectic— proof is that we were able to find the way back.

Even when asleep and inert we were guided by God.

Only thus were we able to awaken longing,

Gather our strength,

And create will.

Because God is almighty

And governs all.

And leaves us no more freedom than to be honest or dishonest, sincere or insincere, true or false.

*　*　*

Everything is predetermined.

Even our steps?

Yes.[2]

Only the direction of the light of our consciousness is not predetermined.

With our consciousness we can look either upwards or downwards.

Because God is almighty.

[1] Max Scheler.
[2] Except when the 'miracle' described later occurs.

254

And good and evil depend only on the direction in which our consciousness is focussed.

If we act with bad intention we are acting in view of the bad, and are dishonest; if we act with good intention we are acting in virtue of the good and are honest.

We are sincere when we express our intentions openly; insincere when we conceal them.

We are truthful when we say only what we know; false when we claim to know what we do not know.

Do you really understand what this means?

Do you know, for instance, that you can lie by silence?

Do you know that alone, in the desert, you are able to lie?

Do you know what it means to have your steps predetermined and to have nevertheless the possibility of choosing between good and evil?

* * *

Who told us?

Where did we find it?

How did we see it?

O God, give it to us that we may give!

Our mind is weak and we have forgotten it.

Smite us with Your justice.

* * *

It is good to pursue that which is real.

It is bad to pursue that which is false, does not exist, is empty and is dead.

Let the dead bury their dead.

This is the rule of the living.

Stern rule; rule of wood in cross; rule for those who must salt the earth. Rule for the preachers of harmony.

And for the others?

Love and understanding.

Thank You, Almighty.

* * *

We are surrounded by falseness; we live among corpses.

We search for truth, we stumble over lies.

It is good to stumble over lies searching for truth,

It is bad to encounter truth and not feel it because we are searching for lies,

It is bad for the wise to pursue justice, for justice is a dead idea. But if the ignorant pursue it, believing in it, they may encounter kindness on their way.

And meantime it is useless to preach the distinction between the living and the dead to those who are in agony.

It is useless, cruel and much more.

It is useful to teach love, because with love, even looking for falseness, truth can be found.

Do you understand now how it is that we are free in spite of our chains?

Only the dead and the false are bound by chains. Nothing can prevent one death from following another. No one can prevent a leaf from falling from a tree when it is dry, and another leaf from budding in due time.

The blind man to whom we gave some coins was destined to receive them, and we were destined to give them.

But the light of kindness that was kindled in the blind man's soul on receiving the love with which we gave them is not written in any book of destiny. Our will is completely free to grant this light according to its own choice.

* * *

Now we will tell you what more we have learned about the riddle of the moral sphinx.

All our steps are predetermined, except when love is allowed to perform miracles.

* * *

Normally every day is the same as the preceding one. Today we do the same as we did yesterday, with very few variations. At least the moral quality of our actions today is the same as of yesterday. What we do today is determined by what we did yesterday. Many things are already predetermined by what we did some years ago.

Yesterday we wronged without noticing it; today we wrong again without noticing it. Yesterday we stinted some coins to a beggar; today we stint them to someone else. And from today it is determined that next year we will continue to do the same. The fundamental theme of the tune of our conduct is always the same, day after day.

While the miracle does not occur.

Not many occur; they are not lavished on us, but they do occur.

Miracles on a minor scale transform to a greater or less degree the fundamental theme of every man's conduct, at certain stages of his life—for instance, in the transition periods between childhood and puberty, between puberty and youth, between the latter and maturity, and between maturity and old age. We are not aware of them, sometimes because these transformations are very slight, or more or less gradual, or because they happen to all men.

But eventually greater miracles may also happen to us that fundamentally alter the moral essence of our behaviour.

These are the miracles of love. They do not happen every day. It is not in our power to alter the course of destiny at every step. If someone is selfish and all his acts bear the stamp of selfishness we cannot expect that two or three times a month he should act with real generosity and disinterestedness, in manifest contrast to the fundamental nature of his other actions. But if the same man is awake, and while his conscience is vigilant he receives a gift of love, this gift may perform the miracle of changing decisively the future course of all his acts.

Such is the immense importance of love.

If we receive it with good will, it may cleanse our hearts of all their impurity and turn us into other springs of harmony.

The childish boast that we are free to do, or not do, whatever we like, is not true. Those who assert this do not know the omnipotence of God. Power over destiny does not belong to man, but to God.

Our conduct always follows the same channel. We always move along the circumference of a circle, and we cannot diverge from it. We are slaves bound to the wheel of destiny. In this the Moslems are right. But from time to time, at certain moments of life —limited, but of great value—God offers us the opportunity of changing the position of the wheel's axis. We shall never leave the wheel, but sometimes we are able to transform it and make it different.

We are not gods, and we cannot change our fate at every step, but it is so arranged that two or three times in our lives we have the *possibility* of changing its course fundamentally.

It is enough that we be vigilant and awake for love to strengthen our will.

"Ask and it shall be given unto you."

The omnipotence of God is infinite for all those who ask with their whole heart.

* * *

The Kiss of Love is the title of the story that tells of the creation of our will.

Everything was different after that kiss.

That which formerly compelled us began to pass us by, leaving us in a surprising immobility.

Only the kiss was burning in our hands.

The little lights that formerly dazzled us continued to shine, but we no longer seemed to see them.

The warmth of the kiss burned us.

And since then we live only by its virtue.

Before, our arms were the sails of a windmill and had no longing to *fly.*

258

Our legs were limbs that only jerked to the beat of a metronome.

Our senses were in constant contention, because their desires were belligerent.

Today we only feel the breath, the music and the call of that kiss.

And our life includes only two stages: the darkness of what was before and the splendour which is after.

Often we fall asleep and seem to lose the feeling of that which sustains us.

Then we are distressed. Again we see the former brilliancy. Again we hear the old 'tic-toc'. Once more we perceive the conflicting calls of our senses. But everything that formerly gave the false warmth of feverish movement, today only produces the coldness of anguish and helplessness.

When we do not feel the kiss, all that formerly was pleasant fills us with dismay.

* * *

Such is the virtue of the kiss of love that we once received in our hands.

Since that moment we also know how to kiss.

And we learned that love transforms all who are awake.

And that all who once have felt the kiss of love have the duty to give it to those who have not yet received it.

* * *

We had no will.

Our soul was in agony.

Then we were told very simply: "Yes, you have will." And we were kissed with the kiss of love on our hands.

Since then we have will.

And our soul is invigorated.

* * *

Now do you know how the will that leads us to God is created?

CREATOR

H E who is able to pray to God the Creator cries like this with all his being:

"O my Father, all that is in me is of Your making; I long to offer You all my deeds. But how can a creature dare to offer something of his own to his Creator Who is Lord of everything? Smite me, O Lord, lest I blaspheme."

He who prays thus, with all the torrent of his blood, speaks not of creation, but of emanation:

"O my Father, my human sight is weak, and delights in the scintillation of Your rays, but is incapable of contemplating Your true light. Lord, You sent forth Your light and created the scintillation. Blind my mortal sight that sees only the scintillation, for I long to see light."

The creationist is drunk with the act of offering to God all that he most values. The emanationist is drunk with contemplation; he renounces everything in exchange for the possibility of contemplating God.

They are two different religious experiences, that give rise to different doctrines.

The creationist maintains that all creation is the work of God. The emanationist maintains that the creation which we know is only a coarse and grotesque parody which germinates in our own mind, and that nothing is important in that creation because when the created is compared with the divine idea from which everything proceeds, only the idea of God has importance.

The ignorant suppose that the doctrine of creation is incompatible with that of emanation, but now you see that this is not so. In each is an aspect of the full truth. But to find it, it is necessary that the doctrine be not only formulated with the head, but also with the heart and bowels.

When only the head works, truth is lost and only the false, which is empty, non-existent, inert, nothing, is seen. Those who philosophise only with the mind stumble onto nothingness.

Every voice has hollow echoes which chill and crystallize; they are echoes from severed heads that speak without the support of the whole body.

One voice says: "Everything is created by God. The world is His great theatre. He who listens is only an actor, and beside him move many other actors. God created the scenery, the decor and the costumes, and even the actors and the drama are His work."

That voice is silent and another is heard: "Nothing is created, but the actors and the drama exist. Everything else, the scenery, decor and costumes, are illusory figments of the actors. Men and their destiny are emanations of the divine mind. But nothing has ever been created, and if illusions appear as creations this is only in the measure in which we re-create ourselves with them."

The two voices cease, and their echo is heard in the head of a corpse: "There is no creation; there is no manifestation. Everything is black around him who listens. The darkness is unfathomable. Nothing exists around him. Nothing except him who listens and his destiny. Only to believe in oneself is to believe in God, because God is oneself."

To allow wisdom to be heard, all the voices of the mind must be silenced and the voice of the heart, which is silence, must speak.

And the great silence speaks thus: "All doctrines are true when they also come from the heart and from the bowels. This is why the doctrines of the saint are always true and those of common man false. There cannot be more truth in the common man than in the service of the saint."

Pilate was common because all his truth consisted in washing his hands, when it is the bowels that must be washed.

All who philosophise for the masses are common men. Only the philosophers of the workshop and the gymnasium know the truth.

* * *

Creationism, the doctrine which finds God in our inner selves, and emanationism, which does not see the high in that which is low, are all truths, when supported by genuine vital experiences.

For each person only one religion is true, because for each person there is only one authentic time and vital experience. For him who has the heart and bowels of a Christian, it is false to embrace Hinduism, and vice versa.

Only a determinate religion is true.

Our voice sounds weak when it tries to say that which should come from a cyclops.

Only one religion is true for you.

Only others are true for others.

But neither they nor you nor anyone is ever free from the obligation of embracing a given, recognized and positive religion, here and now.

Nobody is free to create his own religion, just as nobody can create his own science.

A wise man can delight in physics, another in medicine, and a third in astronomy, but no one can create his own physics, medicine or astronomy.

Only God can create, and all religions and all sciences are creations of God.

* * *

These are mistakes of intellectual pride:

One: to judge narrowmindedly that only one's own religion is the uniquely true one.

No religion is unique in truth.

Two: to look for errors in a religion in order to attack them.

"What we must do—says the voice of a vigilant angel—is not to preach a new religion or correct the church, let us correct ourselves. We would not find so many defects in our religion if we practised it punctiliously. The truth is that our religion has only one defect: ourselves".[1]

The sole truth is not in the outward form of doctrines, but in the inner flame of love and in the radiant light of spiritual contemplation.

Do not confuse absolute sole truth with the relative truths of the intellect.

Every doctrine contains truth and falsehood.

There is no doctrine that is not wholly truthful and wholly false. Falsehood lies in mistaken interpretation, in vanity, in petulance and in the selfishness of those who listen and interpret.

The sole truth is only in Christianity, but Christianity is present in all religions under its purest form of love, submission to that which is high, subjugation to God and harmony.

Truth and relative falsehood are also present in all religions under the exterior guise of dogmatic formulation and interpretation. All dogma is true. But there is no dogma that is well formulated or interpreted.

Language is limited; so is intellect. Love has no limits. The spirit "bloweth where it listeth". God is everywhere.

* * *

How dangerous is evil, for in its extreme forms it resembles good!

We must beware of all our virtues. Evil hides behind them. I was taught this by him who had made pilgrimage to the fountains[2]. It was shown me by evil.

Great temptations come from pseudo-virtues.

Our learning, our knowledge; here we have pseudo-virtue.

We have no more knowledge than that which is given to us.

We should never dare to give more than we have received from God. What does not come from God, comes from the devil.

Let us beware of the devil who is beside us and as near as God.

---

[1] Lanza del Vasto. *Comentary on the Gospel. South. Buenos Aires. 1955.*
[2] An allusion to "A Pilgrimage to the Fountains" by Lanza del Vasto.

But it must not be forgotten that the devil is a chained dog that can only bite us if we go near him.

He who judges like stone, stones; he who judges like water, washes; he who judges like wine, renews.

To judge like stone is to judge with narrow-mindedness, condemning and excluding.

To judge like water is to wash away the bad and let the good appear.

To judge like wine is to vivify everything, with the help of goodness.

Judging in the widest sense, it can be said that our religion is the only true one.

It is well that you should know now that those who write this are practising Catholics.

And our religion tells us that it is the only true one, which should be sustained by the judgement of water and wine.

The Catholic religion is the only true one in the sense that it is the only one within which man can re-bind himself to God *with exact knowledge of the knot which acts as union* and of the agent which forms this knot. There are many ways of re-binding oneself to God and also there are many religions, but Catholicism is the only religion which allows us clearly to recognize the nature of the ways which lead us to this end.

This is the interpretation of water; the interpretation of wine is not within our capacity, because we have not received it. But he who has received water hopes for wine.

Of Heaven

FOR some the highest is truth and for others, goodness. The former do not recognize heaven, the latter know of its existence.

Heaven is the experience of those who take goodness as the object or purpose of knowledge and the culmination of truth. It is denied only by those who think that knowledge has nothing to do with goodness.

Those who are healthy and have eyes to see and ears to hear, know of heaven. The others, those who do not know, are like the sick, the lame, the withered and the blind, who only lean on the crutches of truth and cannot even see that knowledge has no meaning whatsoever unless it leads to goodness.

Therefore to know of heaven, it is necessary to feel that goodness is above truth; that knowledge is something interminable and absurd unless it leads to goodness; and that doctrinary knowledge is only one way of approaching goodness.

It is in accordance with our nature to be on that way. For this we all need a doctrine and a truth. But we must not lose sight of the fact that our aim is goodness produced by truth, the goodness of truth, where the significance and inner meaning of everything is discovered, and where all conflict and doctrinary discrepancy disappear.

When we lose sight of goodness our truth is changed into a weapon of intellectual warfare; once we reach the final stage of truth, which is goodness, we find that what we believed to be material for dispute is in reality a message of harmony, concord, stability and balance.

Jesus Christ said: "Blessed are the peaceful, for they shall be called sons of God" (Matthew 5:9).

What is needed is to be really peaceful. Not with the unreality of an outward decoration or medal, but with the inner quality of internal harmony.

Foolish is he who, without having harmony in himself, denies the celestial world because he cannot see it. He is like someone who denies the beauty of a high peak because he cannot reach it.

* * *

We presume that you have already discovered that truth has no value whatsoever if it is not supported by vital experience and does not lead to goodness.

In practice, the fact that truth actually comes out of life is already a guarantee that it *can* reach the goal of goodness.

A half-truth, a truth without sincerity, honesty or veracity, is nothing but a 'false-truth', nonsense, a dead idea.

To understand the authentic function of truth, we must consider its relation to life and to goodness.

Life makes things true or false, authentic or fictitious.

Life creates the truth and the lie.

Things are what life disposes that they should be.

Our intellectual truths of today are as true as were those of yesterday and those of tomorrow will be.

But in fact there are degrees of quality.

The truth of the stomach is even more relative than that of the intellect. Only in the fire of the heart and the radiation of the spirit can absolute truth be found.

The quality of truth rests ultimately on the nobility, dignity and spiritual level of him who lives it. If the life-experience on which it is based has been purified by honesty, sincerity and veracity, its truth is of the highest quality.

Men have earnestly looked for an absolute and permanent truth in their senses and intellect. It does not exist.

In the world of the senses and of reflexive thought, only the connection between life and truth is permanent.

Life and the truth of the senses and intellect are variable. Only their relation is permanent.

Everything that is not in accordance with this relation is false.

For medieval man it was false to think that the earth moved, for this principle was not in accordance with his experience of life. For us it is false to think that it does not move, for this principle is not in accordance with our experience.

Those who still believe that intellectual truth is absolute may ask themselves: Does the earth move or is it fixed?

The earth has absolutely nothing to do with this discussion.

In reality there is neither movement nor stillness. There is only life.

Life makes movement appear where vital experience discovers it.

We travel in a vehicle. The vehicle moves for us.

If all men were to move in space at the same speed, our experience would tell us that we were all still, and in effect we should be so.

We owe the disclosure of these ideas to the man who in life was called Albert Einstein.

Without life there is no manifestation, and without manifestation there is neither sensorial nor intellectual truth.

For the old Peruvians, Cuzco was the centre of the world; for the old Chinese, the centre of the world was in their country. Our experience of life today is not like that of the Peruvians nor of the Chinese of yesterday, and to us any part of the earth's surface can be its centre, although we prefer to say that it has no centre.

Life has many facets, and each facet has many shades of colour.

Each facet and each shade of life experience has its own dignity or indignity. On this depends the *quality* of truth.

The life experience of those who consider all men in all latitudes to be their brothers and fellow-creatures has most dignity and nobility, most loftiness and sanctity. For this reason and for no other, the statement that the earth has no centre is more true.

But as it is not always easy to decide what type of life is best, so it is not easy to decide whether sensible or intellectual truth is more correct.

In any case sensible truths, or truths of the stomach, are based on the life of the appetites. They consist in the differentiation between that which stimulates the senses and that which does not. The former are considered authentic, the latter false. They are the coarse truths of the passional and common man. They bind to earth and draw away from heaven whoever attempts to mix them with supreme truths.

Intellectual truth is known as logical or gnoseological truth, and consists in equating thought with itself and with exterior things. It is used by the scientist, and some philosophers entertain themselves with it. The riches of the spirit draw us away from heaven when we become attached to them.

The truth of the heart has more dignity than the others, and consists of love. It recognizes goodness as its aim.

The life of the man of heart is a constant struggle to realize the truth of love.

The death of the man of heart is the consecration of his truth.

But even in love there are errors when it is expressed in words. When love turns into phrases, and the phrases become dogmas, its truth becomes relative.

The truth of love is absolute only as long as it is not expressed with a yes or a no.

He who searches for absolute truth must therefore divest himself of the defences of affirmation and negation, and deliver himself without reserve to the revivifying fire of love.

But on this path there are many dangers, and the greatest consists in mistaking dogma for love. Then dogma assumes the external semblance of the absolute, turns against love and lulls it.

Yet doctrines are necessary, and dogmas too, because man cannot dispense with thought.

The great secret is always to consider doctrine and dogma as imperfect expressions of a truth which can be perfectly discerned only with love.

And as a first precaution, doctrinarians and doctrinised should be ready to fling away, as though it were a red hot coal, all dogmatic interpretation that is contrary to love, no matter under what guise it may appear.

Doctrine and dogma are justified only if they are ways leading in the direction of love. They are unstable bridges spanning the abyss that separates us from love, and nothing more. We must look for them and follow them, but be quick to cross over them.

Another danger of love lies in believing that it is already attained when it is still far away. To abandon the bridge of doctrine is as dangerous as to linger on it too long.

In reality, doctrines should never be abandoned, for surpassing them is not the same as putting them aside.

Only he who has genuinely and truly conquered the kingdom of love knows in actual truth what is the legitimate function of doctrine.

* * *

But supreme truth is the truth of the spirit and of real man, and consists in the realization of himself.

Veracity is truth par excellence.

He fulfils himself who is truthful in the highest possible degree in fitting his words to his thoughts, harmonizing his thoughts with his conduct, and conforming his conduct with his inner reality.

To make ourselves what we really are is the supreme way to truth. He who has succeeded in this has attained goodness. He has discovered heaven, and has no more need of truth.

Truthfulness is to say only that which we know and live, and not to pretend to know what we do not know,

It is to live what we feel;

It is to have will;

It is to feel God the Father with the will;

The way to truthfulness is sincerity and honesty.

Sincerity is to think of goodness;

To say what we think, and match the word with the thought;

To express our intention clearly.

Honesty is to love and feel what we think;

To receive the Holy Spirit with love;

To say only what we feel.

Heaven discovered, we live in the truth of goodness, which is the full realization of truthfulness.

* * *

Heaven surrounds us. It is before us, beside us and within us. No, it is not far away in the sky. We have it near us, but it is hidden by the world of illusion.

Our dead ideas and our weak will prevent us from seeing it clearly.

Many people do not know that their own spirit lives eternally in heaven, because they keep it in lethargy. In order to awaken it they need only to build an adequate celestial habitation for it. This is the soul. The souls of all men are not alike. In the majority there is only a miserable rudiment. Their spirit is deeply lethargic.

In others the soul *is* as solid and luminous as a marble palace. Their spirit is awake and conscious that it dwells in heaven.

To develop the soul and awaken the spirit, it is enough to acquire a firm will with the help of love.

The way is the one shown by Him "Who did not come to destroy the law but to fulfil it".

Everyone can verify the presence of heaven within himself and in the world that surrounds him without having to wait for what is called the death of the body. For this it is necessary first to love God with all the fulness of our nature, and our neighbour as ourself. With this love our will is born, and with will we overcome dead ideas. As soon as this has been achieved, the spirit finds itself living in the heaven of the saved.

Many have thought that it is not possible to know anything about heaven, because it cannot be entered except through the door of physical death.

There are many mistakes in this supposition.

That which we call death can lead to heaven, but this is not the only way nor the most certain.

Birth and death are nothing but the two sides of the narrow window through which the lethargic spirit looks at the world. And while we do not build ourselves a healthy and vigorous soul, we are not certain of passing freely to the other side of the opening.

Only the soul can save us from dead ideas.

There are degrees of falsehood. A dead idea is absolutely false. "The State of Justice", "The Ideal of Justice based on this State", "The Progress of Civilization" are dead ideas over which we stumble at every step.

Those who dedicate their lives only and exclusively to the realization of a dead idea, destroy their souls and move further away from heaven.

And Earth

E ARTH is the world of dead ideas. We are tied to it by negative thoughts, emotions and impulses.

Everything negative comes from barriers, divisions and separation. Negative thought is that which comes from the mind only and has no roots in the heart or the bowels. Negative emotion is that which comes from feelings only, and belongs only to sensibility. Negative impulses demand satisfactions which conflict with emotions and thought.

Stay your judgement and pay attention.

The truth of utilitarian science is born of negative thoughts.

Occasionally the heart 'thinks' by itself, and from this are born useless thoughts that have not the consistency of truth. When our 'ground floor' thinks we already know the truth, that truth is being confused with that which gives satisfaction to the senses.

Negative emotion is born from feelings that are rejected by our semi-conscious understanding, and by the part of our nature represented by the word 'bowels' when in a state of disequilibrium and disharmony. It is bred in isolation in a hothouse of ignorance and nourished solely by fantasy. Suddenly it arises, and takes possession of all our being by overpowering and enslaving the mind and bowels that formerly rejected it.

A positive emotion is born with the concurrence of the whole of our nature, and belongs not so much to the sensibility which gives it its form, as to the will which impels it, creating the inner harmony from which it arises. All positive emotion is a form of that love of which it is said: "Thou shalt love with all thy heart, with all thy soul and with all thine understanding".

We can also experience negative emotions with the help of the intellect. They are created by the overflowing fantasy of those who do not control their imagination. Finally, there are negative emotions of an impulsive origin, very frequent in those who have not perfectly regulated their motor, sexual and instinctive centres. Negative impulses are those created by disharmony and lack of balance in the lower centres of the personality.

* * *

Negative emotion is particularly dangerous because it attacks obliquely, and hides behind our most valued virtues. For this reason, he who seeks the benefit of truth must accustom himself to mistrust and suspect his own virtues.

Negative emotion distorts the whole universe, and sets us in the place of its governing centre.

Negative emotion is that feeling which reverses all values and measures them by their relation to ourselves.

The jealous love of him who loves himself in the being of the person he loves; the vanity which makes us proud of our knowledge and of our various abilities; the satisfaction of superiority which we feel when we overcome a vice or attain some moral standard, are all negative emotions.

And they overtake us at every moment.

O how vain we are, even in those moments when we believe ourselves to be most humble!

We obey, and want our superior to be aware of it or we are complacent over the superiority given us by some or other trace of self-control.

Vanity is a negative emotion hidden behind our dearest virtues.

* * *

Negative experiences darken the sky and make us see nothing but the earth. From them is born false personality.

If we measure our personality with the measure of our Brahmanic experience, we will find that falseness forms part of its nature. We always bear it with us, and it is false in the measure in which it darkens the spirit.

But our experience is different, and we think that we can redeem the exterior appearance, reconciling it with the truth, when we become aware that it is deceiving. And we reserve the name of false personality for that which exists without the cleansing effect of self-remembering its role.

The wall of false personality is not difficult to breach, but it is doubly deceptive.

Personality is an ambiguous concept liable to many misinterpretations.

On one hand, the philosophers inspired by Brahmanism and the Laws of Manu consider personality as the sum of the results of negative experiences, which in turn gives rise to further negative experiences in a kind of vicious circle from which we can only be freed by help from a higher level.

On the other hand, positive science[1] maintains in more or less uniform terms, that it is in the aggregate of all the features resulting from *our* experiences that we are differentiated one from another. In personality we find as much of the positive as the negative, and it would be wrong to attribute to it an axiological character.

Historians and the interpreters of antiquity affirm that Christianity has restored the dignity of the human person. By this they mean that Christians have discovered in the person a value that neither the Hindus nor the positive scientists have found there.

Finally, the idealistic philosophers also speak of the person, maintaining that it is the basic value upon which everything else is established and sustained.

So much disagreement can only prove that all, or nearly all, are speaking of different phenomena while giving them the same name. To understand each other, it will be necessary to come to an agreement regarding language.

The idealistic philosophers call 'person' that which we prefer to call 'spirit'—that is, the source from which arises our experience of the valuable. Within each one of us exists this subterranean well, but its water is lost by seeping in many directions. In general, we only suppose the existence of our spirit on the basis of what others tell us. In

---

[1] Here Collin is refering to the objective science that Ouspensky taught.

most of us it is a well which is nearly dry and can be distinguished only with difficulty from our other possibilities. Serious and conscientious work is necessary to mend the cracks and restore our spiritual well. Hence many deny the existence of the person presented by the idealistic philosopher, simply because he who has no spirit cannot find it. And practically speaking, an inert spirit is equivalent to a non-existent spirit.

Christianity gives the name of 'person' to the human being who has not only spirit but soul. In each one of us are powers and possibilities. One of these is the spirit, a power that cannot express itself alone, without the help of another or others. Another power is the soul. No, do not be scandalized. We are speaking of power or force almost in the same sense as physical science. You do not need much philosophical culture to understand us, but on the other hand you will need good will and the desire to understand. Western philosophers have abandoned the concept of power and prefer also to abandon the idea of soul, because they are afraid of embarking on an interminable lexicological discussion. They do well. Because as long as one does not have a soul it is useless to talk about it. All scholastic discussion arises from a few non-animated individuals who, lacking a soul, enjoy discoursing over that which they neither have nor understand.

We can lack soul in the same way that we can lack spirit. In actual fact, all who lack spirit lack soul, because the soul is the power that helps the manifestation of the spirit. This is the reason why the one is mistaken for the other. To continue with the simile of the well, we could say that the soul is something like the caulking of the well of the spirit. Without caulking, all the contents are wasted, the well becomes dry and in no way different to any other dark hole in the desert. A being without soul is something like a being with a cracked soul. Much heat is needed, much friction with the caulking-iron of disillusionment, to restore the caulking of his soul.

This is the opinion of Christianity on the human person. The person possesses dignity and is worthy of respect as long as he has soul. A being without a soul is not a person; it is as a patch of waste land, or straw, or at most a thinking bundle of rags.

According to the teaching of the Gospels, most humans do not possess the dignity of persons. They are not like profitable wheat, but like the weeds that are destined to be burnt.

"... reapers: gather up the weeds first and bind them in bundles to be burnt" (Matthew 13:30).

But each human being can make himself worthy of the dignity of person by building himself an immortal and imperishable soul. He who does not make such a soul, perishes. But he who succeeds makes himself an inheritor of eternal life.

"...but gather the wheat into my barn." (Matthew 13:30).

There was a man who came to the conclusion, based on this teaching, that humanity is divided into two: Christians with souls, and people and blackmen without them. It was necessary to respect the former, but the latter could be enslaved, mutilated and killed. Thus thought an unhappily famous priest called Sepulveda.

The mistake of this way of thinking is first, that only a minimum number of those who are called Christians are so in reality, and in consequence few have the soul that all of them claim to have. And second, that although only a few have the dignity of possessing a soul, every human, person or not, has a second dignity, which consists in being capable of making himself a soul. This is forgotten by the Sepulvedas, or let us say the agents of all tyrannies.

We are not speaking of person in this Christian sense, but of men with soul, whom we prefer to call full and complete men.

A third meaning of the word 'person' is that of the characterologist or psychologist, of positive science, for whom person is that which differentiates all human beings. For a characterologist, the person is the assemblage of traits which distinguishes one human being from another.

We accept the scientific opinion, but add that personality considered in this way is the result of a third kind of force or power, as distinct from the soul as from the spirit. This is the force of our three-dimensional body. In this, our familiar body of head, trunk and limbs, a remarkable activity is continually being produced without the active assistance of soul or spirit. The result of the harmonious activity of body, soul and spirit we call quite simply 'person' or 'personality'. If the result proceeds from the separated activities of the different centres of the body —that is, from the activity which deprives us of the help of the soul and the spirit— we call it 'false personality'.

We cannot separate ourselves from our 'person', and neither should we try to do so. Instead, we can and must rid ourselves of the false personality which binds us to the earth.

No one can liberate himself completely from the level of the earth, but we all can do it to a greater or lesser degree.

To be liberated from the earth means to transcend its influence.

Our earth is the cellular material of our organism. That which we call 'living organism' acts in relation to us like the earth in relation to the planetary order.

God is the Creator of heaven and earth in all their orders, cosmic and human.

In the human order, the earth of our organism continually performs an irresistible cosmic dance which drags and compels us. The power of those movements are as strong as are tectonic and geologic movements in relation to the living nature which covers the surface of the earth. To oppose them is vain, fatuous and childish.

What we should do with our bodily earth is to recognize its influence and transcend it by seeking other forces that can overcome it, because we certainly are not capable of doing so. Living nature transcends the power of the earth by appealing to the energy of the sun, and to the mediating influence of the planets transmitted by their movements. In the same way, we can transcend the overmastering force of our biological organism by appealing to the energy of our spirit and the mediating influence of our soul.

The spirit is our sun; the soul, our planetary world.

The spirit is conscience, in the same way that the sun is light.

The spirit is will, as the sun is vivifying energy.

From that which is above comes the meaning of that which is below. The spirit and the sun give meaning to our earths.

That which is low continues its way although we have no consciousness of it; and when the spirit does not help us with its
consciousness, we can be completely engulfed by that which is low.

The soul introduces the order, harmony and balance necessary for
the spirit to act, in the same way that the planets introduce the order
of the seasons on earth.

God creates spirit, soul and body, but we have freedom to choose
between influences. He who chooses only the influence of the body
remains attached to the earth, enclosed in the shell of false
personality.

The dance continues, the soul awaits and the spirit enlightens.

* * *

Creator of Heaven and Earth,

Creator of the wheels of destiny;

Creator of their points of binding or connection;

Creator of the energy that vivifies them;

Creator of the way that leads to the centre of energy;

Creator of the longing to jump;

Creator of the longing to walk;

Such is God the Father, Almighty, Maker of Heaven and Earth.

THE CHRISTIAN MYSTERY

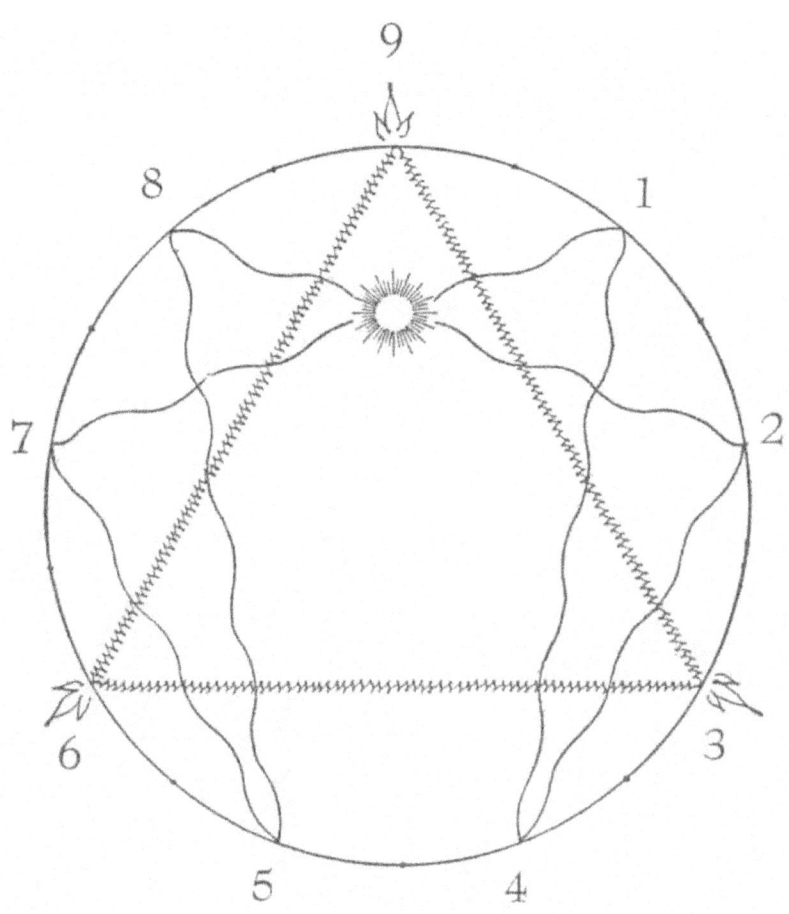

The Mirror of Light and Other Works

FOREWORD TO

THE CHRISTIAN MYSTERY

To those familiar with the vast, clockwork cosmology of Rodney Collin's The Theory of Celestial Influence, this slender volume may arrive as something of a shock. We are accustomed to Collin the synthesizer, the man who could dismantle the solar system and reassemble it as a functioning anatomy of the human soul. But in The Christian Mystery, we encounter a different frequency of his voice—one where the cool precision of the diagram meets the burning intensity of the mystic.

The Enneagram, that nine-pointed symbol brought to the West by Gurdjieff, is often studied as a static map of personality or process. However, in this remarkable text, Collin elevates the Enneagram to its highest possible octave. He does not merely explain the symbol; he enshrines the life of Christ within it.

He proposes that the "Christian Mystery" is not just a historical event or a religious sentiment, but a living, breathing "cosmos"—a distinct entity created by Christ to serve as a bridge between the scale of Man and the scale of the Earth.

What Collin attempts here is a geometric theology. He maps the narrative of the Gospels onto the three internal lines of the Enneagram, revealing them as distinct currents of energy. He identifies the "Way of Decay" (the circle), the "Way of Sacrifice" (the inner web), and the "Way of Glory" (the triangle).

Through this lens, the events of the Passion are not random tragedies but inevitable intersections of cosmic law. When Christ is betrayed by Judas or denied by Peter, we see these not merely as moral failings, but as necessary mechanical points—"crossroads"—where planetary influences (Saturn, Mars, Venus) must be met and transformed.

The audacity of this work lies in its scope. Collin suggests that the life of Jesus was a compression of time—"regeneration," he calls it, "the reversal of time." The thirty years of growth, the three years of ministry, the three days of passion, and the three hours on the cross represent a terrifying acceleration of energy that split history in two. But the text does not stop at Golgotha.

Collin expands the diagram to encompass the entire history of Christendom. The points on the Enneagram that once represented the Virgin Mary, John, or Peter now expand to become entire epochs and civilizations—Byzantium, Rome, the Gothic North. The "ripple" of the Christ-event widens to include the whole of history in a single, simultaneous figure.

Yet, for all its structural rigor, *The Christian Mystery* resolves into a profoundly devotional "Litany for the Enneagram". Here, the scientist steps back, and the worshiper steps forward. We find invocations that blend the astrological with the christological: "O Saturn, give me wisdom... O Venus, give me blood."

It is a synthesis that might seem heretical to the orthodox and sentimental to the occultist, but for the seeker walking the line between knowledge and being, it rings with the truth of a unified reality.

This book is a testament to the idea that truth is not a matter of geography or denomination, but of scale. Collin teaches us that to understand the Christian story, we must see it not as a sequence of days, but as a permanent, eternal structure—a machine for the production of the soul, turning the "Way of Decay" into the "Way of Glory".

I

AND GOD created man in his own image. In his own image created he also nebula, sun, earth, cell and molecule. For his image is a creature with seven natures, living on three foods, and endowed with all possibilities. Such a creature is truly a cosmos.

God is threefold, and through the play of his radiance, his mass and his time, all creatures and all phenomena are brought to being. By his threefold nature, too, they are sustained. For God enters them as three nourishments, without any one of which they perish miserably. Food, breath and light are these three.

In their sixfold play the three god-given foods bring to each cosmos all possibilities and the power of choice. And the six dances of divinity are growth, purification, decay, damnation, healing and rebirth.

All the creatures of God eat and are eaten. What then is damnation? To be eaten of a lower cosmos. What is rebirth? To be incorporated in a higher. Let the cell then be incorporated in man, let man be incorporated in the sun, let the sun be incorporated in God the Absolute. For thus is the whole redeemed, and that which was separated in the beginning shall be made one in the end.

But time—the patience of God—intervenes between us and our perfection. Each cosmos is endowed with a span of life, that other measurement of its size. And the lives of cosmoses are linked as the bird with the tree, and the tree with the seasons. For the life of man is but a breath for the earth his mother, but a wink for the sun his maker.

The redemption of each cosmos depends on the redemption of that higher cosmos which embraces it, makes possible the redemption of that lower one of which it is made. If my heart feels pain, I feel pain: if I feel ecstasy, my heart knows God. For the whole must be redeemed together, and without any part shall none know peace.

But we are too weak to achieve our own regeneration, too brief to share the earth's millenary ascent. What hope then have we? None; save that Christ descended from the stars to create a new cosmos in whose redemption we might share, a cosmos between man and earth, the cosmos of Christendom, the Christian mystery.

II

E VERY COSMOS is endowed with a body and the promise of two other bodies. It possesses a physical body of flesh and blood, already made: a circulation of blood and breath which, made conscious, becomes soul: a heart of flame which, made conscious, becomes spirit. The body is of earth, earthy; the soul is of the planets, airy; the spirit is of God, illuminated. The soul is joined to the body at six places. The spirit is joined to the body at three places. The soul is joined to the spirit at twelve places. This is the divine figure of nine, the image of God.

As the Ram gave way to the Fish, and the Earth entered into its maturity, Christ and the hierarchy were required to create a new image of God among men. Who should generate it? And upon whom?

Molten rock had hardened ages since. Upon the dry rock dew fell, waters formed, molluscs swam. On the edge of the waters reptiles crawled, ferns grew, trees spread. At length through the trees flew birds and butterflies, under them sped deer and tigers. Man was made. Made fire, houses, money, raised crops and herds. Civilisations, each a part cosmos, succeeded one another. Each was generated by the hierarchy. Each reached for understanding, prayed, failed, struggled, left monuments, grew old and died. Atlantis, Egypt, India. Chaldea, Greece and Rome. The world waited and suffered. What next? What next?

First brute mankind was cherished by the Sons of God made sons of men. Later, these were aided by sons of men made sons of God. Together they formed the hierarchy. Hercules, Krishna, Buddha, Socrates. The messengers were multiplied. Many men rose. Yet the masses remained sheep—with or without a shepherd, yet still sheep. Far off, on the heights of the stairway, a door remained closed. There was traffic on the lower flights, yet the door remained closed. What next?

If the Sun is Earth's father, the Dog Star is its King. If the Sun is Earth's growth, the Dog Star is its regeneration. As the Sun to the Earth, so the Dog Star to the Sun. Between Sun and Dog Star a door remained closed. As the Ram gave way to the Fish, and the Earth entered into its maturity, that door opened.

If a king enter at the front door, shall not the maid in the scullery rejoice? If a king enter at the front door, shall not dead bottles be brought from the very cellar to the light? And if the king, loving, spend his seed in that house—what then, what then?

If the Sun were man's God, what then was the Dog Star? A new image of God had to be created, in which men could be redeemed, in which sheep also should be redeemed. Who should generate it? And upon whom? The Father of God should generate it upon the Daughter of Men.

III

EACH COSMOS has a body, a soul and a spirit. Body moves in a circle; 1, 2, 3, 4, 5, 6, 7, 8, 9; soul interlaces between six points 1, 4. 2, 8, 5, 7; spirit describes a triad 3, 6, 9. In their intricate enneagram lies the cosmic monogram.

The body. How does the body of man unfold? Not by years of the earth, but by inner time, the pace it surpasses them. Man falls through time, slowly at first, each minute, each day, each month brimming with change: then faster and faster, till the years flash by indistinguishable, empty of all experience.

Zero, he is conceived. One, brain, heart and bowels distinguish in the womb. Two, he quickens. Three, is born and breathes. Four, grows and crawls. Five, perceives himself. Six, emerges from childhood into the world of men. Seven, marries and begets. Eight, climbs to his zenith, rules, builds, aspires and is terrified. Nine, decays, dies, rejoins infinity. Till, losing its tail of life, nine becomes naught once more.

So with the body of the Christian mystery. Zero, the world lies waiting, a dart flies from the sun of suns. One, a saviour is born of the Virgin Mary in Bethlehem. Two, the gathering of disciples with John in Jerusalem. Three, Christ crucified on Calvary. Four, the dispersal into Asia Minor, land of Mary the Magdalene. Five, the Catholic Church born of Peter in Rome. Six, Christ crucified upon the law; Paul the persecutor. Seven, Christendom. Eight, the betrayal by Judas unto the world. Nine, the end of the world, return to Christ in Majesty, the Second Coming.

At the nine points in the body of the Christian mystery, Christ also set those about whom its faculties should grow. At one, the Virgin Mary: at two, John the disciple whom he loved: at four Mary the Magdalene: at five Simon called Peter; at seven, that other Mary; at eight, Judas who should betray him. And at three, six and nine, he abided himself: at three alone, at six with Paul the persecutor, at nine with his Father which is in heaven.

And in the first image, one and two were measured by years, four and five by decades, seven and eight by many centuries. And in the second, all exist always and everywhere. And the two images are one. For thus is the body of the Christian mystery.

IV

THE SOUL. In man the soul is borne upon the blood, the blood made conscious in its pilgrimage. How journeys the soul of man? Unity is divided into seven parts: between six of them the soul journeys. 1, 4, 2, 8, 5, 7, is the result of that division, and the pattern of that journeying.

One, the cool instinctive bowels; four, the warm flesh; two, the airy movement of limbs; eight, the fire of sex; five, passion of the mind; seven, compassion of the heart. And bearing all it has acquired, the soul journeys on, to one again.

Can you understand that this one of the instinctive bowels is that one at which the parts were distinguished in the womb? That this four of warm flesh is that four of infant growth? That this two of moving limbs is that two of quickening? That this eight of sex is that eight at which man rules and is betrayed? That this seven of compassion is that seven where man mates and begets yet another cycle? If so, begin to perceive the whole.

And the soul of the Christian mystery? One, the Virgin Mary, cool womb of darkness in which the saviour germinates: at four turns to warm flesh of Mary Magdalene, to blood and tears, abandon and repentance. At two, to John the messenger, swift runner for his master, silver-tongued in words not of his own choosing. At eight, borne down with too much seeing, tortured with power and pain, to Judas, betraying yet not blameworthy. At five, to Peter, who smote off Malchus' ear and set it back again. At seven to that other Mary, mother and mercifactress of all men.

Shall then all Christians pass along this path? Shall the soul of each Christian imitate this great pilgrimage? Yes: since the soul of the Christian mystery lies not in time, they shall, in time.

V

S PIRIT is the pure fire, the pure light, the ecstatic bombardment of electrons in every crevice of the universe. It is everywhere. Yet especially it describes a triangle in the being of each cosmos, every man.

What is this triangle of spirit? A flood of divinity. And at each turn in its tide something of divinity turns not, but goes on, goes forth into the unknown.

At its apex, spirit says: "O signature of man, be conceived, go forth into the womb!" At the next angle, spirit says: "O babe, be born, go forth into the air!" At the next, spirit says: "O child, be brave, go forth among men!" And at the apex again, spirit says: "O man, be free, go forth into eternity!" And there is but one apex, and to go forth into eternity is also to go forth into the womb.

For the apex is the zero of generation, the next angle the three of birth, that following the six of maturity, and the apex that nine of death which is yet the zero of regeneration.

The triangle can be called God. For God is spirit, and they that worship him, worship him in spirit. God crosses himself three ways, and a divine signature is cast into the void. That signature is a triangle, that triangle a spirit, that spirit a man.

But there are greater spirits and lesser spirits. What then is the spirit of the Christian mystery? At its apex Divinity said: "O Christ, be incarnated in the flesh of Jesus of Nazareth, go forth into the world a saviour of bodies!" At the next angle, Divinity said: "O Christ, be crucified in the flesh of Jesus of Nazareth, go forth into paradise a saviour of souls!" At the next, Divinity said: "O Christ, be crucified in the church and the law, in pomp and deceit, go forth into heaven a saviour of spirits!" And at the apex again, Divinity shall say: "O Christ, die to the world and men, go forth beyond heaven to him who sent you!" And the Christian mystery shall be consummated, to return again in greater glory.

VI

COMING EVENTS cast their shadows before. Fourteen generations of patriarchs from Abraham to David: fourteen generations of tradition from David to the carrying away into Babylon: fourteen generations of wise men from the carrying away unto Joseph. Since the death of the Minotaur, and since Iknaton gathered the wisdom of ancient Egypt, an unbroken line of preparation.

Yet of this preparation was Christ not born: Joseph was not his father. For men must build only to reach the height where that which is not of man may descend upon them.

And it descended. The figure of the Christian mystery was made.

How to explain that the figure of the Christian mystery is many figures yet one figure?

The figure was created once through the Acts of Christ, a second time through the Acts of the Apostles, a third time through the Acts of the Church. And countless times more.

Yet the many figures are but one figure, as a stone cast into a pool makes a ripple which embraces now a foot, now a yard, and now the whole pool. It is the same ripple, that ripple but the trace in matter of Him who threw the stone.

So at each point of the figure men come and go, deeds are replaced by deeds, as now one and now another drop of water lifts with the current of that ripple. At this point saint succeeds apostle, heretic saint, magician heretic. At that a gospel is built upon a miracle, an order upon a gospel, a cathedral upon an order.

And the whole figure of the Christian mystery, in all its parts, and in all hearts, is unimaginable.

VII

I N THE figure of the Christian mystery, the circle of the body is the Way of Decay, the web of the soul is the Way of Sacrifice, the triangle of the spirit is the Way of Glory.

Take then the Acts of Jesus Christ.

Upon the Way of Decay Jesus lived his bodily life, encountering at each crossroad those who had been set in their roles to await him.

Was born of the Virgin Mary: heralded by John the Baptist and loved by John the Divine: illuminated to his ministry: was given to drink by the Woman of Samaria and cherished by Mary Magdalene: recognised and denied by Peter: transfigured: sustained secretly by Joseph of Arimathea: betrayed by Judas and condemned by Pilate: died and was buried.

Moon, Mercury, Glory: Venus, Mars, Glory: Jupiter, Saturn, Glory. Nine crossroads.

VIII

UPON THE Way of Sacrifice, He did his own work, laboured, suffered, endured, overcame. Was solitary.

He was pursued by Herod into Egypt—silence. Abandoned the Virgin Moon—"Woman, what have I to do with thee?" Fasting, was tempted of the Devil in the wilderness—"Man shall not live by bread alone".

Gathered his disciples—"Sell all thou hast and follow me". Preached upon the Mount—"Blessed are ye when men shall revile you". Passed by Venus—"Her sins are forgiven, for she loved much".

Had mercy upon the people—"The harvest truly is plenteous, but the labourers are few". Healed in secret—"Go straitly and see that no man know it". Acknowledged Mercury—"This is he of whom it is written, Behold I send my messenger before thy face".

Fasting, was tempted of the Devil in the Wilderness—"Get thee behind me, Satan". Was baptised by John in Jordan—"Suffer it to be so now, for thus it becometh us to fulfil all righteousness". Was crucified—"My God, my God, why hast thou forsaken me?"

Descended into hell—silence. Connived with betraying Saturn—"He that dippeth his hand with me in the dish, the same shall betray me". Met Agony alone in the Garden of Gethsemane—"What, could ye not watch with me one hour?"

Washed his friends' feet—"If I wash thee not, ye have no part with me". Stilled their fear—"Why are ye fearful, O ye of little faith?" Drew passionate Mars in his train—"Wilt thou lay down thy life for my sake? ... This night, before the cock crow, ye shall deny me thrice".

Accepted recognition—"Take heed that no man deceive you". Entered into Jerusalem—"All things whatsoever ye shall ask in prayer, believing, ye shall receive". Was sustained by Jupiter—silence.

Met Agony alone in the Garden—"O my Father, if this cup may not pass away from me except I drink it, thy will be done". Was tried before Pilate—"and he answered him never a word". Ascended in glory—silence, silence.

The Wheel of Fortune, Moon, Growth; the Hermit, the Empress, Venus; the High Priestess, the Magician, Mercury; Purification, Strength, Crucifixion.

The Hanged Man, Saturn, Corruption; the Chariot, the Emperor, Mars; the Hierophant, Temptation, Jupiter; Healing, Justice, Ascension.

Twenty-four crossroads. At six he is sustained by men. At twelve he is sustained by God. At twice two he is alone, alone.

At the last he descends into hell.

At the last he ascends into heaven.

IX

U PON THE Way of Glory, he did God's work, was sustained by God, was God.

At the apex Christ departs from God the Spirit, the Spirit.

At the first crossroads on the Way of Sacrifice, "being warned of God", they flee with the babe from Herod's wrath to Egypt. The Wheel of Fortune turns. Begin by abandoning all. A kid for the altar. God the Goat—the fruit of sacrifice.

At the second he is baptised by John in Jordan, "the Spirit of God descending like a dove upon him." Strength from submission. God the Water-Bearer—the dew of Heaven.

At the third he is directed to his disciples. Of God the miraculous draft of fishes. "Fear not, from henceforth thou shalt catch men" . The Hermit, who seeks to be God within universal God. God the fish—he swims within himself.

At the fourth, healing, remission of sins. "Whether is easier to say, Thy sins be forgiven thee, or to say, Arise, and walk?" Both only of God. The Magician, acting of God, creates a new beginning. God the Ram—the effort to begin.

The second apex. A sacrifice is required. An ascension is promised. "And he sent and beheaded John in prison." Christ took his place. God the Son, the Son.

At the fifth crossroads he preaches to the multitude upon the Mount. "Blessed are the poor in spirit: for theirs is the kingdom of heaven". And, "after this manner pray ye: 'Our Father which art in heaven...' ." The veil of the High Priestess was drawn aside. God the Bull—he who abides.

At the sixth the miracle of the loaves and fishes. Which, "looking up to heaven, he blessed, and gave to the multitude". The Empress, nature, handmaid of God, in her plenty. The marriage of flesh and spirit. God the Twins—the pair of opposites.

At the seventh he went to them, walking on the water. "Of a truth thou art the Son of God". The Emperor, he who commands the four elements, for in them is God also. God the Crab—inchoate in the mass.

At the eighth he enters into Jerusalem amid acclaim and palms. "Hosanna to the Son of David, Hosanna in the highest." The ruler. The Hierophant revealed. God the Lion—bold emergence.

The third apex. He is transfigured upon a high mountain. Divine body, pure spirit, timeless with Moses and Elias. God the Father, the Father.

At the ninth crossroads, the Last Supper. "Take, eat, this is my body: this is my blood of the new testament, which is shed for the remission of sins." The Lovers, blood-brothers. Yet he untouched by adoration or betrayal. God the Virgin—who shall conceive.

At the tenth, trial before Pilate. "Art thou the King of the Jews?" "Thou sayest." And all was done as it should be. Justice. God the Scales—most perfect measurement.

At the eleventh, scourging, the crown of thorns, the mocking. "Father, forgive them, for they know not what they do." The Chariot of fire, his who has harnessed both good and evil. God the Scorpion —the knife about to plunge.

At the twelfth he hung upon the cross, was pierced by a spear. "Father, into thy hands I commend my spirit." His betrayer also departed, and went and hanged himself. The Hanged Man. God the Archer—arrow to mark.

The apex once more. Alpha and omega. God the Spirit, the Spirit.

Fifteen crossroads. Twelve with the Way of Sacrifice, three with the Way of Decay. All divine, all of God.

X

P ERCEIVE HOW Christ reversed time.

The body. Man falls through time, slowly at first, each minute, each day, each month brimming with change: then faster and faster, till the years flash by indistinguishable, empty of all experience.

The spirit. Thirty years Jesus grew, studied, learned, foresaw. Three years Christ ministered—what teachings, healings, miracles, communion with the multitude, preparation of his disciples! Three months from the going up to Jerusalem until the end—faster, faster matter is stirred, tighter, tighter is time compressed. Three days of his passion: each minute, each second intent with agony and creation. Three hours upon the cross—"And behold, the veil of the temple was split in twain". Time split. Past, present, above and below were fused. And in those hours a whole great age of man's development was formed.

This is regeneration. The reversal of time. From slow to faster, more potent, dazzling, vertiginous, unbearable. Crack! Ecstasy. God.

XI

C HRIST DIED. Christ lives. The figure grew. Not in intensity but in size, as the ripple expanded. Characters moved to new places for another scale. Others entered. The Acts of the Apostles. The Acts of the Church.

Not thirty years but three thousand. The coiled spring of time, wound beyond breaking point, unwinds again, remaking the Christian mystery in history. In space and centuries.

Its body.

The apex—God, mystery, and the hidden schools of mystery.

From school in Egypt Jesus returned to his birthplace. Where the Virgin Mother Mary stood, now stands Bethlehem, and all it signifies. Peace on earth, goodwill towards men. Christmas, humble nativities.

From Bethlehem Jesus went up in triumph to the capital. Where John stood now stands Jerusalem, place of pilgrimage, prayer, bloodied crusaders, quartered among warring sects, all things to all men according to their being.

The second apex—Christ loving, crucified, ascended, everywhere.

Paul to the Galatians, John to Patmos and the Seven Churches which are in Asia. Where Mary Magdalene stood now stands Asia Minor, land of Diana and Astarte, the Eastern Church, Byzantium.

Peter and Paul to Rome. "Upon this rock will I build my church." Where Peter stood now stands Rome, imperial and eternal Rome, the Vatican and the Popes, the Church Catholic and Militant.

And as between Mars and Venus, so between West and East, Rome and Byzantium, Catholic and Orthodox, two sides of the Christian mystery must wage confederate war till a unity not of time and place be seen again.

The third apex—Paul the persecutor, opposer, fanatic, militant, emissary of schools, martyred and ascended also.

The three Maries to Provence, Joseph of Arimathea to Glastonbury. Where he stood now stands Christian Europe. Monasteries, orders, Knights Templars, chanting in parish church, the devotion of peasants at wayside shrines. Benedict, Augustine, Francis, Luther, more.

Copts to Ethiopia, Jesuits to China, Franciscans to Mexico. Where Judas stood now stands the Christian world. Compound of revelation and betrayal. Courage, martyrdom, love; blood, cruelty, corruption of ancient innocence.

A thousand fantastic sects. Every man's prejudice and imagination armed with Christianity. Yet none to blame: save the being of unregenerate man, for whom Christ came.

The first apex once again—God, mystery, and the schools of mystery, whither the whole circle yearns.

XII

THE SPIRIT of the Christian mystery in time.

At each of the twelve crossroads on the Way of Glory, Christ placed an Apostle.

"The first, Simon who is called Peter, and Andrew his brother; James the son of Zebedee, and John his brother." The first side of the triangle.

"Philip and Bartholomew; Thomas and Matthew the publican". The second side of the triangle.

James the son of Alphaeus, and Lebbaeus whose surname was Thaddeus; Simon the Canaanite, and Judas Iscariot, who also betrayed him." The third side of the triangle.

And these, by their type and deeds, were to point the way at each crossroad, a guide for every man after who shall come there. For such are the saints.

Next, at the first four crossroads were raised the four Gospels. At the fifth the Revelation of John, and at the eighth the Acts told by Paul. As Venus and Mars for ever. Revelation wars with Acts, and Acts wars with Revelation down the ages. And at the other crossroads were raised other scriptures, by fathers, saints, mystics, in those times and later. And all these are organs of the Christian mystery, from which the fine matters of faith and will are poured into the stream of those who pass by, until the Christian mystery shall end.

Buildings and hallowings were added also. On the first side, the shrines of the Holy Places—the Birthplace, the Tomb, the Mount of Olives.

On the second great temples and cathedrals, the domes of Byzantium against the spires of Rome, San Sophia against Notre

Dame, Venusian munificence of Cluniacs against Martial austerity of Cistercians, the eternal struggle and complement of opposites. Lourdes too, and Guadalupe.

And on the third, monuments of sects and beyond sects. Monuments of the return to the mystery of God. Monuments of the inner penetration. Words, books, paintings. Of Luther and Laud, but Blake also and Goethe and Ibsen. No religious words but still the same.

All these are magnetic centres in the body of Christendom. Inns upon the Way of Glory. They evoke the original glory, store it, gather and give it.

And every traveller who passes is judged thereby.

XIII

A ND THE soul of the Christian mystery?
     Ah, the soul!

That is your business.

For the soul of the Christian mystery is made by the passage of Christians along the Way of Sacrifice. Not otherwise can it be made.

How shall we go? How shall we move from the place where we are? In this wise shall you move from the place where you are.

When you are born, say: "God bears me".

When you are at your mother's breast, say: "O Moon, let me depend and know".

When you come the first time to the temptation in the wilderness, know that it is the means of Growth.

When you meet others who belong to the Christian mystery, say: "I recognise God".

When you receive the bounty of nature, say: "God recognises me".

When you feel the warm flesh upon you, say: "O Venus, let me love and give!"

When you see the suffering multitude, see God in them, say: "I love God".

When your sins are forgiven, say: "God loves me".

When you feel song in your throat, movement in your limbs, say: "O Mercury, let me praise and serve".

When you come a second time to the temptation in the wilderness, know that it is the means of Purification.

When you receive the water of understanding, say: "I serve God". When you are reviled, cheated, abandoned, sick, know that it is the means of Crucifixion.

When you go down into hell, say: "God serves me".

When the mind turns, the will stirs, say: "O Saturn, let me understand and do".

When you come to the agony in the garden, know that it is the battle with Corruption.

When you are revealed to yourself, say: "I understand God".

When others reveal themselves to you in judgement, say: "God understands me".

When passion turns blood to fire, makes limbs like air, say: "O Mars, let me dare and destroy!"

When you unwittingly wound, carelessly break, say: "I destroy God".

When illness overtakes you, say: "God destroys me".

When others turn to you, you turn to others, say: "O Jupiter, let me support and bear".

When you come a second time to the agony in the garden, know that it is the means of Healing.

When you suffer pain, say: "I bear God".

When you die, know that it is the means of Ascension.

In the name of Christ, in the name of our Teacher, Amen.

Lent 1952

LITANY FOR THE ENNEAGRAM

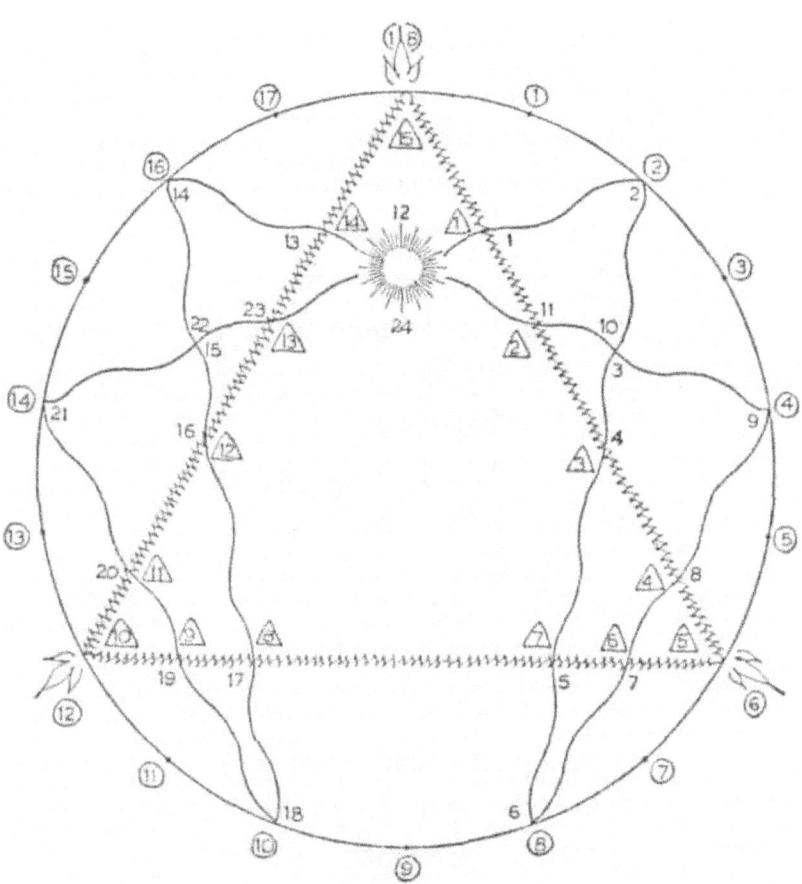

THE CIRCLE

1. I gather my flesh about me.
2. O Moon, give me bowels!
3. I stir in the womb.
4. O Mercury, give me limbs!
5. I come forth into the air.
6. O God, O joy!
7. I breathe and grow.
8. O Venus, give me blood!
9. I watch and wonder!
10. O Mars, give me mind!
11. I come forth into experience.
12. O God, O pain!
13. I hate and mate.
14. O Jupiter, give me compassion!
15. I ponder the meaning.
16. O Saturn, give me wisdom!
17. I decay and die.
18. O God, O self!

1. I gather my flesh about me.
2. O Moon, give me bowels.
3. I stir in the womb.
4. O Mercury, give me limbs!
5. I come forth into the air.
6. O God, O joy!

THE TRIANGLE

1 . God the Goat—the fruit of sacrifice.

2 . God the Water-Carrier—the dew of heaven.

3 . God the Fish—he swims within himself.

4 . God the Ram—the effort to begin.

5 . God the Son—the Son...

6 . God the Bull—he who abides.

7 . God the Twins—the pair of opposites.

8 . God the Crab—inchoate in the mass.

9 . God the Lion—bold emergence.

10 . God the Father—the Father...

11 . God the Virgin—who shall conceive.

12 . God the Scales—most perfect measurement.

13 . God the Scorpion—the knife about to plunge.

14. God the Archer—arrow to mark.

15. God the Spirit—the Spirit...

1 . God the Goat—the fruit of Sacrifice.

2 . God the Water-Carrier—the dew of heaven

3 . God the Fish—he swims within himself.

4 . God the Ram—the effort to begin.

5 . God the Son—the Son...

6 . God the Bull—he who abides.

7 . God the Twins—the pair of opposites.

8 . God the Crab—inchoate in the mass.

9 . God the Lion—bold emergence.

THE FIGURE

1. God bears me.

2. O Moon, let me depend and know!

3. Growth.

4. I recognise God.

5. God recognises me.

6. O Venus, let me love and give!

7. I love God.

8. God loves me.

9. O Mercury, let me praise and serve!

10. Purification.

11. I serve God.

12. Extinction.

13. God serves me.

14. O Saturn, let me understand and do!

15. Corruption.

16. I understand God.

17. God understands me.

18. O Mars, let me dare and destroy!

19. I destroy God.

20. God destroys me.

21. O Jupiter, let me support and bear!

22. Healing.

23. I bear God.

24. Ascension.

THE HERALD OF HARMONY

THE MIRROR OF LIGHT AND OTHER WORKS

FOREWORD TO
THE HERALD OF HARMONY

I n the trajectory of Rodney Collin's writing, one can trace a distinct arc from the intellectual to the emotional, and finally, to the ecstatic. If *The Theory of Celestial Influence* was his map of the cosmos, *The Herald of Harmony* is his hymn to the territory itself. It represents, perhaps, the final distillation of his thought—a text where the complex machinery of the Fourth Way is not abandoned, but accelerated until it blurs into a single, blinding vision of unity.

The work opens with the grandest of pronouncements: "An age is dying away. A new age is coming to birth". For the student of esoteric history, this is familiar ground. We are accustomed to the idea of precessional cycles, of the shift from the Piscean to the Aquarian age. But Collin gives this cosmic clockwork a visceral, biological urgency. He describes the evolution of mankind not merely as a passage of time, but as the sequential awakening of "functions" within the collective body of humanity.

Collin sketches out a sweeping anthropology of the soul. He sees the "First Function" of instinct ruling the cave-dwellers; the "Second Function" of movement driving the nomads; the "Third Function" of emotion building the great religious civilizations; and the "Fourth Function" of intellect culminating in our modern era of science and skepticism. But his gaze is fixed firmly on the horizon, on the emergence of the "Fifth Function".

What is this Fifth Function? In the Gurdjieffian system, the sex center is often discussed as a separate, distinct mind, capable of perceiving a reality inaccessible to the others. Collin, unafraid of the sacred or the profane, identifies this new faculty with the "Mystery of Sex"—not in its degraded, mechanical form, but as the "glorious enjoyment" of God's nature.

He posits that this new age will be characterized by a synthesis, a "Harmony" that reintegrates the fragmented parts of man. It is a bold, almost dangerous prophecy: that the very force which has been the source of so much confusion and suffering is destined to become the instrument of our highest perception.

The text moves with the rhythm of a psalm or a sutra. It challenges the dualities that have plagued religious thought for millennia. Collin refuses to separate the spirit from the flesh, or the sacred from the mundane. In a series of startling paradoxes, he asserts, "This match is God. I blow out God... This spider is God. I kill God".

He pushes his monism to its ultimate conclusion, finding divinity in the "granite" and the "electrons," in the "bank" and the "brothel". This is the "New Christianity" he envisions—a faith stripped of moralizing judgment and replaced with a terrifying, all-consuming awareness.

He even extends this redemption to the ultimate antagonist, commanding, "Get thee behind me, Satan" in a new voice, one that invites the Shadow to "Accept second place... and be redeemed". It is a vision of total integration, where "No thing is evil, but in forgetfulness of God".

The Herald of Harmony is not a work to be analyzed so much as absorbed. It is a transmission of state. Collin is telling us that the "pandemonium" of our current existence is, in fact, God. He invites us to stop struggling against the current of time and to recognize that the "universal symphony" is already playing.

For the weary seeker, caught in the endless friction between 'yes' and 'no', this text offers a glimpse of the resolution—a silence that is not empty, but full of the "ecstatic silence of the Whole". It is a fitting capstone to the work of a man who spent his life trying to harmonize the laws of the universe with the longings of the human heart.

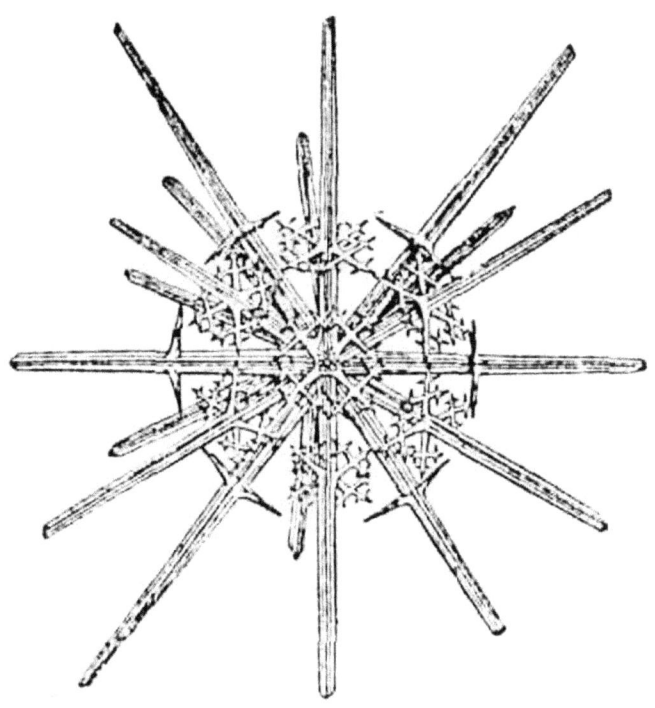

THE MIRROR OF LIGHT AND OTHER WORKS

I

AN AGE is dying away. A new age is coming to birth. What are the signs of a new age?

In the heavens, a new combination of influences. From the Hierarchy, a new generation. Among men, a new function awakened, a new word of salvation given.

For the body of mankind grows as the body of a man grows—one function after another opening in him, each culmination at its appointed age, each fulfilled and transcended by the next. And as in man each function awakens at a certain shining of his stars, so in mankind at a certain shining of the constellations.

As Venus yields to Mars, so childhood wisdom yields to stormy puberty: as the Bull to the Ram, so Egypt to Greece, innocence to paganism, tenderness to strife.

But, unlike a man, whose life goes slowing to its close, for mankind the ages hurry faster by, each more demanding than the last.

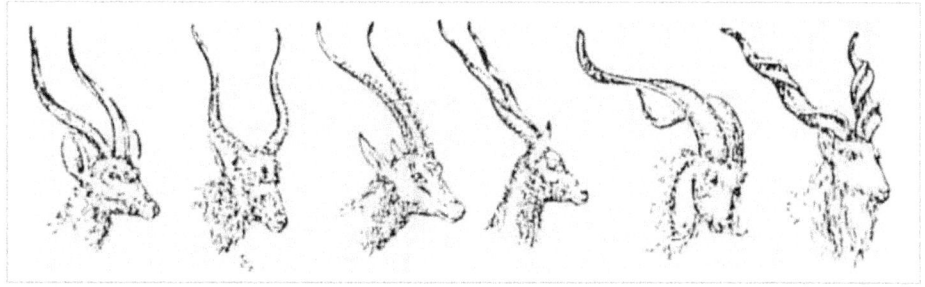

For thirty thousand years, men huddled in their caves as the stars said: "Ruminate". For fifteen more they stalked, trailed, fled, stretched nerve and bow, as the heavens cried: "Hunt". For eight more they cultivated corn, raised temples and pyramids, at the commandment: "Build".

Each was an age. And as each age dawned, a messenger was sent to incarnate the new function and its fulfilment. A hero came, and in him the Hierarchy revealed the next perfection of its plan. Who spoke and manifested the first words of power, we do not know. "Ruminate!" "Hunt!" and "Build!" remain anonymous as stomach, muscle, flesh. Not so the later laws.

For Hercules followed, and with twelve vast labours revealed the next age's cry. "Struggle!" the gods decreed, and for four thousand years men fought, intrigued, took cities and women, lived pagan-proud and fancy-free. So for mankind, lights, liver, blood, muscle and flesh and spleen were slowly sanctified. Drawn towards divinity, divinity revealed in them.

Priesthoods from age on age taught how this function or that should reveal its nature, and man making his varied tissue conscious, be through it shown a way back to his origin. To God.

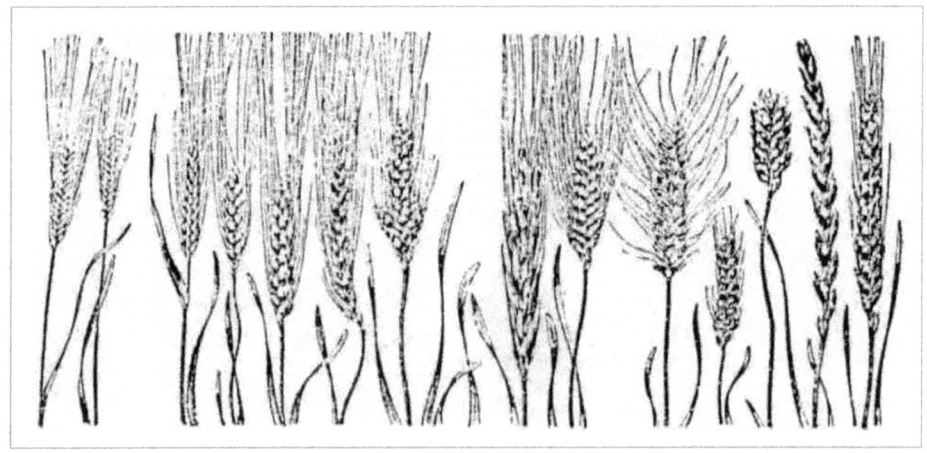

II

A T LAST the heavenly spotlight fell upon men's hearts. The source, the origin, the mainspring of their life. And hearts awakening, responded to the mainspring of the universe, the heart of heaven itself. Made possible the coming of a saviour from that heart.

Christ came. Announced and incarnated the new commandment—"Love".

As Ram gave way to Fish, solar plexus must yield to heart, pagan to Christian, Old Testament to New. Struggle to take be outmoded by love of giving, the gods by God, the manifold by Unity. And passion by love. For sensation of the manifold is passion, sensation of unity is love.

That instant, as all planets conjoined in Pisces, as all organs were shown to swim in spirit, Mankind came of age. A lifeline was thrown to the Earth from the Sun of Suns: seed of the King of Kings was cast thereon.

With the coming of the Hierarchy, Mankind emerged from womb of Earth. With the coming of Christ, Mankind stood straight and recognised the light.

Yet harmony lacked. To one part of man was revealed the hidden secret of the universe—the knowledge that all is one, all life an ocean,

creatures but eddies, separate salvation mirage. And to one organ was given direct sensation of this oneness—love.

But his other members knew this not. Muscles and lungs and flesh and genitals went joyfully upon their ancient secret ways, pursuing their secret separate joys, suffering their secret separate sorrows. Stomach must ruminate, muscle hunt, flesh build, solar plexus struggle. Obeying the words of power of old revealed to them.

So stomach felt union only with what it ate: no food, no unity. Flesh felt union only with other flesh which touched it tingling equally: no caress, no unity. Solar plexus felt union only in the kill: no sacrifice, no unity.

And heart felt universal unity—save with the nerve and tissue which betrayed it.

Thus sprang the inner schism of two thousand years. And if Christ came to announce the commandment—"Love", he no less said to men—"Be crucified". Crucified upon organic contradiction, crucified upon vision unattainable.

For the key of harmony lay hidden twenty centuries.

III

CONSIDER how human Christians received the word of love. Perceiving the future Christ, the devil could have the past. Perceiving high heaven, they invented deepest hell. Perceiving the new incomparable, they turned on the old —at first with bitter words, later with fire and rack.

If love universal were the new revelation, then love erotic was the new sin. If heart were blessed, then liver and lights were damned. If God were one and Christ his only-begotten Son, then Osiris, Astarte, Baal, Zeus, Vishnu and Lao Tse were false; and all their servants, priests, sages, philosophers, magicians demon-driven.

When Elymas the sorcerer withstood their teaching, Paul cried: "O full of subtlety and mischief, thou child of the devil, wilt thou not cease to pervert the right ways of the Lord?" and struck him blind a season.

What else could Paul do? Let converts be seduced? Yet mark the law of multiplication, which with every century magnifies each word and act of the first days a hundred times.

Pass fourteen centuries, and each man who as much as raises a doubt against the doctrine is in danger. From Elymas' blinding springs the Inquisition: ten thousand human bonfires of Jew, Arab, Aztec, making heaven hideous from Toledo to the mounts of Mexico.

And those within the church who differ? Ananias and Sapphira sold a possession, keeping back part the price. Peter accused: straightway the man fell dead. And to the woman coming after said: "The feet of them which have buried thy husband are at the door, and shall carry thee out also". She too gave up the ghost. "And great fear came upon all the church".

What horrors sprang from the fear that entered then! A thousand years go by, and the death of two dissenters has blazed to the Albigensian crusade. Christians rend Christians their fellow-country- men, devastate, torture, loot, set fire to whole villages at worship. Till the very creed is linked with lawlessness.

And man's own private mysteries? Paul wrote: "It is better to marry than to burn", making of marriage a poor substitute for hell, woman the temptress, and sex a shameful and animal necessity.

Across the centuries what sufferings, cruelties, perversions, prostitutions follow! What stifling of creative joy, what load of blasphemous shame! What hideous substitution of filth for beauty!

Yet blame the first Christians not. Now from the vantage-point of time we recognise that blindness which, vision-dazzled, comes after too great light. The immense temptation which they overcame we feel not: the deep seduction of the past—close, warm and comforting— which they resisted. An enormous effort was needed to surpass that past, put away childish things. This they achieved. If harshly, blame them not.

For the key of harmony lay hidden twenty centuries.

IV

I T COULD not be otherwise.

"I come not to bring peace, but a sword."

Sword which severed past from the living present, sex from the living heart, lower from higher, old from miraculous new. The crossbar of that cross.

Thenceforth men lived in an amputated world. In desperate duality. "The father shall be divided against the son, and the son against the father." Hell against heaven, and heaven against hell. Spirit against flesh, and flesh against spirit. Man against woman, and woman against man.

Crusader against Turk. Orthodox against heretic. Catholic against Protestant. Reformation against Counter-Reformation. The Holy City and Grand Babylon besieged each by each.

And man's very heart a battlefield of the Holy War. Tourney of vice and virtue—the symbol of Salvation Psychomachia.

It could not be otherwise.

For the vision was shown, the way to realise it not. Man longed for the newfound light; spurned darkness and its inhabitants, spurned half himself. In vain. Dark female force, rising in witchcraft and troubadours, cathars and courts of love and alchemy, seduced and succoured him. Till, comforted, he turned and destroyed his comforter.

It could not be otherwise.

Love once revealed, mankind hung crucified.

For the key of heaven lay hidden twenty centuries.

V

T HE IDEA of harmony slid slowly in men's minds, unviolent as itself. In music first.

Medieval counterpoint—two voices opposed in image of the time's duality—flowered to cascading chords, intricate weaving of voice and viol in shimmering web of sound. Cool antiphon, response of height to depth in incense-laden vaults, welled to polyphonous splendour of all creatures united in simultaneous praise. Forbidden discords vanished in soaring wealth of sound.

In history next. Florence restored the past. Reconciled Plato with Christ, beauty with love, nakedness with light. Healed the wrong done to the ancient world, resolved the split in time, charmed Venus and Hercules to worship at the Crib.

Next in astronomy.

Cosmic alternative of heaven or hell melted to vision of the Solar Family, to harmony of multiple worlds dancing devotion to their Sun; to music of whirling orbits, spinning spheres. Through toy telescopes, men glimpsed world without end or conflict.

Began to hunger for harmony, longed to redeem the strife. And setting Rose on Cross, endeavoured to join joy and pain, beauty with sacrifice, wed Wanton Nature back to the Son of God.

Passed centuries more. Religion too grew mild. Great faiths met, greeted, acknowledged one another. Wise men saw unity behind the warring sects. Envisaged the harmony of Buddha, Mahomet, Paul. Guessed the great work of Hierarchy, Christ Head of All.

Men dug the buried past, linked race to race, fathomed the depths of space, probed atom's core. Everywhere the clues to harmony. Everywhere hunger for harmony.

But the time was not yet.
Patience! The key lay hidden.

VI

WHAT is harmony?

It is the order by which heaven is ruled, an order not yet manifest on earth. It is the order by which the sun and planets play their parts, infinitely repeating, combining, creating and destroying, infinitely praising God in multiplicity and unity.

"Thy will be done, on earth as it is in heaven."

At the dawn of Greece, the school of Pythagoras studied this heavenly harmony, and compressing its vast vibrations a billion times, revealed and perpetuated it in sound.

Seven notes were found to ring throughout the universe, infinitely echoing from God to rock. The same vibrations—from unimaginable turning of the galaxy to infinitesimal pulse of electrons giving light.

Do Re Mi Fa Sol La Si—the notes ascended, echoed once more to Do, and infinitely on. Between Mi and Fa a half-tone only, cosmic pause, crack, silence, through which might come the echo of higher and lower music, threading creation through itself to unity. Between Si and next Do half-tone again, the leap from one scale to the next, from task completed to next task begun, from end to new beginning.

Mercury, Venus, Mars; comes pause of Asteroids; then Jupiter, Saturn, Uranus, Neptune; and yet another pause transcended into Sun. Thus music of the Spheres.

Chaos, Metal, Mineral; comes aid of Air; then Plant, Invertebrate, Animal, Man; and yet another pause transcended into Angel. Thus music of Nature and the Earth.

Apeman, Caveman, Huntsman; comes help of Hierarchy; then Builder, Warrior, Artist, Scientist; and yet another pause transcended into Saint. Thus the music of Mankind.

Worship of Nature, Fertility, Ancestors; comes help of Hierarchy; then schools of Egypt, Chaldea, India, Judea; and yet another pause transcended into Christ. Thus the music of Salvation.

And each Do sings to Do on every scale; each Mi sings to every other Mi; each Sol to Sols unlimited. For thus is all creation linked, above rings below, below reverberates above.

Till by the Law of Trinity, the notes combine to chords—each three a chord. By chord on chord the moods and worlds are formed. Tranquil, discordant, joyful, terrible—these chords and discords make the music of the universe.

Some are firm-fixed, some hover on the brink of chaos. Great major triad—Do Mi Sol—thunders the majesty of Father, Holy Ghost and Son. Chord of diminished fifth—Re Fa Si—shrieks of the Devil slipping back to nothingness. Others are agony, healing, redemption, death. And all, contained celestially in music of the spheres, extol the marriage musical of heaven and hell.

This is the key of harmony.

VII

MANKIND NEEDS half-a-thousand years to prepare itself. The Renaissance prefigured the Newcomer, as the age of Buddha, Pythagoras, Lao Tse prefigured Christ.

For five hundred years the Hierarchy poured balm upon the wounds, healed, eased the crucifixion of mankind. By art, music, poetry; by charity and science; by revelation of his kinship everywhere.

Slowly the constellations turned. The time approached when all the planets should be conjoined again, an age consummated, another initiated by the Newcomer.

The Hierarchy looked out, chose two messengers, launched East to West the impulse of preparation. The key of harmony and torch of power they entrusted to the first, a Greek. He carried both from Mount Meru to Moscow, there met the second: duplicated the key, kindled the latter's torch. And both moved on, to England and to France.

Everything real is created by a triad. For this reason Great School must appoint two poles in the world, itself the third and hidden one. These two men were plus and minus, light and dark, the male and female of the message.

The Greek destroyer of men's complacency, trickster, magician, hypnotist, juggler of light and dark, new Orpheus, charming his slaves with music nostalgic of beyond. Compassionate sorcerer, diabolic saint; djinn from alchemic bottle, compounding of laws and frailty 'Arabian Nights' delight.

The Russian—firm and invisible. Compiler of wisdom; master of silent experiment, unrecognised effect; new scientist, himself his laboratory, his pupils retorts and their contents, the work transmutation.

Stern guide, most loving friend; austere in the sacrifice of lesser prize, in power perfected jovial. Planter of seeds, the gardener of the soul.

The Greek as masterwork turned cosmic laws to dance—a tide of harmonious movement, bewitching as Maya itself, subtle and difficult as very dance of worlds. By dance broke down men's obstinate separateness; made pigmy passions echo to universal ones; evoked in the world of men a shimmering image of universal harmony.

Soberly, year on year, the Russian taught:

"Find what you want:
Be simple and sincere:
By understanding be freed from illusion and from fear:
Remember yourself—always and everywhere".

"Change destructive emotions into harmony:
Study the laws:
Serve faithfully the work:
Remember yourself—always and everywhere".

Between those poles the lightning arced. "Be drawn to either pole", the Russian warned, "Cling where you are drawn. Don't play between—the current is dangerous". Men misunderstood, piously prayed the poles be reconciled. Some tempted the tension, were shocked. But most heeded the warning, and their little magnets growing polarised, the great field of force was amplified.

Slowly, within this world, a cradle formed; magnetic field for electronic nativity.

VIII

BOTH DIED. Polarity transfigured to the realm of deeds. What was prefigured darkly translated now to light.

The Russian first. Grew old, invisible. Behind the crumbling facade of the body constructed a new edifice, whence HE looked out. Tested his friends in silence; by play of dotage, dared them to disbelieve. And behind his own ruin, contacted Greatest School, was given the script of that which must be performed.

He returned from second exile to the land of his lifetime's work. Called all his friends. And knowing how too much knowledge, like printed paper, is in danger of the fire, declared:

"I abandon the system. Leave explanation—be. What is your wish? 'Tis harmony now we seek. I know not the answer yet: but go to find it".

Withdrew. Enigma. Silence. Invisibly worked. The plot prepared. By casting all perishable upon the flood, and striving mightily to other bank, emerged naked, pure, clean, and utterly reborn. And his friends too lost all they dared. Caught the rope cast from there. Were washed by the waves.

Christ mediating in all.

And before he set his body adrift to disintegrate, with physical tongue last said to them:

"Reconstruct all. Now make all new again. From the very beginning. Thus only harmony may be achieved".

The Russian died: abandoned the Solar System: returned with power to do. Electronically prepared the perfection of his work. Of all his disciples' love, began to create magnetic field as cradle for electronic nativity.

The Greek died also. In a burst of compassion, love and gaiety, which made of his death an Arabian Nights' delight. And joking up to heaven, escaped with but slightest singeing of his wings, a drift of unearthly music echoing in his trail. Was healed. Resumed his right place in spiritual polarity. Triad transformed: translated all effects.

Thus the messengers returned to the ark which launched them forth: their first work done, their second now begun.

IX

COSMIC CONCEPTION coincided with the second messenger's ascent.

Divine mercy flared: impregnated the waiting earth. The guiding constellations wheeled to place. Cells on another scale paired, merged, split, multiplied, the spiritual chromosomes resolving ecstatically to the new age's shape, to pattern of as yet unmanifested harmony.

The clock of new creation began to tick, its time inexorably unrolling from that ecstasy. The web and weft of an age in embryo went knitting up: its organs sketched in: its understanding glimpsed. Its interdependent parts—now single men, now groups—later must grow to nations' beliefs, whole races and their destiny. For what is achieved in little in the embryo, shall be achieved in grandeur in the man.

All this the transfigured messengers must tend.

X

HARMONIOUS BABE must grow in harmony. Its very cells, its assembling organs, bones and flesh sing in the womb of time. And each man, woman, craft and creed that aspires to the future and to God is such a cell, such organ or such bone.

How then shall each member learn to take part in harmony?

First, let each note sound clear and full. Pure in its tone, nor sharp nor flat from imitation, pretence or doubt. Let each type be himself, know his own nature, ring to the vibration God has given him. Let jovial heal, martial be brave, venusian loving; let moon be secret, mercury serviceable, saturn most deeply wise.

Let each craft fulfil itself—artist imagine, scientist deduce, leader bear all. Let each race refind its secrets, each creed its hidden mystery—Christian find Christ, Moslem Mahomet, Buddhist Gautama the Prince.

This is the first rule of harmony.

Second, let each note—remembering itself—listen for the chord. Hear its own sound, ringing with other sound struck simultaneously. Let Do hear itself sound with Mi and Sol. Let Mars hear his note ringing with Jupiter and Moon. Let priest hear his note blend with astronomer's and king's. Till, waking from single notes to wealth of chords, each learn to recognise their infinite variety, taste chord from chord, know the nature of those in which he sounds and why.

This is the second rule of harmony.

Third, let each note accept the key to come, follow the new tonic now revealed to it. Let each type yield to him who unites them all: all craft to the greater truth: all nations to Higher School: all creeds to the Not Yet Born. Each served as tonic in its day and age: each piped the tune once for all humanity. Now fall to other yet equal place—sounding the same, enter a higher key.

This is the third rule of harmony.

And fourth? Faith is the fourth. If note have not faith in the music to be played, in Composer, Conductor and Holy Symphony, what use? Without faith, each note's a pointless tedium. With faith, each note shall know that it is not, has no existence but in the infinite music which evokes it. And knowing this, knows all, to the ultimate inspiration of the work.

This is the fourth rule of harmony.

And all this together is the key of harmony.

All this is freedom from violence and from strife, escape from crucifixion, the integration of heaven and hell.

And by all this, harmonious babe shall grow: shall form and move: and—when the planets conjoin again—be born.

XI

This is the New Christianity. This is the light. Look backwards—but not with longing. Resist seduction—even by the first.

Do you doubt that all now is different?

Hear then the change.

"Vanity of vanities", the old Forerunner preached.

"Glorious enjoyment", the future Choir responds.

"There is nothing new under the Sun", the old one said.

"Let us leap over the Sun then", saith the new.

"Repent, for the Kingdom of Heaven is at hand", the first John warned.

"Rejoice, for heaven's in every limb", exults the next.

"O generation of vipers, how can ye, being evil, speak good things?" Christ cried before.

"O generation of kittens, how can ye, being God's, speak evil?" the echo comes.

"If thy eye offend thee, pluck it out", he said again: "for it is better that one member should perish, than the whole be cast in Hell".

Not so today.

"If thy eye offend thee, pluck out thy offence, and cherish the eye God gave", the command runs now: "for it is better to enter Heaven with a real eye than Hell with an imaginary offence".

The Tempter tried.

"Get thee behind me, Satan", Christ rebuked.

Now speak we fair.

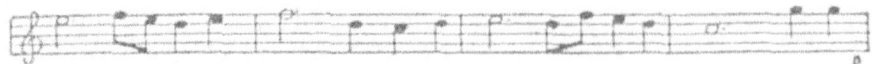

"Accept second place, O Satan, and be redeemed: for 'tis only the lust for first that makes thee Satan."

"And Lord of Harmony, take first place in all my parts: for if thou hast it not, there is no harmony".

So all is made new, all opposite, all redeemed. Then reconstruct all: and rejoicing await the proof.

XII

G OD CREATED all, permeates all, is all. Granite is but the compression of his electrons: who is the devil but his prodigal son?

This match is God. I blow out God. What a joke!

This spider is God. I kill God. What a tragedy!

All that happens is God: all that has happened is God: all that will happen is God.

The bread I eat is God: the saliva which melts it God: the life that leaps thence into my blood is simply God. Where God crosses himself three ways, things come to pass.

God in my bowels. God in my lungs. God in my blood. God in my eyes. God in my limbs. God in my heart. And somewhere in my head a better kind of God. Where God crosses himself seven ways, perfection's possible.

Since God then, in creation, left nothing out, we in regeneration must take all back. Since God from One made Three, from Three Harmony, and from Harmony All, we in the noise of All must rehear harmony, in harmony refind the major triad, resolve that chord to the one note which sounds the universe.

You too are God. Can you please God by coddling his flesh unmindful of his spirit? You too are God. Can you please God in spirit only, punishing his flesh? There is a better way. Make thee a bridge, a conscious soul, this is also God. Know Him in all three worlds, restoring their contents back to Him to whom it all belongs.

At the Fall man forgot God who made him, God of whom his every part is made. Later some men remembered. But in part alone. Remembered their love was made of God's, forgot their anger was; acknowledged spirit's divinity, doubted that of flesh. Avowed this

ad infinitum

teacher to be his messenger, stoned that as Antichrist; worshipped in this temple, desecrated that.

If God pervades all, is he further from the brothel than the church, from bank than shrine? Maybe bank and brothel are sunk deeper in forgetfulness, or maybe not. The distance thence to God is the same zero anyway. Him who forgot remind, him who has guessed confirm.

No thing is evil, but in forgetfulness of God. Money, the godless fount of greed, oppression, violence, robbery, in divine remembrance becomes invisible instrument of the Paraclete. Sex, of itself alone the source of lust, jealousy, possessiveness and rape, in memory of God is glorious enjoyment of his nature.

No thing is good, but in remembrance of God. All things are good, remembering their godliness. For this their godliness transcends their time, change, devilishness and decay. In each this godliness is named the Self. Remember then thy Self, remembering God: remember God, remembering thyself.

Yet remember too that none can merit Him. God not even the angels dare deserve. God alone can give Himself. But this to eternity he does. For such He is.

This is the secret—awfully simple—that the Earth ignores. To ignore it is one thing, to guess it another, to know it a third, a fourth to perceive it, a fifth to be it.

This last achieved, the Herald of Harmony can return to Him who sent him, his mission done. This last achieved, the universal symphony shall be drowned in ecstatic silence of the Whole.

Know then our present pandemonium as God:
our future harmony as God:
holy unison as God:
silence as God:
Self as God:
God:
God:
God.

THE MIRROR OF LIGHT AND OTHER WORKS

EDITOR'S AUTOBIOGRAPHICAL NOTES

Robin Bloor was born in 1951 in Liverpool, UK. He obtained a BSc in Mathematics at Nottingham University and took up a career in the computer industry, initially writing software. From 1989 onwards, he became a technology analyst and consultant. He has thus been a writer of a kind ever since. In 2002, he was awarded an honorary Ph.D. in Computer Science by Wolverhampton University in the UK.

He currently resides in and works from Austin, Texas in the USA. In 1988, after drifting through several Work groups, Bloor met and became a pupil of Rina Hands. Rina was a one-time associate of J. G. Bennett, a student of Peter Ouspensky's, and later, a pupil of George Gurdjieff. Following Gurdjieff's death, she remained part of J. G. Bennett's group for a while. Subsequently, she formed groups both in London, where she lived, and in Bradford in the North of England – initially in conjunction with Madame Nott.

She was both an accomplished movements teacher and an inspirational group leader. She died in 1994 and is buried next to Jane Heap in a cemetery in North London. The author acknowledges the following individuals, who – whether they realize it or not – were of assistance in writing and publishing this book, and to whom he is grateful: Rina Hands, Derek Sinko, Paula Schmidt, and Stephen Aronson.

OTHER BOOKS FROM THE KARNAK PRESS

- Gurdjieff's Hydrogens Vol 1: The Ray of Creation by Robin Bloor
- Gurdjieff & Kundabuffer by Robin Bloor
- Readings, Prosaic and Poetic by Robin Bloor & Paula Schmidt
- Sayings From The Gurdjieff Work by Robin Bloor
- Notes on Beelzebub's Tales Volume 1: The Arousing of Thought by Robin Bloor
- The 1931 Manuscript of Beelzebub's Tales by G. I. Gurdjieff
- The Revised Version of the 1931 Manuscript by G. I. Gurdjieff
- Beelzebub's Tales: Book One, Side by Side Comparison by G. I. Gurdjieff
- Beelzebub's Tales: Book Two, Side by Side Comparison by G. I. Gurdjieff
- The Herald of Coming Good [With Notes by R. Bloor] by G. I. Gurdjieff
- The Search For Meaning by Stephen Aronson
- As Inside, So Outside, As Above, So Below by Stephen Aronson
- Sacred Dances by Nella Liska
- Rodney Collin by Terje Tonne

All books are available on Amazon

The Mirror of Light and Other Works

www.ingramcontent.com/pod-product-compliance
Lightning Source LLC
Chambersburg PA
CBHW061553120626
46550CB00004B/1471